D0054259

HOW FAR DO YOU WANT TO GO?

HOW FAR DO YOU WANT TO GO?

Lessons from a Common-Sense Billionaire

JOHN CATSIMATIDIS

Matt Holt Books
An Imprint of BenBella Books, Inc.
Dallas, TX

The events, locations, and conversations in this book while true, are recreated from the author's memory. However, the essence of the story, and the feelings and emotions evoked are intended to be accurate representations.

Matt Holt is an imprint of BenBella Books, Inc.
10440 N. Central Expressway
Suite 800
Dallas, TX 75231
benbellabooks.com
Send feedback to feedback@benbellabooks.com

Printed in the United States of America
10 9 8 7 6 5 4 3 2 1

Library of Congress Control Number: 2022034459
ISBN 9781637743430 (hardcover)
ISBN 9781637743447 (electronic)

Copyediting by Lydia Choi
Proofreading by Kellie Doherty and Ariel Fagiola
Text design and composition by Aaron Edmiston
Cover design by Brigid Pearson
Cover image © Shutterstock / Francois Roux
Printed by Lake Book Manufacturing

I have had a very fortunate life, and the privilege of meeting many very interesting and important people along the way. They have made a difference in my life and gave me the wisdom to succeed. This book is dedicated to all of them for enriching my life. But most of all, this book is dedicated to my wonderful mother and father, who brought me to this great country at the age of six months (six months too late for me to be eligible to run for President), my beloved children, AJ and John Jr., and the love of my life and great partner, Margo, my sunshine, who makes me smile every day.

CONTENTS

Top: John Catsimatidis speaking at Federal Hall.

Bottom: Mark Simone, John Catsimatidis Jr., Margo Catsimatidis, John Catsimatidis, AJ Catsimatidis, and Newt Gingrich.

Introduction

AMERICAN SONG

It was a magical night in New York City.

How could it not be? I was surrounded by a couple hundred of my closest friends. Just as important, I had lured them all to an awe-inspiring location kitty-corner from the New York Stock Exchange, a place where most of these people had never been before. I'd passed this old building a thousand times, maybe ten thousand. But only once had I ever stepped inside. I'd known this spot was important in American history, but I hadn't been quite sure why. Until recently, I'd had no idea how many world-changing events occurred right here.

What can I tell you? I learn something new every day.

This was the Federal Hall National Memorial, site of the first capitol building of the United States of America under the US Constitution. It was here, in 1789, that General George Washington was sworn in as our nation's first president. This was where the first US Congress met, back in the days when Congress actually conducted important business for the nation instead of remaining frozen in semipermanent gridlock. The Bill of Rights was ratified on this very spot, setting out our most precious rights and freedoms. The Judiciary Act of 1789 was passed here, establishing our federal court system, which I'm thankful for. Mostly.

So why isn't every schoolchild in America taken on a guided tour of Federal Hall?

The truth is that the memorial, historic though it is, has often been overlooked in recent years amid all the sights and sounds of New York. This is no one's fault exactly. The National Park Service, which runs the place, has plenty of other things to worry about and is always squeezed for cash. The World Trade Center site, just a few blocks to the west, has soaked up a lot of attention since 2001. And on this special evening, as I caught up with old friends while making new ones, the domed main hall seemed a little dowdy, to tell you the truth. The artifact displays, including the one with the George Washington Inaugural Bible, looked like they'd last been updated when I was a child. The entire building, which went all the way from Wall Street to Pine Street, felt like it needed a vigorous scrubbing with one of those steel-bristle brushes my mother used to use. Clearly, Federal Hall was crying out for some love.

That was exactly the point of getting all these people out on this warm summer evening. If such an important piece of American history needed attention, what were we waiting for?

....

I was prepared to write a hefty check to help with renovations. But I knew that bringing Federal Hall into the twenty-first century couldn't be a one-man crusade. This was an American national treasure, after all. We needed lots of people involved. Thankfully, Mack McLarty, who was Bill Clinton's White House Chief of Staff, had already talked to Newt Gingrich, the former Speaker of the House of Representatives. Both men are friends of mine, and both are genuine patriots, whatever you might think of their individual politics. Now, both of them were on board. I loved the fact that Mack's a Democrat and Newt's a Republican, and both were lending their voices (not to mention their gold-plated contact lists) to such a worthy cause. There should be more of that in America—people working together across our many national divides. While Mack and Newt recruited others in Washington, I focused on people I knew in New York. I was confident: once we got people inside this overlooked cradle of democracy, they, too, would want to help.

It was a typical Cats crowd.

Political people. Media pros. Folks I'd done business with over the years. Young people. Old people. Liberals. Conservatives. Catholics, Protestants, Jews, and others. Greeks and non-Greeks. Random characters I'd met along the way. Friends of my daughter, Andrea (we call her AJ), and my son, John Jr. Friends of my wife, Margo. Just another night in New York City, where you can bump into just about anyone. Some of the guests had sex appeal, bringing glamour to the occasion. Some, like me, had *checks* appeal, willing and able to give to a worthy cause. Whoever you are, bring what you have—that's what I say!

Newt, who'd started his career as a history professor, gave a rousing speech about the first principles of our nation, tying those timeless concepts to the wild politics of today. To keep things balanced and interesting, he was then interrogated on stage by Sam Roberts, a terrific reporter from the *New York Times*. A woman from the National Park Service spoke about the staff's ambitious plans for the future of the memorial, and Donna McLarty, Mack's wife, reported on the ex-senators and ex-congressmen who were already signing on. The two women helped to focus the evening. Newt and Sam traded friendly jabs.

As I listened to all of this a few feet off the stage, an idea suddenly occurred to me.

We have some amazing people in this country of ours, yet we live at a deeply divided time. Virtually everything is sharply politicized. There's almost nothing everyone can agree on. But maybe we had a moment here. It seemed to me that we might.

When all the speeches were over, it was my turn to step on stage. I thanked everyone for coming. For what must have been the hundredth time, I marveled at the inspiration all around us. I didn't ask anyone for money or practical assistance. That would happen later, I knew. But I did make one request.

"What I'd like to do now," I said, "is I'd like to invite everyone to stand and join in singing 'God Bless America.'"

People don't normally sing at fancy social gatherings in New York City. I could see some of the guests looking at each other, slightly uncomfortable for a second or two. But only a second or two. What I was suggesting must have fit the mood and the venue. This was a special night and a special location. Wasn't Federal Hall where our country began to define itself? Wasn't George Washington's Bible right over there? In ways that still ought to matter, this piece of public real estate helped us figure out who and what we are as a nation.

I could hear feet shuffling. I could hear wooden chairs slide against a hard, dull floor. Then, in ones and twos and threes, people stood and smiled. And they started to sing.

"God bless America, land that I love."

I knew a little about the history of this stirring anthem. It was written by Irving Berlin, an immigrant not so different from me, who'd come to the United States from Russia at age five. Berlin wrote the words and music in 1918 while serving in the US Army at Camp Upton in Yaphank, New York, about sixty-five miles from Federal Hall. But he put the song aside because he didn't believe it fit well in *Yip Yip Yaphank,* a musical revue he was writing at the time. Not until 1938, with the rise of Adolf Hitler, did Berlin, who was Jewish, believe the time was right to resurrect the song. It was introduced by the singer Kate Smith on her radio program on Armistice Day.

I'm not sure how many of the people in Federal Hall knew that story. But they understood the feeling behind it, which was impossible not to share. Their voices filled the grand, domed hall.

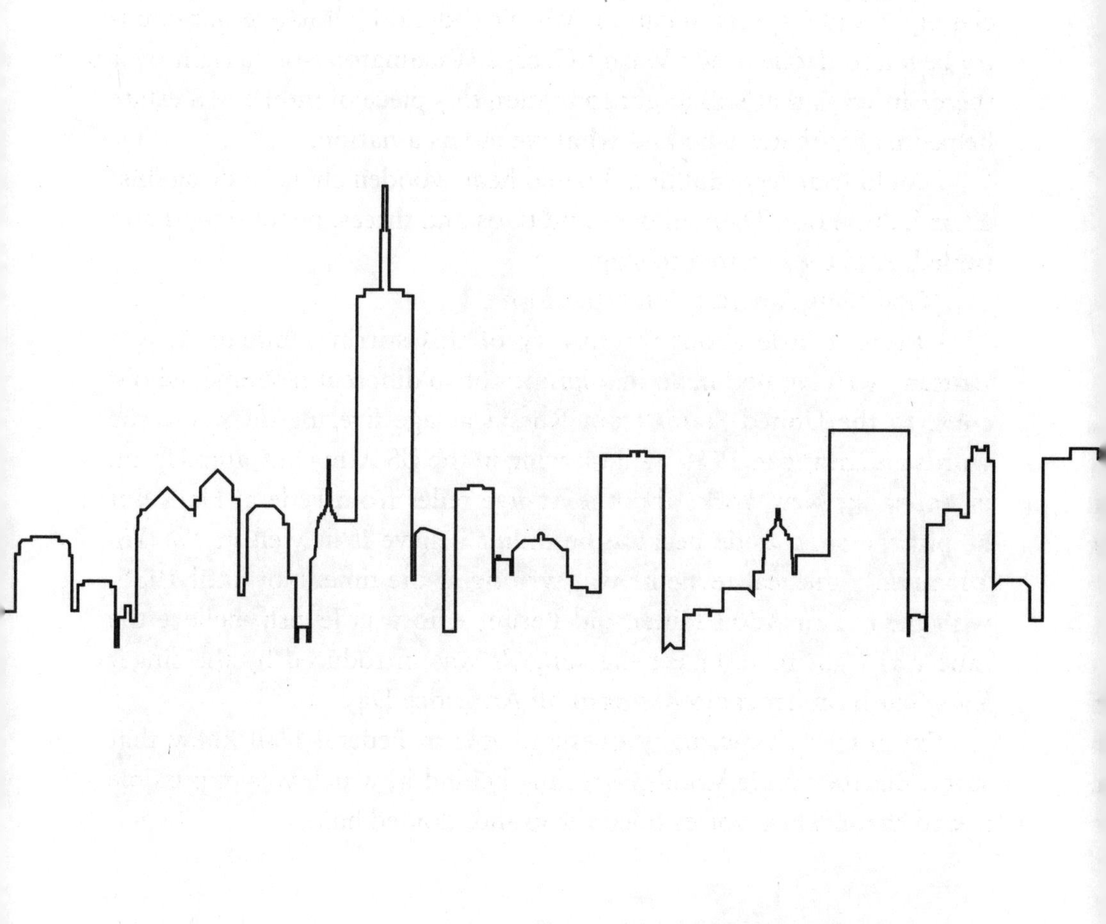

The lighthouse (top) and shoreline (bottom) of the island of Nisyros.

1

TELL ALL

I didn't speak a word of English when I first arrived in America.

Actually, I didn't speak a word of anything, unless you count "goo-goo-gaa-gaa" and a loud, piercing "waaaa!"

I was six months old.

Born on a tiny Greek island, traveling across the ocean, the circumstances were different back then, but the concept was the same: our dreams were what got us here. My parents never considered themselves poor or oppressed or downtrodden. Why should they have? They had ambition. They had hard work. They had each other. And they also had me, their first and only child, a brand-new generation to carry their dreams forward. America was the land of opportunity. Lucky for us, we were here.

That was the world I grew up in: twentieth-century immigrant New York. My life began with learning English; making friends; playing stoopball, stickball, and Johnny-on-a-Pony on the sidewalks of West Harlem. Obeying my parents and studying hard, like a dutiful child should. Climbing through public school and Greek school and all-boys Brooklyn Tech. Learning to hustle, learning to lead, picking up side jobs along the way. Buying my first car. Getting my college diploma—*almost*. Disappointing my parents by walking away from a promising professional career. Then turning a small grocery store into a sprawling New York empire that boasted some of supermarketing's proudest names. Discovering that I liked doing business and had a knack for it. Who knew? Expanding the business. Expanding the business some more. Meeting Father Alex and rediscovering what it means to be Greek. Realizing that the sunshine of my life was sitting right beside me. Starting a family with her. Getting into aviation, energy, real estate, insurance, and investments—and why stop there? Learning to count in millions, then in billions. Diving into politics. Getting to know congressmen, senators, and presidents—*really* getting to know them. Rising to the highest levels of the Democratic Party, then rising to the highest levels of the Republican Party (how many people can say that?). Giving millions and millions of dollars away. Thinking of running for mayor, then actually doing it. Constantly promoting new causes and favorite candidates and other things I care about. Convening the *Cats Roundtable* on the radio. And after all those years on the move, still trying to figure out exactly where I stand.

That's my story, and I'm sticking to it. In the pages that follow, I will share it all with you: the thrills, the excitement, the sense of adventure, and the wonderful people I have gotten to know and the distances all of us have come. There are twists and turns and lessons learned, and they are still flying at me. What a wonderful accident of geography and history: none of it could have happened anywhere but here and now. And I'm not done yet.

For a long time, people have been suggesting that I write a book, to tell *my* story *my* way—as only I can tell it.

"Your life is the stuff of drama and mythology," my friends keep saying to me.

"What kind of drama?" I ask. "Comedy or tragedy? What kind of mythology? Greek or American?"

Some of both, I'm sure. It's the tale of an immigrant pip-squeak, a scrappy city kid who reaches the highest heights of the American Dream and still keeps reaching for more. I've engaged with some fascinating people and made some beautiful friends. I have countless stories to tell. Some of them, I know, are genuinely inspiring. I've seen the looks on the faces of children and adults, and sometimes even reporters, when

I lay this stuff out. God knows my mind is constantly racing forward, always filled to the brim.

But if I'm going to tell my story right, I figure I might also sound an alarm about some things that need fixing. I don't like how divided our nation is—the way liberals talk only to liberals, conservatives talk only to conservatives, and both sides refuse to listen. That's no way to do democracy right. It certainly wasn't the vision created by my Greek ancestors or spelled out at Federal Hall. I understand where the conservatives are coming from. Getting the government out of people's business. Enhancing the values of hard work and opportunity. But, come on, guys—you gotta have a heart! And I understand where the liberals are coming from. Looking out for those who are still struggling. Trying to give everyone a fighting chance in life. But you can't wreck the system that created the wealth you are so eager to redistribute! Both those outlooks have worthwhile insights and policies to share. These days, I don't think of myself as a Democrat or a Republican. I'm just a common-sense billionaire.

I had a dream the other night. I was a character in the movie *Planet of the Apes,* the original and still the best of the series. I was walking along a river. I wasn't sure where I was. Crazy stuff was happening all around me. Then I looked up and saw the Statue of Liberty. I knew I was in New York, the center of everything, that place of endless possibilities, where the future really does live in your head and your hands. That image focused me. It motivated me. I knew it was time to take care of business, time to get busy writing this book.

Snatches of my story have been written here and there, in newspapers, magazines, and business reports. My name pops up in gossip columns and on the *Forbes* richest lists. And yet none of that coverage has ever quite captured the story right. Not the story behind the story. It's never been told the way it should. But now, it will.

"The unexamined life is not worth living," the ancient Greek philosopher Socrates supposedly said. The truth is we don't know if Socrates really said that. The great teacher didn't write anything down. All we have to go by are the reports from Plato and other star students. But I'm inclined to believe what they say. I like examining things, my own life included. That's how I improve myself. That's what I've always done: look at the situation, whatever it is, turn my brainpower on it, and then try to solve the issues that I find. That's how I built my businesses. That's how I've run my life.

The American Dream, I discovered somewhere along the way, doesn't come with an instruction manual or a page at the end that says, "Okay, you can stop now. You have arrived." I know my copy doesn't. I've done a lot and seen even more. But I'm still that immigrant kid who thinks this is the greatest country ever. I still believe in the promise of America. I still believe the best is yet to come. But I'm getting ahead of myself already. This story doesn't start in New York City or Washington. It doesn't start in a supermarket. It doesn't start with Republicans or Democrats. It starts in the middle of the Aegean Sea, in the turquoise waters between the lands of Greece and Turkey, a long, long time ago.

Hold on tight now. The wild journey begins.

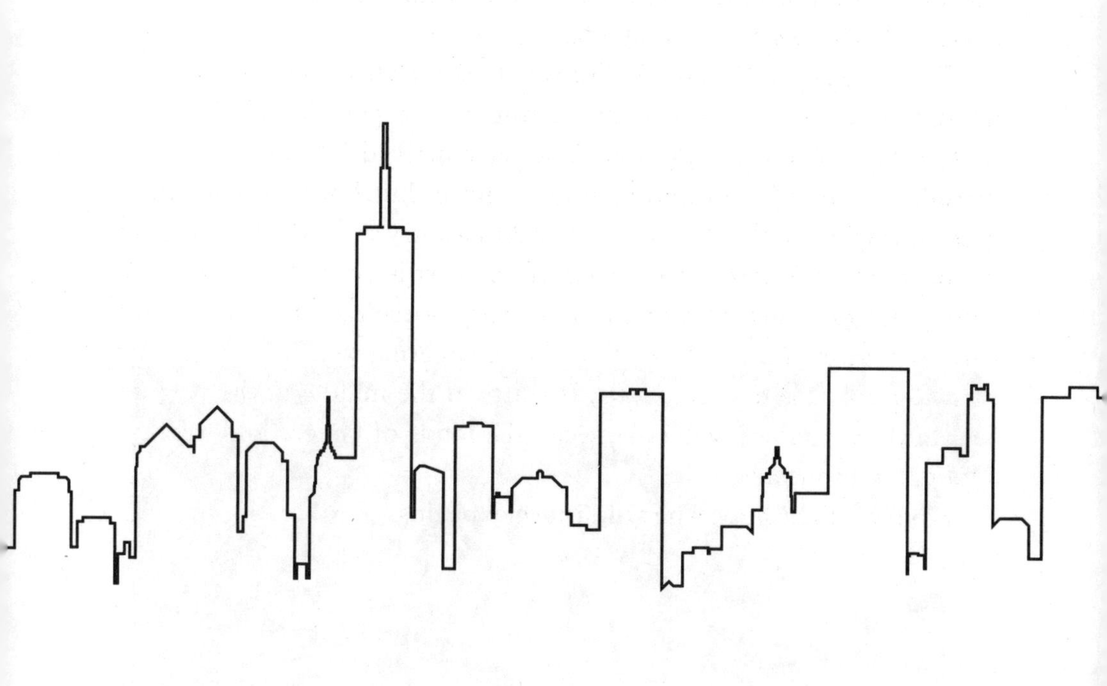

The wedding of Andreas and Despina Catsimatidis on the island of Nisyros in 1947.

2

LUCKY STRIKE

The Greeks have stories to explain everything, and I do mean *everything*.

There's a famous story in Greek mythology about Nisyros, the rugged but beautiful little island in the Aegean Sea where I was born. The hero of this story is Poseidon, the fearless god of the sea. During the epic battle between the gods and the Titans, Poseidon frantically chases after the giant Polyvotis, finally catching up with him on the island of Kos. It is there, in a flash of righteous fury and fortunate aim, that Poseidon supposedly chops off part of Kos with his three-pronged trident and hurls the chunk of rock and earth at Polyvotis, smacking the fleeing giant in the back of the head and sinking him to the bottom of the sea.

Poseidon's lucky strike became Nisyros.

Believe that story if you want to. Many Nisyrians swear it's the honest truth. All these centuries later, the locals will tell you they can still hear the defeated giant sighing inside the island's still-active volcano, which of course everyone calls Polyvotis after its eternal and unwilling inhabitant. Poor giant!

That volcano—the flames, the heat, the smoke, the tar-and-ash aroma—looms over everything and everyone on Nisyros. Always has and always will. The volcano isn't currently spewing lava, but it has erupted at least thirteen times in recorded history. It's also a cause of the island's many earthquakes. With an active volcano on such a small island, it's impossible to forget how powerful nature is and how unpredictable life can be. Clearly, some forces greater than ourselves influence our destinies.

Life is just different when you come from an island like that.

Nisyros is far less developed than the Greek islands you've probably seen in person or on tourist web sites. Barely five miles across, it is part of a chain of small islands, the Dodecanese, scattered like pepper flakes between the vibrant coasts of Greece and Turkey. There's a small harbor, some cliffs, and a few modest farms. The unspoiled terrain is dotted with churches, forts, small white houses with blue windows, and, along the seventeen-mile coastline, a handful of small tavernas serving fresh squid, octopus, and other delicious creatures pulled that morning from the sea. Everybody knows everybody.

The people of Nisyros love their island, but they don't like change. "We want our island the way it's always been," they say, and they mean it. The population has shrunk over the decades as people have migrated, mostly to America. But other than that, Nisyros has stayed pretty much the same. The people fish and farm and love talking with friends and family late into the night.

The island has had a tumultuous history, and that makes the people appreciate the calm and quiet even more. The Minoans, the Mycenaeans, the Dorians, the Persians, the Athenians—they all took turns invading and occupying Nisyros and the other islands of the Dodecanese. So did Alexander the Great, whose powerful armies arrived in 332 BC and hung around until 164 BC, when the growing Roman Empire finally shoved them aside. Compared to Alexander, the Romans were almost gentlemen. Soon after the death of Jesus, Saint Paul and Saint John brought Christianity to the region, where the new religion quickly took hold. Doubt that? Try counting all the Byzantine churches on Nisyros. It's a big number. I promise you that.

Next came the Turkish army of Suleiman the Magnificent. He didn't look so magnificent to the local folks in the 1520s when he overran the whole island chain, instituting nearly four centuries of iron-fisted Ottoman rule. The Italians grabbed the islands back in 1912.

When World War I broke out, Greece and Italy found themselves on the same side as France, the United Kingdom, and the United States. The Italians even invited France and the United Kingdom to use the islands as a staging area for naval operations—and, thankfully, the Allies won. World War II didn't unfold so well, however. After Italy invaded Greece in October 1940, the Greek army pushed the invading Italians back into Albania. But the Nazis roared the following April, overrunning the Greek defenses in just a few weeks. And though Italy surrendered to the Allied powers in September 1943, the Italian occupiers didn't leave the islands immediately. They liked it there. It wasn't until years later that the British tossed out the Italian occupiers, finally returning Nisyros and the other Dodecanese islands to their rightful owner and protector: the proud republic of Greece.

I don't remember any of this firsthand, not even our island's long-awaited liberation and return to Greece. I was inside my mother's belly that spring. But I'm pretty sure, even from my warm and cozy spot, I could hear the church bells peal. That's why, all these years later, I still like to joke that I was conceived an Italian and born a Greek. Given the way the calendar fell, that's no lie. In early December 1947, when my mother became pregnant with me, Nisyros was still in the hands of the Italians. Nine months later, on September 7, 1948, when I finally burst into the world, kicking and screaming and wondering, *What's for lunch?*—our island had been liberated by the British and was finally, officially Greek, as was I.

A few hours after I was born, my father, Andreas Catsimatidis, took me to the house of his mother, who hadn't been well. He carried me into the bedroom and handed me to my *Ya-Ya,* which is what Greek children call their grandmothers. Without a word of prompting, she said to my father, "A new Yiánni Catsimatidis is born." That was her late husband's name, Yiánni—Greek for John. And that night, my grandmother died. That very night. She was happy the whole day long.

Those are the kinds of people I come from. Their lives are truly the stuff of sweeping narrative.

My mother's name before she got married was Despina Emmanouilidis. She often went by the nickname Despo. Her family, like my father's, had deep roots in Nisyros, though my mother's upbringing was very different from my father's. My father's family members were simple island people—fishermen, farmers, carpenters, other tradesmen—who worked hard and mostly stayed put on Nisyros. My mother's family, on the other hand, moved back and forth between the quiet island and the more cosmopolitan Turkish city of Constantinople, modern-day Istanbul. Educated and relatively well-to-do, the Emmanouilidises had close ties to the Greek Orthodox Church. My great-great-grandfather on my mother's side was a chancellor of the Ecumenical Patriarchate of Constantinople, a top aide to the leader of the world's Orthodox people. His son, my great-grandfather, John Zannis, was an Orthodox priest. My great-grandfather and his wife, Despina, whose name my mother would later take, had three daughters—my grandmother Irene and her two sisters, Marigo and Eftihia—along with their brother, Nickolas. But life for Turkey's Greek minority grew tense. A lot of wild charges were being thrown around. My great-grandfather was accused of being a terrorist. He was no terrorist—he was a dedicated parish priest defending his Greek flock at a time of intense prejudice. But when things grew unbearable, he fled with family to Nisyros, finding peace and safety on the quiet island of their ancestors.

You know the song "If I Were a Carpenter"? My grandmother, Irene Zannis, married a hardworking young carpenter from Nisyros. Emmanuel Emmanouilidis was the carpenter's name, and she loved him dearly. They had three children—my mother Despina and her two brothers, Charalambos and Yiánni, also known as Harry and John. The island was as starkly beautiful as ever. But there were few good jobs there, especially for a young man who needed to support three children and a wife with tastes etched in Constantinople. Fortunately, there was another option. In those years, many young men from Nisyros were leaving the island—not for Turkey, but for the promised land of America. There, not only were the factories hiring, but so were the ports, restaurants, and construction companies. Anyone willing to work hard, it was said, could land a job in America, live cheaply with other Greek immigrants, and send plenty of extra money back home.

Young Emmanuel decided to make the trip. He already had two brothers in New York City who agreed to sponsor him. He could stay with them until he got settled, and they would help him find work.

And so my grandfather went.

After a tearful goodbye at the dock in Nisyros, he boarded a small boat to Kos and then a slightly larger boat to the larger island of Rhodes and then on to Athens, where he boarded an ocean-going passenger ship bound for New York. His wife and children missed him immensely, but even the young ones understood. Papa was gone for the good of the family. He'd send much-needed money and be back as soon as he could. Maybe one day before long, he would even gather up the family and they could join him in America. But until that time came, Grandma Irene and her three children would carry on as best they could. My grandmother was a real matriarch, a proud and serious woman who considered it her duty to keep a tidy home, provide clear guidance for the children, and hold her head up high. She wasn't the only one with these such burdens, and she wasn't one to complain.

Soon enough, just as she expected, an envelope arrived on the mail boat.

Inside the envelope was a wad of American money, enough to get my grandmother and her children through the month. But there was something else in the envelope. It was a postcard from America with a glimmering photo of New York Harbor and the famous Statue of Liberty. But, oddly, nothing was written on the back of the card, and no note was inside.

My grandmother wasn't quite sure what to make of that. Why didn't her husband tell her how he was doing or what kind of work he had found? He was never a strong writer, but it was still strange. In any case, she didn't have much time to worry over it. She was too busy raising her children and getting through the day.

Then, almost exactly a month later, another envelope arrived.

Another wad of American money. Another Statue of Liberty post-card. No note, no signature, and no return address.

A month after that, a third envelope came on the mail boat. Same thing. By then, people on the island were talking. Nisyros is not a place of many secrets. My grandmother didn't like talking about the envelopes from America or the mystery of her husband's life there. God forbid the family name be tarnished. She made it her business to say that everything was fine. Her husband was off in America, supporting his family on Nisyros—what else did they need to know? She smiled and shrugged and got on with her business and dreaded the questions when they came up.

And so it went, month after month, year after year. Money, a postcard, and that was all.

Of course, there were whispers around the island, and my grandmother heard some of them. Maybe her husband was part of *nýfes tis nýchtas,* the Greek Mafia in America, the so-called "godfathers of the night." Maybe he'd married another woman across the ocean and didn't want his first wife to know. In times of stress, the imagination can run. Anything was possible, my grandmother knew, but she chose to not dwell on it.

She missed her husband. She focused on raising her daughter and her sons. She would keep the family together, whatever that might mean.

....

As the years rolled on, my grandmother Irene sent my mother to high school and then to the big island, Rhodes, for college, where she studied to be an elementary school teacher. These were the years between the two world wars. The islands were under the rule of the Italians. As my mother was studying to be a teacher, she met a young man who was a friend of her brother Charalmbos. She and this boy immediately hit it off. As she studied education in Rhodes, he dreamed of studying law in Athens. He wasn't from a wealthy family, but he was smart as a whip. She knew he would make a talented lawyer. She wasn't earning money of her own yet, but she had some jewelry she'd gotten from her mother. Piece by piece, she sold the rings and the necklaces, gladly sharing the money to help pay her true love's law school bills.

They wrote love letters back and forth, sharing their dreams of the day they would finally be reunited. When he began his apprenticeship with a prominent lawyer in Rhodes, she knew that day was coming soon. Finally, they decided to marry. They set a date for a big engagement party, a Greek tradition that can be almost as lavish and high-spirited as the wedding itself.

When the day finally came, the house had been painted. The musicians had arrived. The drinks were already flowing. The food was out. The guests were laughing and talking and greeting each other. A few had even begun to dance. Despina's youngest brother, Yiánni, was dispatched to the dock to wait for the future groom to arrive.

But when the boat reached the island, the groom was not on board. Instead, the captain handed a letter to Yiánni. "This is for your sister," the boat captain said. "Do not read; just deliver."

The young brother understood immediately what a bad turn this was. He hated to imagine the reaction he was about to receive. But he knew he had to walk back to the house and deliver the letter, and that is what he did.

News on Nisyros has a way of traveling faster than life does. By the time Yiánni reached the house, word of the absent groom had somehow beaten him there. The guests looked stricken. The musicians lowered their instruments. It seemed that even they could tell something was wrong. When the bride's brother walked into the living room alone, everyone understood.

He handed the unopened letter to his sister, just as the boat captain asked him to. She said nothing. The ashen look on her face said it all. She opened the envelope and slid the letter out. She couldn't possibly have read more than a line or two.

"Dear Despina," the letter said, "I am sorry to tell you that there will be no wedding. I have met someone else. She is the daughter of the lawyer I have been working for in Rhodes. I am very sorry to tell you this."

Somewhere around the second or third sentence, my mother collapsed on the floor. She was helped into her bedroom, where she lowered the curtains, shut the door, and, so the family story has it, did not emerge for more than a year.

. . . .

On an island as small as Nisyros, among a people so insular, there are not many choices in the search for love. Sometimes magic happens, and two people will find each other, thrilled at their good fortune and matched for life. Usually, however, the families—by which I mean the mothers—push the process along. Sometimes that produces happiness and sometimes not, though it must be noted that no system triumphs 100 percent of the time.

But a case like Despina's offered special challenges for my grandmother. For one thing, her daughter had wasted a lot of time on a suitor who turned out to be unreliable. She wasn't getting any younger. And there was another very real issue: Despina was her mother's only daughter, and the oldest child, too. According to the customs of the island, until she married, none of her younger siblings could. Despina didn't have any younger sisters, but she did have two brothers, both of whom had fiancées by then and were eager to get married. Now, all they could do was wait.

And that wasn't the end of it. Since those two couples couldn't marry, neither could the fiancées' brothers. As everyone on this very small island quickly calculated, Despina and her self-imposed solitude were standing in the way of at least ten identifiable weddings, freezing the lives of those couples tragically in place.

People were understanding at first. But as the months rolled on and a year turned into two, the injustice of the situation became increasingly unbearable. Finally, my grandmother spoke up.

"You have a choice," she told her daughter. "You can't stay like this forever."

Then she laid the options out.

"You can go into the convent," she told her daughter.

No sound came out of Despina's mouth, but her face held a silent gasp as her mother pressed on. "If a girl has a religious vocation, that relieves her of the obligation to marry. If you become a nun, your brothers can marry, and so can all the others waiting in line."

My grandmother took a breath and continued.

"There is, however, another possibility," she said. "I have identified a man you can marry if you would like to do that. His name is Andreas Catsimatidis. His family comes from Nisyros. They are good people. We know them. For sixteen years, since 1931, young Andreas has lived by himself on a small island in the sea. The island is called Kandelioussa. He tended a lighthouse there."

The island, which the Italians controlled until they were evicted by the British, was really just a piece of rock in the water, completely uninhabited except for this man and some goats. "He fished for his food," my grandmother said. "A boat would come by every so often and deliver supplies to him. With the money he earned, he helped to support his sisters, Calliope, Anna, and Eftihia, and other family members, too. Sixteen years is a very long time."

Now that that the Italians were gone, my grandmother said, he was back on Nisyros and ready to take a wife. "I must tell you," my grandmother cautioned. "He is not your social equal. Nor your educational equal. But he is a good man, and he will be a good husband to you."

Despina just stared and said nothing for a moment, weighing the two options laid out for her: life in a nunnery or life with the lighthouse man. "I will marry the lighthouse man," she said.

Plans were made quickly. Houses all over Nisyros were painted and decorated. Massive platters of food were cooked and brought in.

And for eleven weekends that fall, weddings were held in churches all over the island.

Despina looked beautiful in her wedding dress. Her groom, Andreas, received a gray wool wedding suit from his brother in America. Each of the brides following my mother would get her own white dress, but that gray suit was passed on, one by one, to the next ten grooms. Sleeves were shortened. Sleeves were let out. Torsos were tightened. Torsos were released.

Whatever it took to get those grooms and their patient brides down the aisle—that is exactly what occurred that fall.

My mother's story, recounted in the book *Eleven Weddings and a Sacrifice*, became a bestseller in Greece.

Top: John Catsimatidis with his mother, Despina, and father, Andreas.
Bottom: John Catsimatidis's father, Andreas Catsimatidis, when he was a chef at Longchamps restaurant in New York City.

3

CITY KID

When my father was up in years, I brought him to visit Ellis Island, the legend-ary immigrant-receiving center in New York Harbor, just north of the Statue of Liberty. From 1892 until 1954, twelve million men, women, and children passed through that bustling facility, the final stop on their often-perilous journeys to brand-new lives in what to them really was the New World.

It had been many decades since my father had made the bold decision to leave tiny Nisyros and travel with my mother and me to America. But I knew hardly anything about the journey that had gotten us here. I thought that taking my dad to Ellis Island might spark some memories. I certainly didn't remember the trip myself. I just knew what a special place Ellis Island was for many immigrants of my father's generation: truly sacred ground.

"Pop," I said, as we stood in the island's dazzling Great Hall, now the centerpiece of an immigration museum. "Look around. Does any of this look familiar to you?"

My father shot me one of those glances that fathers sometimes direct at their sons—half loving and indulgent, half *Don't you know anything?*

"What do you want from me?" he asked. "I've never been here before in my life. We came through Idlewild," he said, using an old name for the John F. Kennedy International Airport.

As my father patiently explained, I was six months old when he gathered up my mother and me. We took a boat from Nisyros to Athens. From Athens, we flew to London, where we had to go through our first round of immigration clearance.

Finding our papers in order, the British officials put us through a medical screening to make sure we were also in good health. This included a smallpox vaccination for little me. Unfortunately, the nurse made a mistake and gave me an adult dose of the vaccine, ten times what an infant is supposed to receive. My tiny body reacted violently. I had trouble breathing. My temperature shot up to 105 degrees F. I started turning an eerie shade of blue. My parents panicked, my mother especially. It seemed their little angel would never make it to America.

I was pumped full of fluids. Frantic doctors and nurses hovered around. My mother did her best to restrain her hysteria. And then, incredibly, everything was all right. My fever subsided. My breathing returned to normal. My color came back. I was smiling and giggling and ready for our next flight. The crisis passed. Deep down, I must have had a strong inner constitution, and no amount of medical malpractice could stop me. So off we went to New York.

Just not directly. They didn't have so many nonstop flights across the Atlantic in those days. We traveled first to Montreal, a flight that kept us in the air for more than fifteen hours. In Montreal, our papers were checked again—no more inoculations, thank God. Then we were allowed to board our final flight, the one to what was officially named New York International Airport but that everyone called Idlewild after the Idlewild Beach Golf Course whose property the new airport was built on.

Our journey from Nisyros to New York City hadn't been an easy one. After all, I'd almost died in London. But on balance, it was a whole lot quicker and a lot more comfortable than the nightmarish, high-seas adventures that many immigrants were forced to endure, though they may have had stirring memories of Ellis Island that my parents did not. Ultimately, the most important thing was that we had finally arrived. Our papers were stamped one last time, this time by US immigration personnel. We made our way into the international arrivals terminal. And our new lives as Americans were finally about to begin.

"It was an amazing feeling," my father assured me that day on Ellis Island as he filled in some of the missing details. "I was just so happy to be in America. Your mother was, too. I don't think you had any idea where you were. But you knew you were somewhere special. I could tell. You were looking around with those big brown eyes of yours. Even you could tell we had arrived."

....

In America, almost everybody came from someplace else. My parents' reason for coming to America will sound familiar to anyone whose family didn't arrive on the *Mayflower*. It might even sound familiar to the descendants of America's very first immigrants. Life was tough back home, and they dreamed of a brighter future in the land of opportunity. Greece was still pulling itself up from the aftermath of World War II. On our little island, job prospects were just about nil. My father couldn't count on the Italians anymore as he had in his lighthouse days. So my parents followed the same dream that had lured generations of immigrants to the Land of the Free, the same dream that is still attracting immigrants to America today. My father's father, Yiánni Catsimatidis, had made the trip in 1913. Two of his brothers—his older brother, Nick, and his younger brother, George—had come in the 1920s, even as the United States enacted immigration acts limiting the number of Greek newcomers. His older sister, Calliope, and younger sister, Anna, had left Piraeus in Greece aboard the SS *Vulcania* and arrived in America three weeks later on February 10, 1948. Many other men and some women from Nisyros had also come. My father's brothers and sisters had been urging him to join them. They convinced him that America was the future, a place of endless possibilities, a genuine place of opportunity for those who dared to come.

In those days, someone had to sponsor you, promising to cover the rent if you didn't pay it and be responsible for you. Nick and George agreed to sign on the dotted line. My father didn't have a job lined up, but I don't think his brothers were too worried about his work ethic or his sense of responsibility toward my mother and me. He was the kind of man who would do whatever was necessary—and I do mean *whatever*—to take care of his family.

His brothers had already found us a three-bedroom apartment in a walk-up at 512 West 1Thirty-Fifth Street in the West Harlem neighborhood in Upper Manhattan. Uncle George lived in the same building. Uncle Nick lived in the building next door. The rent was $47 a month, and if the landlord had tried to raise it to $48, I promise you my father would have started World War III. My father went looking for work right away.

There wasn't much call for lighthouse tenders in New York City in the late 1940s—or non-English-speaking carpenters. My father spoke fluent Greek and Italian but knew hardly any English at all. Still, he was willing to start wherever he had to, and that is what he did. He applied for a job at Longchamps, a white-tablecloth restaurant on Lexington Avenue and Forty-Second Street across from Grand Central Terminal, and got the only position he qualified for: busboy. But he didn't complain. He was happy to be in America, happy to have a job (or two), and happy to be getting on with our new lives.

My father would leave home every weekday morning at ten o'clock and ride the subway to Forty-Second Street. He'd work the lunch rush and the dinner rush, then be back home late, usually by ten or ten thirty at night. It was a long day, but that's how it went every Monday to Friday. Then, on Saturdays and Sundays, he worked as a waiter in the Italian restaurants of Astoria, Queens. The owners there, like most of the patrons and other employees, were from Greece or Italy. My father didn't need to speak English to take orders or communicate with the kitchen help. The one thing he didn't know, however, was the meaning of a day off. The same way my father had dedicated himself to supporting his family in Greece, toiling away on that lonely lighthouse island—that's how he took care of my mother and me. To say he "lived up to his responsibilities" is a completely inadequate description. He gave us his everything.

My father was always looking for ways to earn or save a buck. He rented the third bedroom of our apartment to another new immigrant from Nisyros. Dino Ralis, our tenant, would go on to build a major insurance agency in Astoria, Queens. But when he first arrived in New York City, Dino lived with us. He paid my father $8 a week, which included my mother's home-cooked meals. "What's the difference?" my mother asked with a shrug. "Feed three people? Feed four people?" It was all the same to her. And Dino's money covered more than half the monthly rent.

That was the kind of family we were.

We lived frugally. My mother made sure of that. She made soap in the bathtub. She made her own Greek yogurt, just like she had back home. I suppose you would have called us poor. I can see that now. But I certainly had no sense that we were deprived in any way. I don't think my parents did, either. We always had food on the table. And there was never, ever a time that any of us went to bed hungry. That was a point of pride for my father. We didn't live any differently from the way our neighbors did or my father's brothers did—or the way anyone else in our little universe on West 1Thirty-Fifth Street did, for that matter. We were in a new country. We were living new lives. The future looked bright.

One of my very first memories is of my father taking me to Grant's Tomb on Riverside Drive and 122nd Street. President Dwight Eisenhower was there that day. The great World War II general who was elected to be America's thirty-fourth president was honoring Ulysses S. Grant, the great Civil War general who became the nation's eighteenth president. I had no idea about any of that history. But I understood that my father considered it important, and a huge crowd turned out that day. There would be other days that would stand out, but mostly what I remember about my father was that he was almost always at work. Meanwhile, my mother took care of everything at home, including me. How much did my mother love me? Like only a mother who had struggled through heartache could. After she and my father got married, they were eager to start a family. They figured they had waited long enough. By then, my mother was thirty-seven years old.

My mother never discussed those past difficulties when I was a child, but she always behaved like a woman who was deeply, deeply grateful that her dream of being a mother had finally come true. Her love for me was infinite and never ending.

She peeled my grapes. That's no exaggeration. When I was a boy, she peeled my grapes so I wouldn't have to peel them myself.

Literally, she peeled my grapes.

I know that sounds over the top today. But in our family, that's what it was like being the only child of Andreas and Despina Catsimatidis. My mother didn't work outside the home. Her twenty-four-hours-a-day responsibility was taking care of my father and me. My father used to tell a story to illustrate how dedicated to me my mother was. It isn't a true story—I don't think so, anyway—but in it, a mother has a very bad son—so bad, in fact, that he is about to chop off his mother's head. As the young brute raises his long-blade knife and prepares to swing, his mother gently admonishes him: "Be careful, my son. Don't cut your hand."

My mother would laugh at the story, but she never denied that it made a certain kind of sense.

She played with me in Riverside Park. We went for walks on the campus of City College, which was just down the block from us. It is fair to say she was an overprotective mother, but that was her way of showing love. Sometimes we took the subway to visit my father during his midafternoon breaks from work. The three of us would meet at a Horn & Hardart automat down the block from Longchamps. I'd have a Coca-Cola and a peanut-butter-and-jelly sandwich for a grand total of twenty-five cents. Afterward, we'd sit at a table in the half-empty restaurant and just talk. Those were big days for us. It was like my mother and father were dating again, and I got to come along. For me, those afternoons were special.

The one thing my parents never did was look back. As far as they were concerned, Greece was the past. America was the present and the future. That's how things were going to stay. Language was the barrier the three of us had to overcome whenever we left the apartment. At home, my parents spoke Greek to each other and to me. They called me Yiánni. Sometimes, when they didn't want me to understand what they were saying, they used a dialect from Nisyros that had elements of Greek, Italian, and Turkish. The words sounded to my young ears like "a-fi-de-foe-da-fa." If I weren't Greek, I might say it sounded like Greek to me. It left me slow to learn English.

What little English I knew, I was picking up from the cartoons and other shows I watched on a five-inch, black-and-white Emerson TV in the living room. I learned English from Daffy Duck, Popeye, Bugs Bunny, Dick Tracy, Koko the Clown, and the puppets Kukla, Fran, and Ollie. They may not have been official New York City public school teachers. But they got me talking, and I am forever grateful to them for that.

When I was five years old, I started kindergarten at PS 192, the Jacob H. Schiff School. The school was named after a German-born banker and philanthropist, an immigrant from an earlier generation whose granddaughter, Dorothy Schiff, was the owner and then publisher of the *New York Post*. The building was on West 138th Street, across from City College's Lewisohn Stadium, a grand-looking amphitheater with Doric columns that looked like it could have easily stood in Greece. The school's slogan was aimed at human uplift: "Never let it rest until our good gets better and our better gets best."

At PS 192, I wasn't Yiánni anymore. I was John. There were hardly any other Greeks in our school, but there were plenty of other immigrants, Irish and Italians especially. At that time, Spanish speakers—mainly Puerto Ricans and Dominicans—had also begun to move in. I was a skinny kid with a shock of thick, black hair and a bundle of insecurities. Insecure that I wasn't smart enough. Insecure that my English wasn't good enough. Insecure that the other kids had more and knew more than I did. Insecure that I didn't really belong. Lots of children feel that way, immigrant children especially. I know that now. But at the time, being just five, I didn't look at the other kids as fellow immigrants with similar worries about not fitting in. I thought I was the only one.

Embarrassment can be an overwhelmingly powerful emotion when you are young. For me, there were some uncomfortable moments when I didn't understand things. Even today, I am amazed at how deeply those moments affected me, so much that I can still conjure them up vividly in my head. During an Easter egg hunt in the school yard, I took eggs from the wrong spot, and the teacher yelled at me. I didn't mean to cheat. I just didn't know. Another day, in first grade, I was accosted by three older boys on my way into school. They didn't have any weapons. But they grabbed me and took the fifteen cents I had in my pocket to buy lunch. When I got to the school, I was crying. My teacher asked what was wrong, and I explained as well as I could.

"Were the boys colored?" my teacher asked me.

"No," I said.

"Were they Spanish?"

"No," I said.

These were the questions she asked.

"Were they oriental?" she continued.

"No."

"Were they White?"

"No."

My teacher looked totally confused. "What were they then?" she said.

"They were Black," I said, not understanding, with my limited grasp of English, that "colored," at that time, was another word for "Black."

My family was certainly tight, but I wasn't raised to be especially prejudiced. In West Harlem, we were surrounded by all of God's creatures, people of every imaginable race, religious belief, and ethnic group. Everyone's family was a little different, but I wasn't taught to look down or look up at anyone. To my eyes, we were all the same even though we did look different. There was nothing wrong with that. It was just a fact. Blond hair, brown hair, brown skin, white skin—what difference did that make? They were just trying to get through life, pretty much like we were. My public elementary school turned out to be an ideal place for me to face my insecurities and find my own place in the great human diversity that was mid-twentieth-century New York.

I was always a bright kid, despite my shaky English, and I actually got pretty good grades. I was never in major trouble. Talking in class,

backgrounds and stories similar to mine. It wasn't that I felt uncomfortable in public school. But these kids were almost like family. We studied together, played together, sang in the choir together, and rode the bus together. We were rarely apart. It was like having a roomful of brothers and sisters, something I wasn't used to as an only child. It stuck with me. I knew almost immediately: many of those boys and girls would remain my friends forever. I wasn't a good baseball or football player. I wasn't the most handsome boy in the class or the most charming. I was none of that. At that age, I was still worried about people liking me. But I was as much a part of the class as anyone, and that gave me a genuine sense of belonging. It was like these were my people, and I had come home.

Everything at GAI went according to a careful routine. From nine o'clock to noon, we learned in English. Then we had lunch. From one to four, we were taught in Greek. The curriculum was definitely more demanding than in public school. The teachers—Mr. Olson for fifth grade, Mr. McDonald for sixth grade, Mrs. Panagiotapolis for seventh and eighth grades—believed in homework, drills, memorization, and writing essays. They really did teach us to think and to learn. And it stuck with most of us.

Of the thirty boys and girls in my class at the Greek American Institute, I am still in touch with all but one or two today.

Our teachers weren't overly preachy. That wasn't the Greek Orthodox way. But religion was definitely part of the curriculum at our school. No one ever suggested I might have found a vocation—I was never going to be a priest—but when we were in seventh grade and twelve years old, my classmate John Bilious and I did sign up to be altar boys at Annunciation Greek Orthodox Church on West End Avenue and West Ninety-First Street. The church was originally built for Presbyterians in the early 1890s with its square-corner bell tower, four illuminated clock faces, and gargoyle gutter-spouts. When the Greeks took over in 1952, they'd made it their own, preserving the John La Farge stained glass and the 1,200-seat sanctuary but adorning the walls with saintly portraits and icons. Serving Mass there could be intimidating.

I don't believe John and I were ever recognized for our extraordinary piety or our careful attention to ecclesiastic detail. But we wore snappy robes and belts and learned the basic altar-boy moves. And there was one day I can never forget. We were doing well enough at Mass on this Sunday morning. We walked behind the Holy Table, not in front of it. We carried the lighted candles and the lanterns at the appointed times. When we passed the large crucifix, we were sure to always make the sign of the cross. But as the priest droned on and on in his Epistle and Gospel readings and his never-ending homily, the tedium was simply unbearable. John and I were bored out of our skulls, not to mention hungry. Neither one of us had eaten breakfast yet.

As the priest was reciting the Creed and we were supposed to be cutting up the bread for Communion, John and I were eating the loaf instead, one small slice at a time. Cutting. Eating. Cutting. Eating. Until almost all the bread was gone.

When the priest finally said, "*Proskomen, ta Agia tis Agiis*" (Let us attend the Holy Gifts for the holy people of God), there were no such Holy Gifts for the faithful to attend. John and I had eaten them.

When the priest realized what we had done, he was not one bit understanding. It was all he could do to refrain from reaming us out in front of everyone. He rushed through the end of the service and then fired us both as altar boys. But he did hire us back. Good altar boys, even hungry ones, were hard to find.

John and I stayed friends for years after that, and not just because of that memorable experience. He was a fun, warm-hearted boy, the only member of our GAI class who's passed away so far.

....

Even as a kid, I was interested in business. I would read the stock table in the newspaper along with the baseball box scores and joke with my father: "I'm going to become a millionaire." I'd also say, "I am going to become a pilot, a *pilótos*."

My father got a kick out of that. In Greek, many words sound almost the same. Instead of saying I was going to become an *aéro pilótos*, he would substitute *aero* for *aério*, which is Greek for passing gas. He would tell everyone I'd be a farter when I grew up. That drew major laughs around our living room.

I couldn't stay at the Greek school forever. In the fall of 1961, soon after I started eighth grade, my teacher told me I should think about applying to Brooklyn Technical High School, an academically rigorous all-boys public school in the borough's Fort Greene neighborhood. "Your English and language skills aren't the greatest," she told me, "but you are very strong in math and science. Brooklyn Tech would be a good place for you." To their credit, the teachers at the Greek school really did take an individual interest in each of the students.

But you couldn't just go to Brooklyn Tech, where the curriculum focused on science, technology, engineering, and math. Along with Stuyvesant High School and the Bronx High School of Science, Brooklyn Tech was one of the most selective public high schools in New York City—maybe even in the nation. To get in, you had to pass the SHSAT, the Specialized High Schools Admissions Test. Most people who applied weren't going to be admitted. But those that were would often go to Ivy League colleges and other prestigious universities after graduation.

Six of us at the Greek school took the exam in hopes of being admitted to Brooklyn Tech. The other five were all accepted immediately, a tribute to our school's rigorous standards. I got a letter from the Brooklyn Tech admissions office that said, "Thanks, but no thanks." The letter did mention something about a waiting list, however.

It wasn't that I'd been so focused on attending Brooklyn Tech. George Washington High School was on Audubon Avenue and West 193rd Street, a much shorter subway ride than going all the way to Brooklyn. But when my five friends got in and I didn't, I was devastated. Everyone would find out, I knew. The whole thing would be humiliating.

Then my Uncle Nick had an idea. He reminded my father that the new principal at the Greek American Institute, the man who had taken over from my mother's old teacher on Nisyros, was my father's first cousin. He spelled his name differently, with a K instead of a C—Katsimatidis. But screwy spellings were a frequent occurrence when US immigration clerks, at Ellis Island or elsewhere, were translating names from Greek to English. The point was that, no matter the spelling, we were still related to cousin Katsy-with-a-K.

Uncle Nick went to see him.

"It's not right that John didn't get in," Uncle Nick said.

The GAI principal wrote a letter to the principal at Brooklyn Tech, saying what a promising boy I was and urging the school to find a place for me. I'm not sure if his letter did the trick or if I would have floated to the top of the waiting list anyway as other rising freshmen chose to attend Bronx Science or Stuyvesant or some other school instead of Brooklyn Tech. All I knew was that I got in.

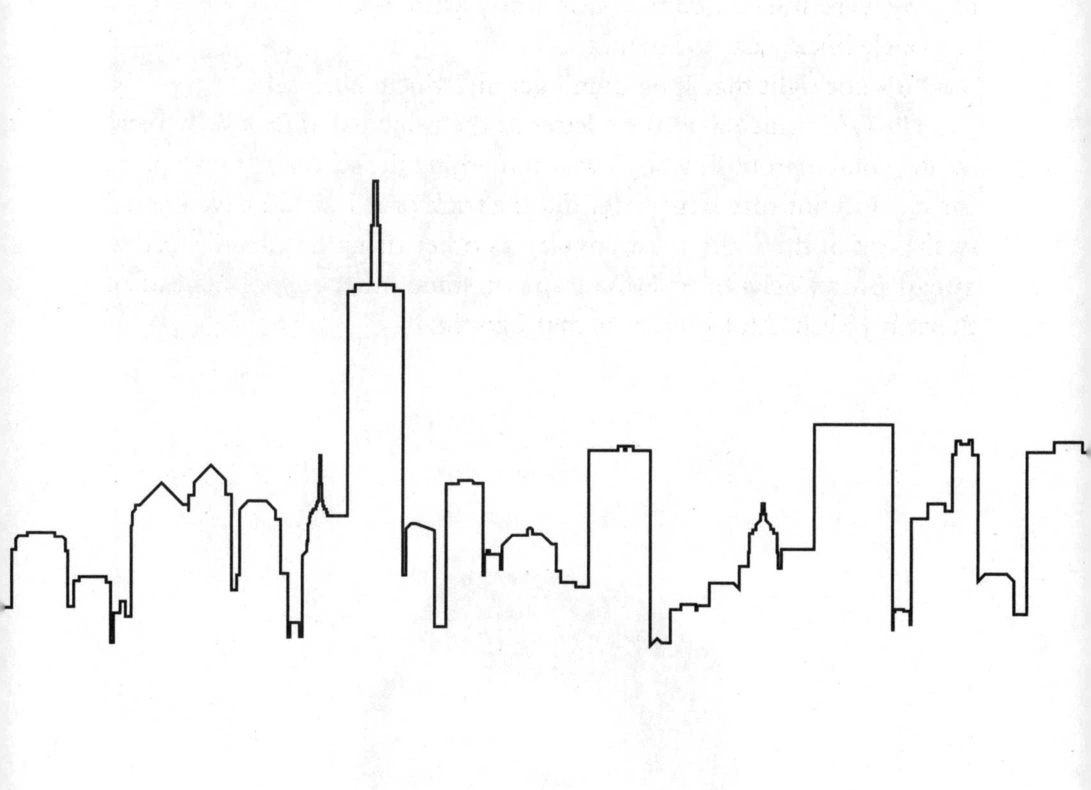

Top: The Brooklyn Technical High School reunion of the Class of 1966 on April 29, 2006. *Bottom:* Young John Catsimatidis.

4

TEEN SPIRIT

The old country was new to me.

In the summer of 1962, when I was about to begin attending Brooklyn Tech for ninth grade, my father took three weeks of vacation. He had never done anything like that before. As far as I could recall, he'd hardly had a single day off. But he told his bosses at Longchamp and at the Italian place in Astoria that he was taking his wife and teenage son to the place that we had come from in Greece.

This was the first time any of us had been back to Nisyros since we'd moved to America in the spring of 1949. I had no idea what to expect. Since I had left Nisyros at six months old, I had no memories at all to go by. We flew on a brand-new airplane, a Boeing 707, from New York to Frankfurt and then Frankfurt to Athens. Finally, we got on a boat to Nisyros.

For me, those next three weeks were a life-changing experience.

I got to spend time with my grandmother Zannis, who the kids called *Ya-Ya*—the Greek nickname for grandma—and she was everything I had heard she was. Warm and loving, friendly and respected by everyone. No one ever mentioned my grandfather's absence from the island, certainly not to me. Before this trip, my generous mother had been sending overstuffed boxes from New York, and *Ya-Ya* was the one who would receive them and pass out the goodies to everyone. I remember watching as my mother had carefully packed those boxes filled with lollipops, hand-me-down clothing, and notebooks for the children. Sports socks, some pens, maybe a transistor radio for the adults. For years, people had been stopping by *Ya-Ya*'s house to see what Andreas and Despina had sent. Now, everyone seemed happy to see us.

I met many cousins, but the one I especially connected with was Manos, my mother's brother's son, who was born on August 4, 1948, making him a month and three days older than I was. I say I "met" Manos, but that's not exactly right. He and I had already met, actually. You could even say we were close. I had heard the story from our relatives in New York. They loved telling it. Apparently, when Manos and I were babies on Nisyros, my mother couldn't breastfeed due to complications in her pregnancy. Aunt Popi, Manos's mother, cheerfully pitched in and breastfed the two of us together. While Manos suckled at one breast, I went to work on the other. I never did hear which one of us had which side. Or maybe we traded off. I don't know. But everyone loved the image, and you can't get much closer than that. When Manos and I finally reconnected as we were both about to turn fourteen, I could tell immediately: he was the boy I would have been if my father hadn't packed us up and taken us to America. I felt like we had never been separated, like Manos and I were almost twins.

"You want to learn how to swim?" he asked on my second day in Nisyros.

"Sure," I said.

"Nisyros style?"

I had no idea what that meant. "Okay," I said.

I soon discovered exactly what Manos meant. My cousin pushed me off the pier and hoped for the best. He stood and waited, staring into the clear-blue water, to see what happened next. If I had gone down to the bottom and not come up, I'm sure he or one of the other boys would have jumped in to save me. Thankfully, I didn't sink. My arms starting waving. My feet started kicking. I got one mouthful of water and panicked a bit. But then I somehow collected myself. I stopped flailing so violently. I got my head above the water. I learned how to swim right then and there. From that day forward, I have been a firm believer in the Nisyros theory of swimming instruction: the original sink or swim.

Manos took me everywhere. He collected a big mob of cousins and friends and included me in everything. We pulled fish and octopus out of the Aegean and ate them right off a wood-fired grill. We climbed up a cliff for a picnic with a couple of girls. We started to, anyway. Somehow, Manos got the job of hauling the watermelon. He complained so much about how heavy it was, we never even made it halfway to the top. We couldn't disappoint the girls, though, so we found a grassy spot for our picnic and whacked the watermelon there. That was the kind of summer it was.

Nisyros was different from New York City in a thousand different ways, but none of them was more striking than this: on the island, everybody's home was everybody's home. I was family there, even if most of the people had never met me. So all local privileges were extended to me, despite how totally lame my Greek was.

I'd just spent four years in Greek school. My parents still mostly spoke Greek at home. But I certainly didn't talk like a native. Being exposed to the language since birth, I thought my Greek was stronger than it was. But in truth, I never felt like it was a problem on Nisyros. Almost all the young people spoke some English, as did a lot of adults. In those years, lots of people were going back and forth to America. Somehow, everybody understood, and no one made fun of me. If the roles had been reversed, I'm not sure the kids in New York would have been so kind.

Mostly, we just had fun.

I met my cousin Irene, who was friendly and hung out with us, and a couple of cute girls. But it was a beautiful dog named Blackie I really fell for. We had a heart-pounding drama one day when Blackie fell down a well. He was stuck down there, wailing so loudly that adults and children began to gather around. I had no idea what to do. Then someone suggested I tie a rope around Manos. Slowly, I lowered him into the well. He didn't waste a minute once he got to the bottom. He scooped up the frightened Blackie and called up to me. It took all the strength I had, but I managed to pull them both up to safety.

That might have been my life's greatest achievement until then.

I'd brought some baseballs and a couple of bats in my suitcase from New York, as well as a portable shortwave radio. I gave the other boys some tips on pitching and hitting—real American fun—after Manos taught me to swim and we'd pulled Blackie from the well. A couple of the boys got really good really quickly. We broke three windows at the school.

I had brought the shortwave mainly to keep up with the Yankees season while I was away, the only way to do that back then. But the big news coming out of the radio's scratchy speaker wasn't the Yankees campaign to keep the Minnesota Twins from grabbing the American League pennant. Instead, I heard on the Voice of America newscast on August 5 that Marilyn Monroe had died. I ran to share the report with everyone. People seemed genuinely shaken and sad. Even on a tiny island so far from America, they all seemed to know Marilyn as a sexy Hollywood star who had played dumb blonds in the movies and was quite possibly having an affair with President Kennedy—maybe his brother Bobby, too.

All the people on Nisyros loved John Kennedy. Many of them had pictures of the young American president framed in their living rooms. To the Greeks, he was a savior, opening America to the modern era, deserving of respect around the world. If he liked Marilyn—well, so did they.

I was sad when our trip came to an end and it was time to return to New York. Manos promised he would come to visit, maybe even come to stay. It wasn't that I really wanted to remain on Nisyros or move to the island for good. I knew that wasn't my future. I had things to do in New York. But that summer, as the adventure of high school grew near, I had a far better sense of where I came from and, therefore, a far better sense of who I was.

• •

Brooklyn Technical High School was two subway trains and a million miles from our familiar stretch of West 1Thirty-Fifth Street. The building was a constant hub of activity, like a busy brick beehive looming over Fort Greene Park. The place was massive. It was twelve stories tall and took up half a city block. It had every kind of classroom, lab, and special program you could imagine. The six thousand students came from all five boroughs of New York City and many different races and ethnic groups. But all the students had two things in common: they seemed uniformly bright and studious—and not one of them was a girl. The academic demands were rigorous. We had courses like astronomy, botany, and, even back then, computer science. Every night the teachers piled the homework on. Everyone had to declare a college-style major such as civil engineering, biological sciences, or architecture.

In a high school so huge and diverse, there was no way the teachers and administrators could keep a close eye on everyone. That was the job of the SOS, or Safety Order Service, sometimes called the Service Squad. I joined this elite crew in my freshman year. We were three hundred students responsible for maintaining order, keeping things running smoothly, and enforcing the rules. That was a huge load of responsibility to put in the hands of teenage boys. But surprisingly, we mostly lived up to it. We weren't exactly junior teachers or guidance counselors. I certainly wouldn't have called us prison guards. But we played an important role in helping to run the school.

Brooklyn Tech had a lot of rules—no running in the hallways, no hats in the classroom, no dungarees, no smoking within a block of the school, for instance—and we were on the lookout for violators. Where to line up for morning assembly. Which door to enter the cafeteria. *No, you can't go up the down stairway!* What kind of pass you needed to wander outside the classroom during second period. We had to know the system and exercise sound judgment in enforcement.

William Pabst was the principal, and no one questioned his authority. But out in the hallways and in the schoolyard, we were the front lines. It was all very military. We had badges and ranks and a clear chain of command. Like everyone else, I started as a squad man with little influence or authority. But if you showed leadership potential, you could rise through the ranks of the SOS. By junior year, you might become a corporal or a first lieutenant or second lieutenant. I ended up as First Lieutenant Catsimatidis. Tony Piccolo was my second lieutenant. Herb Henkel, the captain of the SOS, went on to become the CEO of the global industrial conglomerate Ingersoll Rand. I'm sure he learned many of his moves in SOS. The whole experience really did teach us to lead. It made me a lifelong believer in universal public service. If every kid in America spent six months performing some kind of public service, just imagine the nation of young leaders we would have.

Holding so much responsibility taught us valuable life skills. You couldn't just be a hard-ass. Everyone would hate you. But you couldn't be a pushover, either. You'd get no respect. You had to learn the difference between serious and trivial, and you had to learn the persuasive power of personal relationships. Yelling wasn't nearly as effective as making people *want* to behave. I tried to be helpful to the students and the teachers. I tried to make sound judgments. I took it all very seriously.

With so much power in the hands of students, it was amazing how seldom it got abused. We had the right to stop and question anyone. Once you got promoted, you could even assign detention. If one of the SOS guys abused his authority, though, he got a good talking-to from his superiors. If it happened again, he'd get bounced.

In my senior year, I was in charge of sixth period. I had eight or nine people under me. The teachers came to *me* for assignments. I learned leadership at a very early age. When you say, "Charge!"—do all your people follow you? How do you make sure they do? Leadership was a talent I didn't realize I had inside me. It just happened, and I was good at it.

....

My father was always interested in politics. He would sit at a table for a meal and talk politics for as long as anyone would listen. He knew the players and the issues. He had strong opinions about everyone and everything. Often, it was Greek politics, which I had zero interest in. To me, that was the past. But when the talk turned to America, the topic came alive. My father was a mostly left-wing Democrat. He hated Richard Nixon and, like most Greek immigrants in those days, loved John Kennedy. And so did I.

President Kennedy was part of a new generation. He upset the apple cart. And that appealed to me. I liked that Kennedy had the courage to say we were going to the moon and then immediately got busy sending us there. That turned out to be a very smart idea. A tremendous amount of technology was developed as a result of the space program. NASA spun off thousands of high-paying engineering jobs. We are still living with the benefits of that. Without space, America wouldn't be the world's leader in technology.

I didn't have any real plans for the summer between my freshman and sophomore years at Brooklyn Tech. My next-door neighbor, Robert Stewart, was in pretty much the same position. Our parents didn't like the idea of our just hanging around all day. It was my father who suggested that we go down to the office of our local congressman and see if we could volunteer.

"I'm sure they'll pay you exactly what you're worth," he teased Robert and me.

Our congressman was a Democrat, of course. There weren't too many Republicans in those days on the Upper West Side of Manhattan, just like there aren't too many today. The congressman's name was William Fitts Ryan.

Ryan was a well-connected New York politician and definitely a bright guy. His father, Bernard Ryan, was a judge on the New York State Court of Appeals, appointed by Governor Franklin D. Roosevelt. The son graduated from Princeton University and Columbia Law School, served in the Pacific as an Army artillery lieutenant during World War II, then ran for Congress as a reform Democrat. By that summer, he was a reliable champion of civil rights and an early opponent of the Vietnam War.

Robert and I did what my father suggested. We went down to the congressman's office and said we wanted to volunteer. Neither one of us had any agenda other than getting our parents to quit bugging us. We didn't have any issues that we were all that interested in. We didn't do it for the money. We showed up just wanting something to do and hoping it might be interesting. Ryan's people agreed to hire us for the price of a cup of coffee and all the water we could drink. I don't remember anyone saying that explicitly, but that was pretty much the deal. We worked in the district office making copies, stuffing envelopes, and fetching coffee for the staff. We also got an up close view of politics and government, especially of all the people who came in and out of the office asking questions, looking for favors, pushing issues, wanting things from the congressman. I found all of it fascinating. I loved that feeling of being on the inside.

When the congressman was home from Washington, we went to events with him and watched him interact with the people. He was very popular with the voters in his district. He seemed to like Robert and me.

. . . .

All through high school, I had part-time jobs. Some of them, after my foray into the political world, even paid money.

Everybody I knew had a job. Why wouldn't I? The men often juggled two or three jobs, the way my father did. Some of the women worked, too. And those who stayed home with the children probably worked at least as hard as those who toiled in an office or a sweatshop. The teenagers had part-time jobs at night, on weekends, and in the summer. I don't remember anyone even questioning that. Work was just part of living the way I grew up. In a community as tight as ours was, the jobs often came through relatives or family friends.

At one point, I worked in a hardware store that was owned by a quasi-cousin of ours, John Georges. Fort Washington Hardware, the store was called. It was on Broadway in the 160's. With Mr. Georges standing over me, I learned how to copy keys, mix paint, run a cash register, and talk to the customers. It was a good experience. Years later, his son would come to work for me.

There was a Sloan's supermarket down the block from our apartment. I got a job there. It wasn't exactly a job—more of a money-earning opportunity. There were no regular paychecks involved. In those days, supermarkets didn't hire delivery people. What you would do was stand next to a checkout line. You'd put the groceries in a bag. Then, you'd politely ask the customer: "Do you want it delivered?" Many times, the person shopping would answer yes. You'd get a tip for the deliveries. Fifty cents was about the going rate. Sometimes the people would also give you their empty beer and soda bottles to return to the store for the deposits. It was there I got my first glimpse of the supermarket business, but I didn't really learn that much about groceries. What that experience taught me was how to hustle.

You had to be friendly. You had to be energetic. You had to deal with all kinds of customers, the friendly and the grumpy ones. You had to learn their little quirks and expectations. You had to learn to smile. The tips were always better if you smiled. You had to look at the whole thing like a challenge and adventure. Whatever else you did, you didn't show up to fail.

Looking back at those years, I can see how both my parents put me in a mindset to succeed in the world. My father did this mostly through the example of hard work. He had a goal: to support his family and give them every opportunity. He worked days, nights, and weekends to achieve his goal. He never bragged about it or acted like it was any huge sacrifice. But his example was unmistakable, and I embraced it thoroughly, hardly realizing that I had.

My mother was more verbal and more direct. She believed in the power of pressure and example. "Look at how successful that other boy is," she would say. Sometimes it felt like she was breaking my balls. But the need to achieve was planted deeply in my brain. And there was always the lingering notion that I must never bring shame to the family. "Whatever you do," my mother often warned, "don't ruin the family name. You'd better not do anything to embarrass the family."

Embarrass the family in front of whom? The neighbors? The relatives? The people back in Greece? I never knew, and my mother never said. But the need to not do that followed me around like a cloud. Being a failure, I understood, would be a big embarrassment to the family. And I learned from my mother that I should never let that occur.

Accompanying that warning was a road map to success. Hard work and integrity would deliver me there, I was constantly told. That was what my parents believed in. It was also part of the great American Dream. Both my parents tried to live it every day.

Like many immigrants of their generation, they were bred for this. Born in Constantinople into a family of churchmen, my mother knew how people judged each other. Tending his lonely lighthouse to support his sisters and his mom, my father knew the importance of duty and work. They both possessed a powerful sense of their responsibilities in the world. When they became parents, they naturally carried that on. My dad did what he had to for his family. My mother did what she had to for her family. I went to school every day. That was my job. I was expected to perform it responsibly. Later, I would go to work with the same sense of purpose and drive.

....

Eventually, the time arrived to figure out what was next for me.

Brooklyn Tech was a college-preparatory high school. Almost all the graduates went on to a college or university. I took the SAT with the rest of my Brooklyn Tech classmates and hoped for the best. Clearly, the language deficit I had grown up with hadn't entirely disappeared. Even after all those years of American schooling, I scored a near-perfect 780 on the quantitative section but a highly unimpressive 480 on the verbal part. My school grades were excellent, though. I just hoped there'd be an admissions officer somewhere who'd focus on that or be impressed enough with my math-and-science prowess or understanding enough of the immigrant backstory to let me in somewhere. Then I had what I thought was a bright idea.

In junior year, as the guidance counselors started talking to us about college, I got it into my head that I might like to go to the US Air Force Academy, located in Colorado Springs, Colorado. I wanted to fly airplanes—be an *aéro pilótos*, not that other thing—and the Air Force Academy seemed like an excellent place to learn. To get into the Air Force Academy, my counselor told me, I needed to be nominated by a senator or a congressman. The minute I heard that, a light went off in my teenage brain. I knew Congressman Ryan. I assumed he liked me. I knew that if I asked, I could at least get a meeting with him.

He couldn't have been more friendly when I was ushered into his large office and told him what I had in mind. But he had a counterproposal for me.

"Have you considered West Point?" he asked me.

He reminded me that the US Military Academy, the premiere service academy for the entire US Army, was located up the Hudson River in West Point, New York. Competition was stiff, he warned me. But the education was excellent. The tuition was zero. I'd be commissioned as an officer upon graduation. And most important of all, he'd be willing to nominate me.

I loved America. I knew about West Point from television. I told him I'd absolutely go. West Point seemed like the perfect place for me. It had one other advantage, the more I thought about it: it would get me off 1Thirty-Fifth Street. I liked our neighborhood. It was where we lived. We had friends and family there. But even I could tell it was a ghetto. West Harlem definitely wasn't an upscale area in those days. Everyone who lived there dreamed of escaping and going somewhere nicer. I saw West Point as a way for me to escape.

But it wasn't to be.

When my parents learned about all this, they yelled and screamed. They begged me not to go. They were totally opposed to the whole idea, my mother especially.

It had nothing to do with politics or the military or the Vietnam War, which was heating up at the time. It had to do with my being an only child. They wanted their son closer to them. They didn't want to give me up. Going to West Point would mean four years on campus and then a five-year obligation to the Army after that.

Both my parents cried. My father stared glumly.

"It's wrong," my mother pleaded. "Don't do it."

In the end, I turned down the appointment to West Point and applied to New York University instead. I couldn't bring myself to break my parents' hearts. I figured I would major in engineering and join the Reserve Officers' Training Corps (ROTC). That way, if I wanted to, I could still be an officer in the Army.

NYU, whose main campus was in the University Heights section of the Bronx, hadn't been my first choice. But I tried to console myself. Several of my Brooklyn Tech friends were going there, too, and I liked being with my friends. Just getting the West Point nomination had fueled my confidence and ambition, even if I had no clear professional direction at that point in my life. I knew NYU was a respectable college. I was an only child, and in the end I knew that I hated the way it sounded when my mother cried.

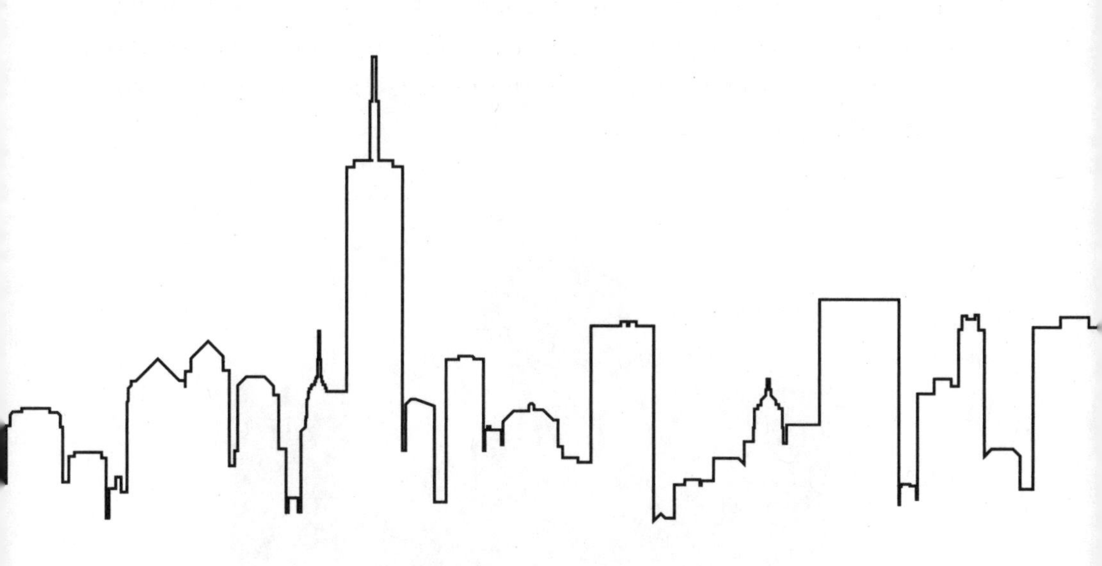

When John did not go to West Point and went to NYU, he went into their ROTC program.

5

HIGHER ED

I had big plans for the summer.

High school was behind me. College was waiting in the Bronx. I fully expected to park myself on the couch in the living room and watch television for the next three months. I'd worked hard at Brooklyn Tech. I had earned top grades and risen to the upper ranks of the SOS. School had been my job, and I had done it well. I'd even wrangled a nomination to West Point. Though I wasn't going, you certainly couldn't blame me. Talk to my overprotective parents about that. And come September, I figured, I'd be cracking the books again. NYU wasn't yet the high-prestige university it would become in future decades. But it was a respectable private commuter school that attracted its share of bright students from in and around New York.

Didn't I deserve a lazy summer to catch my breath? I wish someone had mentioned that to my mom.

Without even asking me, she marched over to our neighborhood grocery store on West 137th Street. Broadway Supermarket, the store was called, though the "super" part makes it sound a little grander than it was. The store was owned by a young guy we called Cousin Tony, who was in his mid-twenties at that point. Like Mr. Georges at the hardware store, Tony wasn't technically our cousin. Or maybe he was; I don't know. But he was a fellow Greek immigrant and, at the very least, a close family friend.

"You got a job for my son?" my mother asked Cousin Tony. "He's a high school graduate now." I guess that was the strongest argument my mother had beyond the fact that Tony was family, more or less, and that I was my mother's son.

I gather Tony wasn't overly thrilled to take me on for the summer. But he told my mother he would let me help around the store. One dollar an hour would be my pay. I don't think my mother negotiated very hard. She came straight home and announced I should show up at Tony's store bright and early the next day. She seemed so happy that I would be freeing up the couch space, I didn't have the heart to argue with her about my busted leisure plans. I just shrugged and said I would go see Tony in the morning.

In those days, I had a knack for aiming like a rifle at whatever I was doing, whether it was working in a grocery store or lounging around the living room. Without thinking twice about it, I could easily go from extreme to extreme. That was just my personality. And once I started working with Tony, I forgot about my lazy summer entirely. In fact, I worked seven days a week and didn't utter a single word of complaint.

Cousin or not, Tony was quite the demanding boss. He was too cheap to have a conveyor belt. But now he had me, carrying the sodas and the beers up from the basement and making sure the coolers were fully stocked. I filled the dairy case with milk, butter, yogurt, and eggs. I straightened the canned goods and the cereal boxes and paper towels. I made sure the ripe fruit was at the top of the pile and the overripe fruit was carefully hidden somewhere below. When the store got busy, I'd stand at the front of the store, helping cashiers pack the bags with groceries. And I was also the store's security guard. If somebody was trying to steal something, I'd grab the thief and make him put the item back. I had no precise job description. I did whatever Tony asked me to do and whatever needed to be done. I got along with the customers and the other employees. I enjoyed having somewhere to go every day. I definitely liked earning money—even my entry-level wage.

It was Tony's store. He was the boss. But he and I got along beautifully. Everybody loved Tony, the women especially. He was a good-looking, blondish guy from northern Greece, six or seven years older than I was. I learned a lot from him that summer, things I had no idea would later become important to me. Tony knew how to run a grocery store, and he was a generous teacher. He'd started out as a fruit man, and he still had a big stand outside. He was always focused on ripeness and on price. He believed in communicating clearly with the customer, using large, hand-lettered signs to announce whatever he was pushing that day. If the wholesale market had cherries—or apples, or apricots—at an attractive wholesale price, he'd buy a big load, lay out a nice selection, and post a huge sign: "CHERRIES 19¢ A POUND!"

Tony was a born merchandiser, a marketer, someone who was thinking constantly about the best ways to sell the items in his store. Working with him, I was exposed to that kind of thinking.

I did get a little irritated when I found out that the cashier was making $1.10 an hour, ten cents more than I was. *With all I'm doing, she's earning more than I am? She's pushing buttons on a register while I'm breaking my back and helping Tony run the store?* But I never brought it up with Tony. I just tried to put in as many hours as I could.

I had it in my mind that summer to learn how to drive. But driver's ed was expensive. Private driving lessons cost $27 an hour. With Tony's $1 an hour, I had to work half a week for just one hour of driving. But I was going to college in the Bronx in September, and I thought that that would be a much better experience if I didn't have to take the subway and could drive up there. I knew there'd be a lot of rich kids at NYU, students who came from Scarsdale and Stamford and other fancy suburbs like that. I knew enough about life by then to understand that 1Thirty-Fifth Street wasn't ever going to compete on campus with Scarsdale and Stamford. But having a car, I thought, would at least get me in the game.

What the game was, I had no idea. But I was pretty sure I wanted to be in it.

So I took my paltry grocery earnings and invested in driving lessons. I still needed my father's help buying a car. But he stepped up even better than I could have hoped for. Since I was a baby, he'd been paying $6 a month for a life insurance policy. By that summer, the cash value of the policy was north of $800. He cashed in the policy and bought me a blue 1962 Buick Special, a four-door hardtop with bucket seats, power steering, a Dual Path transmission, and 155-horsepower V6. It wasn't a cool Mustang or a Corvette like I imagined those suburban college boys would be tooling around in. But sitting behind the wheel of that Buick, I believed I could go just about anywhere. The car was mine, and it gave me a sense of freedom I had never experienced before.

I wasn't entirely sure what to do with it, but I definitely liked the way that freedom felt.

....

I liked NYU, though being a day student and living at home wasn't quite as exciting as I imagined going off to West Point would have been. But the Bronx campus—the College on a Hill, people called it—was actually quite beautiful. Overlooking the Harlem River, University Heights certainly had gorgeous views. The professors were learned. The other students were bright. Engineering felt like a good fit for me, and I dove right into the freshman requirements. World history. English literature. The basic sciences. As I had planned, I signed up for Army ROTC.

I wasn't the only Greek guy on campus, though the three or four others all came directly from middle-class families in Greece. There was one Greek girl who caught my eye. I thought about asking her out, but somehow I never got up the nerve. I was right to expect a lot of rich kids, and some of them actually turned out to be nice. One of my good friends—we're still friends now—was Jonathan Farkas, whose family owned the Alexander's department stores. His father donated enough money for the university to build two or three new buildings. How could I compete with that? I didn't even like telling people I lived on 1Thirty-Fifth Street.

It sounds silly now, I know. But that's how I felt at the time. Most young people want to fit in. I certainly did. Occasionally, I tried too hard and regretted it. There was a pretty girl I was getting friendly with. I wanted to impress her. So I told her I lived at 200 Central Park South, a modern white-glove building at Seventh Avenue and Central Park South, the fanciest address I knew. She believed me. Why wouldn't she?

She believed me, that is, until a few days later. "I went to 200 Central Park South," she told me. "The doorman didn't know who you were."

Busted!

I made some excuse about fill-in doormen, but it was probably better that things ended right there. Imagine if she and I had really started dating. How do you bring a girl to meet your parents where you don't really live if you can't even get past the doorman?

My '62 Buick actually served me pretty well, even if some of my buddies were driving home to broad-lawn suburbs in foreign sports cars while I was circling the West 130s, dodging the alternate-side-of-the-street parking signs.

My mother, being my mother, noticed that last detail.

One day that fall, as I was heading back and forth to NYU, my mother announced that she was going out to get a job. She had never worked outside of the home before. My father never expected her to. She'd stayed plenty busy looking after him, me, our apartment, our renters, and assorted relatives, neighbors, and friends. The news caught us all by surprise.

"You don't have to," my father told her.

"I know," she said. "I want to."

The reason she wanted to, it turned out, was my Buick and me. "I'm going to work to pay your garage bill. You should put that car in a garage."

And she did. She was hired as a seamstress at a blouse factory in the Garment District. Sweatshops, they called those places, on account of the long hours, tedious work, low wages, and lack of air conditioning. It was the kind of place where many immigrant women worked, the first stop on what they hoped, sometimes in vain, would be a gradual climb up the American career ladder.

She started working and went every day for two full weeks. At the end of two full weeks, her take-home pay was $28, which was exactly the monthly fee for my space in the parking garage. I made her quit. I could not see my mother working two full weeks to pay for my damn garage bill.

I still get tears in my eyes every time I think about that.

. . . .

A couple of my Brooklyn Tech SOS friends also signed up for NYU ROTC. The closest was Eddie Salzano, who'd been SOS Captain my sophomore year. We all drilled together and played war games. With my SOS training, I felt confident about being a leader. I always wanted to be the hero, the one with the ideas and the skills to execute them, no matter what challenge we faced. During a training exercise at Fort Dix, New Jersey, a few of my guys and I almost single-handedly captured an entire competing company. That gave me a tremendous thrill.

But as my fellow students and I were playing at war, the real thing was growing larger and darker in Vietnam. We all realized that it was people our age doing the fighting and the dying over there. As the war raged on, so did the anti-war protests and demonstrations on American college campuses, including NYU's. The marches on Washington. The Students for a Democratic Society. The passionate debates in and out of the classroom. It was a dicey time to be part of a military-officer training program. But there I was, every Tuesday morning, walking up the hill in my ROTC uniform. After a while, I really wasn't sure what any of that stood for or even what I believed.

I stuck with ROTC until the end of the school year, and then I gave it up. I was nineteen years old and didn't have many deep opinions of my own. I was living at home, commuting to campus, and taking things as they came. But when I asked myself, "Is this what I am going to college for?" the answer, I decided, was no.

I didn't grasp it at the time, but that was an important fork in the road for me. I never lost my own appreciation and respect for the military. Still, it never had the same call to me again. I knew others who served, even in my own family. Antonio Mavroudis, who also came from Nisyros and lived across from us on 1Thirty-Fifth Street, was a Boy Scout who later joined the Army as a gung ho young man. When he came home on leave, his uniform shirt was covered with medals and ribbons. He was promoted to major before he was killed at twenty-four in Vietnam.

I am still friends with his brother, John Mavroudis.

Antonio was one of 58,220 American men and women lost in that war, but his death hit me hard. I guess it was the first time I experienced the death of a friend or someone close to me. I'm not sure he or anyone knew what exactly we were fighting for. We were told by the politicians in Washington that it was to stop communism. But where and how? In Vietnam? In North Korea? In Cambodia? In Thailand? Why one place and not another? That was too many lives to lose without clear answers.

I knew this much: if I had gone to West Point or completed ROTC, I'd have been fighting in the war, too. Seventy members of the West Point Class of 1970 were killed in Vietnam. I would have been in the center of the action. God knows what would have happened to me.

For a long time, I stayed away from politics.

....

Our tenant Dino had long since moved out of the third bedroom in the apartment, and we'd found a new renter to replace him. My mother's brother, Yiánni Emmanouilidis—the one who as a boy carried the letter from my mother's runaway groom—had also come and gone. He'd moved into an apartment at Eighth Avenue and Forty-Fourth Street with four other men from Nisyros. Uncle Yiánni—Uncle John—then sent for his oldest son, Manos, my beloved cousin, near-twin, and long-ago breakfast mate.

Manos, like me, was now out of high school. His father wanted him to go to college for architecture. Manos said he was more interested in marine engineering. His father had an answer for that: "I tell you what. You can forget both of them. Come to America. Now!"

Manos seemed up for the adventure, and I was thrilled to hear he was finally on the way. He'd been promising in his letters to visit ever since my summer on Nisyros. Manos and I picked up exactly where we'd left off. He had the same cheerful spirit and the same boundless energy. Only this time, I was showing him my world, not the other way around. We went out at night together. I showed him how to use the subway. We drove around in the Buick. But Manos, like all new immigrants, didn't come to New York to vacation. He came to work.

Pappoú, our grandfather with the postcards, took him to the Port Authority Bus Terminal to meet another man from Nisyros. The man owned a restaurant on the second floor. The restaurant owner hugged and kissed Manos like he was greeting a long-lost nephew, though the two of them had never met. The man then told Manos to start bussing tables and get busy at the dishwashing station.

"So I'm hired?" Manos asked in Greek.

"Of course," the restaurant owner said.

Manos would work the night shift, the restaurant man explained, 10 PM to 6 AM, and would receive no pay for the first two weeks. "That will be your training period."

When Manos raised a quiet objection to the no-pay part, the man raised his hand as if he were going to strike my cousin, and Manos got quickly to work. I didn't see all this myself, but Manos told me about it after three nights at the restaurant.

"John," he said, "you have to find me another job."

I had a friend who owned a factory in the Astoria section of Queens, a neighborhood that was quickly filling up with Greeks by then. I took Manos to Twenty-First Avenue and Thirty-Fifth Street, Superior Manufacturing, where they made gears for the US Army and the space program. The owner told Manos he'd get $1.25 an hour for sixty hours a week—and the pay would start immediately. Six months later, Manos, who barely spoke English, was promoted to assistant foreman, supervising sixty people on the factory floor.

That didn't surprise me at all.

. . . .

Cousin Tony and I stayed close as I made my way through NYU. I'd stop by the store to talk with him when I was in the neighborhood. I'd help him out on weekends and during summers when he needed it or when I needed a few extra bucks for the car. Over time, he became like a big brother to me. He'd give me advice and listen to me grumble about my parents or my teachers or my dating opportunities. If I wanted to take out a girl, Tony would lend me his car, a new Pontiac Bonneville that was about half a block wide and much cooler than my Buick Special. Tony's wife kept wondering where their car was, but Tony always shrugged it off and said to me, "Don't worry about that. I have everything under control."

Tony knew about a lot of things, not just the grocery business.

Even though I was busy with my schoolwork, I always needed money and never stopped working on the side. I discovered I could make a few bucks—maybe more than a few—buying little products and selling them on the street. My inner entrepreneur was coming out. I'd load the trunk of the Buick with whatever I was selling and head out into the neighborhood. I wasn't nervous talking to people. I liked the challenge of closing a deal. As it turned out, I was natural salesman.

I sold touchtone phones before the phone companies had them. I knew a guy—that was how a lot of stories began back then. I knew a guy who sold me the phones by the dozen. I'd jack up the price, then sell them one by one on the street. Touchtone phones weren't the perfect product. New York City still had an analog phone system that didn't recognize the tones. "The phone won't dial out yet," I had to caution my prospective customers. "Right now, you can use it as an extension. But you'll be ready when New York Telephone puts the push-button service in."

People have always liked being ahead of the curve.

"It's coming soon," I promised.

The pitch made sense because a lot of people had visited the Radio Corporation of America's pavilion at the 1964 World's Fair in Flushing, Queens, where the futuristic telephones had caused quite a stir.

I tried a couple of other products. But aftershave lotion was my real success. I bought the bottles from a guy for $2 each. In a neighborhood like West Harlem, there were always guys looking to sell stuff. If you paid attention and kept your head about you, you could get some good deals from them. I resold the bottles of aftershave for $4 or $5 each. These were knockoffs with brand names that had a familiar ring to them but weren't exactly the real thing.

Russian Leather. That was one of my best products. I would speak to my sidewalk prospects as if I was sharing something confidential with them, the way a sales person at B. Altman or Alexander's might mention an upcoming friends-and-family sale to a loyal customer from the Upper East Side. I'd say, "You know *English* Leather. But have you tried *Russian* Leather? I think you'll like it very much."

It was marketing, pure and simple, and I had a talent for it. I was buying and selling, the foundation of all business, and it was working for me. The vast majority of the customers were very happy with the product. I never got in trouble. I always sold out. The customers were eager to see me again. They wanted more. I was making money. I was a little businessman. The trunk was my store.

I only remember one real complaint. It was from a friend of mine who bought a bottle of Russian Leather from me. Constantino Gil was his name. He was from Spain. "What's in that stuff?" he wanted to know. "I had to take two baths to get it off."

He was laughing as he said that to me. So maybe he was just giving me a hard time. Or not. I didn't let it worry me. I just kept selling. Tony had taught me well.

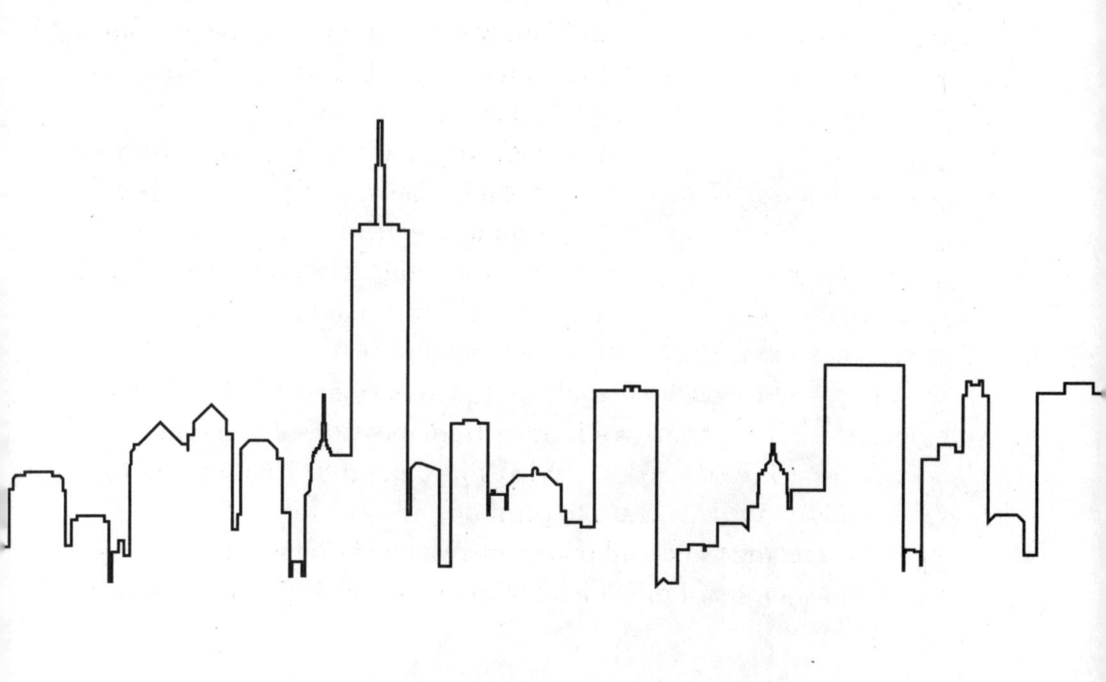

John Catsimatidis in his first grocery store.

6

GREEN GROCER

Thirty-seven blocks south of his market near City College, Cousin Tony owned a second grocery store. This one was on Broadway between Ninety-Ninth and One Hundredth streets, right next door to a popular kosher deli restaurant called Bernstein's.

Tony thought he was being clever when he named the store Seven-Eleven. At that point, the 7-Eleven convenience stores had thousands of franchise outlets all over America, but they hadn't yet moved into New York City. Tony had the bright idea that if he slapped that name on his grocery and spelled it in a slightly different way—Seven-Eleven instead of 7-Eleven—the Dallas-based quickie conglomerate would have to pay him a big pile of money to get the New York naming rights back. It was a hairbrained idea—total nonsense. But that wasn't Tony's biggest problem. His biggest problem was that he didn't own this second store alone. He had a partner, his mother's brother: his uncle Nick Hatsis.

Tony couldn't stand being in business with Uncle Nick, and from all I could tell, the feeling was entirely mutual. Every day that passed, I was waiting for the two of them to come to blows.

If Cousin Tony bought twenty cases of oranges, Uncle Nick would say, "Why did you buy so many? They're gonna go rotten!" If Tony bought ten the next time, his uncle would be just as perturbed: "They were a great price! Why didn't you buy twenty?" All this bickering wasn't helping the business. They couldn't agree on anything. The employees and the customers could sense the hostility. Tony was the one I was talking to, and I knew the situation was driving him nuts. The store, for those reasons and others, wasn't doing nearly the business it should have on such a busy block.

In the fall of 1968, Tony came to me: "I swear I'm gonna strangle my uncle," he said. "You have to take my half of the store."

I was still a junior at NYU, working on my degree in electrical engineering. Part-time work was one thing. Helping out in Tony's store or selling aftershave from my trunk—that wasn't the same as co-owning a real business. I knew how hard Tony worked. But I had to admit I was still intrigued. I was also willing to work hard. I knew something about the grocery business. I was twenty years old. I certainly had no lack of confidence. But there was one large problem standing in my way: I had no money.

"So how am I supposed to pay for this?" I asked Tony after he had brushed aside all concerns about my youth, my lack of experience, and my responsibilities at school. It turned out Tony was so eager to get away from his uncle, he had already thought about the money part.

"You'll pay me nothing," he said. "Not right away. You'll sign some notes and pay me over time from what you'll make on the store."

I took it all in. I understood nothing was certain. But I liked the idea of having my own business that didn't operate out of a car. I knew some people in the grocery business. They weren't all geniuses. I said to myself, *How hard can this be?* That was about the extent of my careful deliberation. I told Tony yes.

He had me sign ten notes for $1,000 each—a total of $10,000. I would pay one every month. That was the full cost of my half of the store. And just like that, I was in the grocery business. Of course, I had no way of knowing whether I was going to make enough to pay Tony back. But confidence and youth are a powerful combination. All I had to do was get to work.

I showed up the next morning. I kept my mouth shut. I began to learn the business from the owner's side. I never had a single argument with Uncle Nick.

I used what I had, which was some good old American know-how and some New York common sense. If the customers bought a lot of bananas, we'd stock more bananas and display them up front. If the people turned up their noses at kiwi, we'd skip the kiwi next week. Nick didn't fight me on any of this. He just seemed happy that I was in there making decisions, and I wasn't yelling at him. In three months' time, I turned Seven-Eleven around.

How did I do this? I don't think it had much to do with expertise. When Tony first made Nick a partner, Nick knew zero about running a grocery store. And when Tony sold his share to me, I didn't know any more than Nick did when he started. But from the start, I was a good communicator, in large part thanks to my SOS days at Brooklyn Tech and my experience selling aftershave on the street. Have an idea. Know what you want. Let everybody around you know. I could see immediately that the store needed marketing, which is really just another word for communicating with the public. We had to tell the people what we were selling and why it was good. Obvious, right? We also had to communicate with the employees if we wanted them to be on the same page as we were. If we did both those things, I knew the store would be a success.

It worked. By New Year's, we were making enough so that Uncle Nick and I could each pay ourselves $500 a week. In cash. That was a lot of money in 1969.

From that experience, I also discovered something important about partnerships. You know why partners argue? They argue when they are losing money and start blaming each other: "It's your fault!" "No, it's your fault." When you're losing money, you argue. The best way not to argue, I figured, was not to lose money.

Now that Uncle Nick and I were making money, what was there to argue about? By summer, nine months after I'd come on board, he and I were each taking home $1,000 a week. And I couldn't have been happier with myself. I had money in my pocket. I had money to pay back Cousin Tony's notes. I had gas in the Buick. I was starting my senior year in college, still keeping up with my schoolwork, and already felt like a success. So much so that I started thinking seriously about what I was going to do after graduation when I finally had my electrical engineering degree.

Electrical engineers at that time were making $129 a week. Compared to what I was pulling in at the grocery store, that didn't sound so exciting to me. I liked running a business. I didn't want to take a pay cut.

The answer seemed obvious to me. I should skip engineering, say no to the skimpy paycheck, and go into the supermarket business full-time.

Unfortunately, when I mentioned this to my immigrant parents, it was like telling them I wanted to go to West Point all over again. My father yelled. My mother cried.

And through all of that, I'm not sure which one of them glared at me with more disappointment.

"We sent you to the university to become a *hamali*?" my father thundered. That's a Turkish word for someone who carries crates on his back, a common laborer. My father didn't mean it as a compliment.

"Why, why are you doing this?" my mother pleaded with me.

She had the idea that I was throwing away not only my education but also the family's whole life-changing journey to America. I tried to tell her that the truth was exactly the opposite. Why work for someone else when I could have my own business? Wasn't that the essence of the American Dream?

She just shook her head and told me I had no idea what I was talking about.

But I had grown in the past four years. I wasn't a schoolboy anymore. I'd learned some lessons. I was a businessman. I'd built my confidence. I had a better idea of what was important to me.

This time, I followed *my* dream.

Not only did I push full speed ahead in the grocery business. Not only did I apply for exactly zero engineering positions. I also stopped going to classes in my final semester and didn't bother to graduate. I left NYU eight credits short.

I'm not exaggerating when I say how very deeply disappointed my parents were. Looking back, I can even understand where they were coming from. They didn't like the choice I was making, but this time their disapproval didn't stop me. With such a heavy load on my shoulders, however, I had to make this grocery idea work. I knew that failure wasn't an option. I follow that thinking today.

. . . .

With my attention focused full-time on the store and the profits flowing steadily in, Nick and I found the happy partnership that had eluded him and Tony. We really had no issues at all, and things ran smoothly—until one afternoon the following year when I wasn't in the store. Nick got into a disagreement with a neighborhood tough guy. The tough guy was hassling one of our workers. Nick intervened. Hostile words were exchanged. Threats were made.

As the man stormed away, he snarled one last time at Nick, "I'm coming back for you."

By the time I returned to the store the next morning, I'd heard all about the incident and had a handgun in my jacket pocket. That in itself wasn't unusual. In those days, all the storekeepers in the neighborhood had guns. When the man who'd threatened Nick returned just like he said he would, I was ready for him. I didn't wait for him to find Nick in the basement. I didn't hesitate a second. I walked straight over to the man. I pulled the pistol out of my jacket and pressed the steel barrel against the man's head.

"You come within three blocks of this store again," I said calmly but directly, "I'm going to blow your head off."

He didn't say another word.

He turned around and started running. Out the door. Up Broadway toward One Hundredth Street and beyond. Moving so quickly I couldn't see where he went. Some people might say that I'd had an unnecessarily aggressive reaction, but I believed at the time it was justified. Upon reflection and with years of experience, I realize now that this was not the right thing to do. But Mr. Tough Guy never came back again.

However, Nick didn't want to return to the store, either. That's how much the whole experience had rattled him. He just wasn't comfortable in the store anymore. Truthfully, I don't think he ever got the same thrill operating a business that I did. I ended up buying his share and started running the place solo. By then, I had already set my sights on a second location, this one a dozen blocks south on Eighty-Seventh Street, just west of Broadway, between a garage and the Four Brothers restaurant. My father had recently retired from Longchamps, where he had been for twenty-five years. Now, although he'd been so opposed to me abandoning engineering for the grocery business, he found himself with time on his hands, and he agreed to come work with me. I put him in the original store so I could turn my attention to creating a new supermarket that would be truly my own, right from the start.

I needed a name for the store on Eighty-Seventh. I certainly wasn't going to call it Seven-Eleven. By then, Tony had already discovered that his fat payday from Dallas was never going to materialize. I wanted a name that made people think of apple pie and vanilla ice cream, something unmistakably, unapologetically American. Having the right name, I believed, was crucial. I wanted a name that people could identify with, a name that would make the customers smile.

The name I came up with was Red Apple.

To my ear, Red Apple said it all. It sounded fresh. It seemed wholesome. It was easy for anyone to remember and to pronounce, which matters in a city as diverse as New York. As far as I was concerned, the name said exactly what I wanted to say as an immigrant, as an American, as me. And the store became an almost instant success.

There were three main pieces to this, and all of them were common sense: focusing on the product, keeping the customers happy, and getting the employees to work well together. It sounds so simple, laying it out like that. But those three principles, I came to see, really are the foundation of building a successful business—any kind of business in any field. As the leader, it was my job to make sure all three of those principles remained front and center every day of the week. If the product wasn't pleasing or we didn't deliver what the customers were looking for, they would shop elsewhere. If the employees didn't feel engaged and appreciated, they would turn surly and drive the customers away. Either way, the business would suffer.

And I was the one who had to set the tone. If I behaved like a leader, I discovered, people would follow me. A lot of this went back to SOS at Brooklyn Tech. Those skills kept coming back to help me. When you say, "Okay, guys, *charge!*"—it's nice if they actually charge.

I just kept thinking of ways to make the store better. I never had any shortage of ideas.

I had learned some of the basics at Seven-Eleven. But Red Apple was my opportunity to show my stuff. I am proud to say that many of the ideas we tested in that store would become standard in the industry in the decades to come, copied by myself and others many times over. I had hunches. I had beliefs. But I had no real proof that any of it would work until I tried it.

Perhaps my biggest idea was being open when people wanted to shop. Again, it sounds so obvious. I never understood why our competitors didn't get there first. But in those days, most supermarkets shut their doors and closed for the evening at eight or nine o'clock. Many nights, we stayed open until 1 AM. New Yorkers worked all kinds of crazy hours. People liked knowing that they could stop at the neighborhood supermarket and buy what they needed on their way home. And it paid off. We did half the store's business between 9 PM and 1 AM.

We also opened on Sundays. In those days, New York City had what were known as blue laws. Stores weren't allowed to be open on Sundays. If you were open when you weren't supposed to be, you took the chance that a city inspector might come around. More often, it'd be the local cop who would see the lights on and the doors open.

They wouldn't arrest you. Instead, you'd most likely get a $5 ticket if you were found doing business on Sundays. And that was okay with me. It was just a cost of doing business in those days. When you grow up the way that I did, you get to know the way things are done in the real world. Sometimes, you just do what you think is best and deal with any issues later.

Another way I made sure my stores stood out from the competition was by cashing customers' checks. In those days, New York City supermarkets took two forms of payment—cash and checks. But at my places, we went the extra mile. We didn't only accept checks to pay for groceries. We cashed peoples' personal checks like a bank branch would.

Our competitors thought we were nuts. "You'll regret that," we were warned over and over again. "You'll have so many worthless checks, they'll be bouncing up and down the aisles." You know what? It almost never happened. And the convenience turned our neighbors into our customers. People came in to cash their checks after banking hours. While they were in the store, they'd pick up some groceries. They liked the convenience. They got used to the store. They got to know the employees. Of course we became their supermarket. Where else would they go? They appreciated the trust we had in them. They kept coming back.

We knew our customers. They were nice people. They lived or worked in the neighborhood. We accepted their cash. We accepted their food stamps. We cashed their checks. We treated them right, and they noticed.

I swear the Citibank branch at Eighty-Sixth and Broadway was starting to look a little empty. I think we were cashing more checks than the real bank was.

....

There was always tough competition in the supermarket business. We were never the only place to shop for groceries in the neighborhood. Those were the days of medium-sized supermarket chains, and there were lots of them in New York City. Key Food. Sloan's. Food City. Associated. Names like those. The Food Emporium, which A&P owned, came a little later. Shopwell. Many of them were larger than we were, bought in greater volume, and had lower prices than we did.

But for us, it wasn't only about price. It was convenience and familiarity and being nice to people—just doing what it took to make the customer happy. It was all personal. I was always in the store. I liked to stand up by the registers or walk the aisles. I wanted to be in the middle of wherever the action was. It made the store feel alive, and it made me feel alive. Being on the scene—letting the employees see me, letting the vendors see me, letting the customers see me, nurturing all those relationships—that was the foundation of the business we built.

From the start, we worried less about revenue than about giving our customers a fair price. We worried about making the customer happy. My attitude was that if we did the right thing by the customer and made the customers happy, eventually we would succeed. Pretty soon, Red Apple was doing brisk business, and I was making another $1,000 a week.

You cannot underestimate the value of knowing your customer. You become a part of people's lives. We were smaller than other stores, but at Red Apple you could still buy about 80 percent of what you needed—from meats to ice cream. We listened. We had our ear to the ground. When our local Woolworth's closed and W. T. Grant shut down, we started carrying frying pans, spatulas, and all sorts of non-food items. Soon, we were part general store. We were your place to go. And all of that worked to our advantage. Customers felt comfortable coming to the store, and they kept coming back.

Over time, that store on Eighty-Seventh Street, like the first store at Broadway and Ninety-Ninth Street, took on a greater meaning in our shoppers' lives. It wasn't just a supermarket. It was a social center, too. Busy neighborhoods need these gathering spots. The customers knew the employees. The employees knew the customers. Everyone knew me. But Meeps probably deserves some credit, too.

Meeps was the store cat. She was black and white, like a tuxedo with four legs and a tail. She was always around. She loved to be petted. She would slink around the aisles, often rubbing up against the legs of friendly shoppers. Everybody loved Meeps. If the customers didn't see her, they would ask, "Where's Meeps?" They would ask that even before they asked, "Where's John?" And Meeps's friendliness wasn't limited to humans in the neighborhood. Over her lifetime, Meeps, let's just say, got around. She had more than one hundred kittens, which we gave away to our customers, who then became even more like family. Soon, their shopping lists included constant supplies of cat food. I still keep Meeps's picture.

My business intuition was paying off, and I was just getting started.

I learned a lot from that store. And there was no reason, I told myself, that I couldn't apply those lessons to other stores, other blocks, and other neighborhoods. If they worked at Eighty-Seventh and Broadway, why wouldn't they work five blocks to the north or ten blocks to the south?

Each corner was different. I understood that. Some blocks were richer. Some blocks were poorer. The ethnic mix was always shifting in New York. But people need groceries, and all we had to do was create the right kind of store for them. A neighborhood store just had to reflect the neighborhood to be a seamless part of it.

John Catsimatidis with Perdue Founder and Chairman, Frank Perdue.

7

STOCKING UP

As the business started taking off, one thing was missing from my life.

A life.

I was working so many hours every week, I hardly had time to live one. I worked and slept and then went back to work, and I did that day after day after day with hardly any time off. The only exception, the only time I carved out for myself, was late Saturday night.

Make that early Sunday morning, since I didn't turn out the lights at the store on One Hundredth Street until midnight on Saturday. But when I would finally lock the door and pull down the security shutters, my next-door neighbor, Robert Stewart, would come by the store with his girlfriend, a pretty, dark-haired young woman named Liba Korn. The three of us would head into the night, hitting the bars and clubs of Manhattan until 4 AM.

Those few hours, from just past midnight until the bartender announced "last call" a few minutes before four—that was my time to forget about the supermarket business, my brief chance to relax and unwind. Soon enough, I knew, the sun would be rising over the Hudson River again. My alarm clock would ring. And all the demands of running the business would be front and center again.

Liba was nice and outgoing. Robert was funny and up for anything. Together, they were the full extent of my social life, and I appreciated their openness to letting me tag along.

We went out together, week after week, for nearly a year. Then, one Saturday night, just after midnight, Liba turned up at the store right at closing time. This time, she was alone. I could see that she'd been crying.

"What's the matter?" I asked her.

"I broke up with Robert," she blurted out.

I couldn't believe it. They'd seemed like the perfect couple to me. As far as I could tell, they got along great. "What happened?" I asked, genuinely concerned.

I was shocked by the answer, though maybe not as shocked as Liba was: "Robert told me he is gay."

I did not see that coming any more than Liba had. But that Saturday night, it wasn't all three of us hitting the clubs of downtown Manhattan. It was just Liba and me.

By this point, we knew each other fairly well. Her family had come over from Germany when Liba was ten years old. Her mother was Catholic. Her father was Jewish. Liba was two years younger than me, and she was definitely smart. She ran the pension department for a small insurance company. I liked the way she answered the phone when I called her office—very efficiently. "Pension department," she'd say with authority.

The girl exuded competence.

"I need your help," I told her one day. That's all it took for her to come work for me in the office above the Red Apple store. We still had two stores, but I had started thinking seriously about opening many more. Liba became the company's cash comptroller. She was a whiz with numbers, and she set up a system to keep careful track of what was going out and what was coming in. And we still had fun going out on Saturday nights.

....

I had to build a team. If I wanted to grow this business beyond two small stores and a dozen employees, I knew I couldn't do it alone. I needed help. I needed people around me who were smart, loyal, hardworking, and dedicated to the business—people who knew more than I did, a lot more. That last point was especially important. As hard as I was working, as quick as I was to catch on, I couldn't know everything. That was one of the leadership lessons I had learned back at Brooklyn Tech: you need your people in place. They were your eyes and ears and, if you were lucky, part of your brainpower, too. I felt like I had already learned a lot about how to operate a small supermarket—how to stock the right items, how to take a personal interest in the customers, how to keep the costs under control, and so on. But I didn't want to stop there, and that meant having the best team I could assemble. If I could run a store or two, why couldn't I run ten or twenty or one hundred? With the right people around me and the right systems in place, I was sure I could.

We didn't have what you might call a formal hiring process. There were no headhunters or employment agencies involved. People could just apply for jobs in one of the stores—as a cashier, a butcher, a delivery person, whatever it was. I interviewed the applicants. I asked some questions. I mostly went by my instincts and hired the ones I thought would be good. Most of the time, I was right. Many of those people are still with me today. But beyond those important early hires, I understood I also needed a core group of people working with me in the office, a small headquarters staff, people I could really depend on as I tried to grow Red Apple.

Liba was already there and doing a great job keeping close track of the cash flow. I was focused on the future. I then hired a bright young woman named Margo Vondersaar to work as my administrative assistant. Margo came from Indianapolis, Indiana. She had moved to New York to be a ballet dancer. I still remember the first day she walked into the office on Eighty-Seventh Street. Blond hair. Bright, blue eyes. Clear Midwestern accent. Twenty and a half years old. Wearing a green corduroy suit with a beige turtleneck sweater on an especially steamy afternoon in the city. This was the summer of 1972. I was impressed by the story she told me.

Like me, Margo came from an immigrant family of modest means, though her people were Russian and Polish, not Greek. She and her older sister, Jeannette, had been studying ballet since they were little girls and were recognized as two of the top student dancers in Indiana. When Margo was twelve years old, she was invited to dance with Russia's legendary Bolshoi Ballet, which had come to perform in Indiana. It was a huge honor. Margo was the youngest of all the dancers asked to perform. As soon as she graduated from high school, she packed a few belongings and came to New York City, where Jeannette had earned a place in the prestigious Harkness Ballet. Margo arrived with one hundred bucks in her pocket. The next day, she won the lead in an off-Broadway show, and she was on her way.

Margo dove into the New York ballet world with the same vigor she'd shown back home. But just as her dance career seemed to be leaping forward, she began experiencing terrible pain in her knees. The injections she received hardly helped at all. Now, she had to face the difficult reality that her future probably wouldn't be on stage with a ballet company in New York.

Sidelined from her long-dreamed-of dance career, she was babysitting for her nephew, trying to figure out what might come next. At the Red Apple supermarket near her sister's apartment, the butcher said to her one day: "Hey, the owner of the company is looking for an assistant. He's starting to grow the company. Would you be willing to apply for the job?"

It had to pay more than babysitting for her nephew, which she was doing for free. Margo made an appointment and came up to the office to speak with me.

She said she could type eighty words a minute and had never been scared of working hard. "Before I left Indiana," she said, "my father warned me. 'You'd better have a skill. You might get injured and not be able to dance.' My mother can type 120. I'm not that fast. But I think eighty words a minute should be fast enough for a supermarket, don't you think?"

As someone who barely typed at all, I had no idea how fast eighty or 120 words a minute might be. But I liked her cheerful attitude and offered her the job.

We had a tremendous amount of work to do and very few people to do it. There were seven people in the two-room office: Liba, Margo, Mike Seltzer (our accounts-receivable comptroller), John Riley (our buyer), Art Ferry (our perishables manager), Ira Weiss (our operations manager), and me. Liba sat at a desk just outside my office. There was a window between us so she could wave me over when she had a question, and I could do the same when I needed her. Margo had a small desk next to mine. Ira was mostly out running around. Sometimes I had to run over to the store on Broadway and Ninety-Ninth Street, but my father kept things over there mostly under control. We were all working hard trying to open store number three.

With a group that tight and that small, no one was shy about expressing ideas or opinions, Margo least of all. "You are the most disorganized person I have ever seen," she told me the very first week she started working, and she was just getting warmed up. She knew nothing about the grocery business, but she started studying how things worked and began to learn. She told me one day, "Now I wake up every morning and my brain hurts more than my knees do. That's progress, I think."

Everyone had four or five jobs at once, which is often the case in small companies. Liba wasn't just our comptroller. She handled a lot of the paperwork and record keeping—basically anything that had a dollar sign attached. She had a real talent for seeing trends, good and bad, and anything that needed my attention. It was the same with Margo. From the very beginning, Margo did a whole lot more than type and answer the phone. She printed up the weekly specials on our ancient copy machine. She dealt with the vendors and the salesmen who came by. She punched in every can of beans for every store. This gave me time to do the things that I needed to.

I spent a lot of time in those early days dreaming up marketing ideas, planning our next expansion, and trying to understand how an early IBM computer could help to run a supermarket company. All three were crucial to our growth. The computer part may not sound like much today. But back then, I was a revolutionary in our industry. Nobody was running a supermarket like that. I was certain that, as we grew, technology would give us big advantages over the other guys.

We didn't have a lot of marketing money, but we cooked up ideas to connect with the regular customers and to bring new ones in. Sales on special items. Newspaper advertising campaigns. Handbills. If something worked, we did it again. If it didn't work, we pretended we hadn't done it the first time. No one ever went home at five o'clock. While I was up in the office writing my computer code, Liba was running her latest spreadsheets, and Margo was on the floor downstairs pulling items forward on the shelves so both sides of every aisle looked 100 percent full. That's just what we did, all of us. We worked. Eighty or ninety hours. But it was fun, and we were building a business, and we could see the growth right in front of our eyes. Margo and Liba both kept telling me I was a genius at business. After a while, I started believing them.

....

One night in February after work, without a word of warning, Liba said to me: "So . . . are we going to make plans?"

I didn't have any idea what she meant. "Plans for what?"

"Getting married," she said.

"Getting married," I repeated, hardly stopping to give the question a second thought. "Sure. Okay."

Honestly, the idea hadn't occurred to me. Work was what I had been thinking about. Not marriage. It wasn't that I was necessarily opposed to getting married—it was more like I didn't have a position on the topic. I definitely liked Liba. I didn't want to lose her. We had fun together, and she was there with me every day as an important part of the company. Other people I knew were getting married. It seemed like a normal thing to do. I couldn't think of any real reason *not* to get married. There was really only one impediment, as far as I could see: my parents. They hadn't said anything directly to me about it, but I knew without even asking that the minute they'd hear I was marrying Liba, all hell would break loose.

The issue wasn't Liba's personality or her intelligence or her decency. They hardly knew her and certainly hadn't heard anything bad about her from me. The issue was where she and her family came from. Liba wasn't Greek. My parents had always just assumed that when their only son got married, whenever that might be, he would of course marry a Greek girl. Not only were my parents dead set on my marrying a Greek girl—they had an even more specific idea. They really wanted me to marry a girl from our little island, Nisyros. To them, a mixed marriage would have been with a girl from Kos, the next island over. I didn't realize it yet, but my mother even had her eye on potential candidates.

There were two sisters from Nisyros: Nikki and Kiki. I had first met them when I was fourteen. My mother wanted me to fall in love with one of them. Their mission, as far as she was concerned, was to lure me away from Liba. But things were moving quickly. Liba wasn't waiting around for any of that.

"We have to buy a ring," Liba told me.

"Okay," I said. I didn't know how these things were supposed to go. But Liba seemed to know. We went to a jewelry store and bought a ring for $1,200. We went Dutch, putting up $600 each. That meant we were engaged. I figured that should calm things down long enough for me to catch my breath and figure out what I wanted to do.

But Liba had momentum on her side, and she kept moving forward.

"Now we have to set a date," she said.

That sounded a little abrupt to me, one degree more real than I had in mind and certainly faster than I was hoping for. "We're engaged," I told her, hoping that would suffice and buy me extra time. It didn't. We set a date. It was just a couple months off. We didn't plan a big wedding or invite hundreds of friends and family or even tell my parents. Who needed World War III? Before I knew it, the day arrived. We went downtown and got married in the wedding chapel at the municipal building across from City Hall. There were four of us—Liba, her mother, Liba's friend Rita Hudes, and me. Rita and my new mother-in-law were the witnesses. Liba and I both said, "I do." Then the four of us went to lunch at Lüchow's, a famous German restaurant on Fourteenth Street.

Only after we got back home did I tell my parents. As expected, they were devastated. Totally devastated. So devastated, in fact, that things were uncomfortable, with my mother especially, for a good long while.

Liba and I got busy being a married couple. We moved into a nice one-bedroom apartment at One Lincoln Plaza. The rent was $728 a month, which was very high at the time.

"How are you going to pay the rent?" my friends asked, knowing I had also been paying the rent on my parents' penthouse apartment, where I had lived until I got married.

"It's okay," I shrugged. "I'll work harder."

I was doing well and expecting to do only better. I figured I'd find a way to afford everything.

....

I needed allies wherever I could find them. One of my best early ones was the chicken man, Frank Perdue.

Frank passed as a celebrity in the retail food world. CEO of Perdue Farms, a large poultry marketer based in Salisbury, Maryland, he had spent his whole life around chickens. His parents, Arthur and Pearl, had started the family company, but it was Frank who made the Perdue name famous. He did this by appearing in a series of TV commercials where, in his own super-nerdy way, he extolled the virtues of his birds and ended with the same memorable tagline: "It takes a tough man to make a tender chicken."

Frank didn't look so tough when he came to see me one day. He was a skinny little guy with a squeaky voice and a problem he was hoping I might help him solve. By then, Frank was doing big business everywhere across the Northeast—except in New York City.

"Nobody in New York will take my chickens," Frank said to me. "Not one supermarket chain. They're scared." And for good reason. Rumor had it that his competitors were people of highly questionable character.

Frank said he understood that I had an independent streak. "You're the New York maverick, I hear," he said.

"*Manhattan* Maverick," I corrected him. "Just one borough."

I'm not sure if Frank got my New York humor. I'm not even sure if Frank understood what a borough was. But as Frank spoke, Margo was sitting in her usual spot in the cramped office where I could see her but Frank couldn't. I could tell she was listening carefully and trying to decide what she thought of Frank's sales pitch, which he delivered in a meandering, folksy way.

"People like my chickens," he explained. "We've developed our own specialized chicken feed that includes marigold blossoms. You know marigold blossoms?"

I nodded that I did. That nod was a lie.

"They give a golden-yellow hue to the skins of the chickens," he went on. "No one else has that."

Finally, Frank got around to his point. He said his problem in New York stemmed from a labor-organizing campaign at his plant in Accomac, Virginia. The United Food and Commercial Workers Union was trying to unionize the Perdue Farms facility—so far without success. In retaliation, Frank said, a union vice president had urged supermarkets in the New York area not to sell Perdue products. The stores didn't want trouble with the union, so they were saying no to Frank's birds.

I didn't want trouble, either. But I also felt bad for Frank. I told him I had checked out his chicken and was indeed impressed. I looked over at Margo. She nodded a silent yes. I told Frank we would take his chickens, even if no one else would.

He ultimately settled the labor dispute and got his birds accepted virtually everywhere, including New York City. But I don't think he ever forgot the support we gave him. He would be a loyal vendor for decades to come.

....

In those business-building years, there was always something going on. Around the time that Frank Perdue came to see us, we were finalizing plans to open store number three. This was a big deal for the company, the biggest financial risk we had taken yet. I had found a location on Broadway between Eighty-Second and Eighty-Third streets. The building was owned by the Zabar family, whose legendary gourmet deli, Zabar's, was a little south of us. This was a far pricier stretch of Broadway than the locations of our first two stores. Everything I had, I put into this new location. Financially, the stakes could not have been any higher. If store number three failed, I could also kiss stores one and two goodbye.

I knew we had to open the store with a bang. I wanted to be sure everyone in the neighborhood knew that Red Apple had arrived. We needed an extravagant grand opening.

I hired a band. I ordered a couple thousand Red Apple balloons. I dreamed up a list of enticing food giveaways. I somehow convinced Margo—I'm still not sure how I did this—but I somehow convinced her and her friend Emily Segelstein (her dad, Irwin, was president of NBC Television) to put on clown suits and hand out those Red Apple balloons. We were all in.

. . . .

The store opening was everything I hoped it would be.

The weather was perfect. A giant crowd turned out. People kept streaming into our newest Red Apple, walking the aisles and perusing the fully stocked shelves. I thought the store looked great. The employees seemed pleased, too. I walked out to the sidewalk, where Margo and Emily in their clown suits were frantically handing out the red balloons.

As I took this all in, I couldn't have been prouder. The band was still playing. The sidewalk was packed. And every direction I looked—up Broadway, down Broadway, across Eighty-Second Street—I could see Red Apple balloons in the hands of happy people, bouncing up the thoroughfares of the Upper West Side.

"Now *that's* marketing," I said to myself.

. . . .

I had three stores up and running, and I wasn't done. Our small staff did their job, but I still needed more help growing. I made a point of connecting with talented people who were willing to give me guidance and advice.

One of my earliest and most important mentors was my first lawyer, Sam Stein. Sam had his own firm, Stein & Rosen, and his family was also involved in the supermarket business. They were smart and big-hearted people. Sam's brother Lou was chairman of Food Fair, a large supermarket chain. And besides practicing law, Sam owned a wholesaler in New Jersey called Filigree Foods. Sam was not only my grocery business mentor. He was also my lender.

When I was ready to expand the business, and every time after that, Sam would call up his controller and say: "Give John more credit. He wants to open up another store."

The experiences I had at my first stores kept serving me well. Within two years of my decision to expand, I had ten stores, mostly along Broadway: besides the Seven-Eleven at Broadway and Ninety-Ninth Street and the Red Apple at Eighty-Seventh off Broadway, we had Red Apples at Ninety-Sixth Street, Eighty-Eighth Street, Eighty-Second Street, and other locations.

Those stores fed a lot of hungry families. They kept a lot of people employed. They helped stabilize some rougher blocks on the West Side of Manhattan at a difficult time for New York. I was learning lessons about business that I hoped would carry me for the rest of my life. Sure, I'd disappointed my parents, but even they had come around.

I was twenty-four years old.

I was earning $1 million a year.

SUNDAY, OCTOBER 16, 1977

The Columbus Avenue Festival.

8

HIGH FLIER

I always knew I was born to fly.

I made paper airplanes when I was little. One time, I wrapped a bath-towel cape around my shoulders and jumped for hours off the living room couch. I loved macho flying movies like *Task Force*, *Dive Bomber*, *I Wanted Wings*, *The Dawn Patrol*, *Battle of Britain*, and *The Bridges at Toko-Ri*. It's no wonder that I dreamed in high school about attending the Air Force Academy. I'd seen the leather jackets that bomber pilots wore. What could be cooler than that? I had to put that dream aside—and West Point, too—when I agreed to stay home and go to college at NYU in the Bronx, but I never shoved flying out of my mind. I just experienced a brief ground delay. Even with two feet planted firmly in a growing and successful grocery business, I couldn't imagine spending my whole life on the ground. And I didn't have to. In 1975, when I was twenty-seven years old, I was earning enough money that I could afford to take flying lessons and consider buying an airplane of my own.

And so I let the real fun begin!

One glorious afternoon in May, I drove across the Hudson River and up toward the New Jersey–New York state line. Out past the aging factories and the close-in suburbs, I found my way to tiny Ramapo Valley Airport, now long gone, where I signed up for flying lessons. Just driving out there lifted my spirits. Once the instructor and I climbed into the single-engine trainer plane—I in the pilot's seat, he immediately to my right as copilot—I didn't have a care in the world. Why should I? I was gazing across farms and sprouting subdivisions. The clouds were down below us. We were soaring above everything. And the flight instructor was calmly explaining everything to me. Flying really wasn't so hard, it seemed. You just had to pay attention. And what a reward you got! Those clouds looked so soft and perfect, I swear I could have landed on top of them.

It was peaceful up there. It was quiet, too, except for the low hum of the engine, which was soothing in its own way. I quickly signed up for more lessons and got used to that feeling in a hurry. No matter how rough a day I was having, the sun was always shining at ten thousand feet.

I took enough lessons and logged sufficient flying time to earn my student license and to figure out what kind of airplane I wanted to buy. It was a Cessna 206, a rugged single-engine aircraft that you could load with half a dozen passengers and fly for one thousand miles. The station wagon of Cessnas—that's how the 206 felt to me. It was a highly forgiving aircraft, even with a newbie pilot at the controls.

Having only a student license meant I couldn't fly solo. But that was okay. I was happy to have a licensed pilot sitting next to me in the copilot's seat when I flew. Most of the time, that was Cliff Cawley, who had thirty or forty thousand hours of flying time to his name. The way I figured it, this guy was good enough to stay alive for all those hours. Why not have him sitting in the copilot's seat, watching everything I do? Clearly, he was someone who liked coming home alive. We definitely had that in common.

Every time I flew, I gained confidence and improved my piloting skills. Cliff made suggestions that were almost always useful. We made short trips and some longer ones, too. Cliff and I were in Orlando on business one day, and before we headed back to New York, I decided I wanted to fly to Cancún, Mexico. We thought nothing of it. Orlando to Cancún wasn't much more than a two-hour flight straight across the Gulf of Mexico. But as we headed over the open water, my imagination kicked into overdrive. And not in a good way. *This airplane has only one engine,* I recalled. I looked down at the huge expanse of water, and suddenly marine biology was a topic of great interest. *I wonder how many sharks are down there.*

Then, of course, I started hearing things.

A ping. A bump. A growl. Every few minutes, the engine sounded funny to me. *Hmm*, I thought to myself. *What was that?* Then I'd look down and still see no emergency landing strips—just water, water everywhere. After what seemed like forty-seven hours over the choppy Gulf water, but was really more like an hour and a half, I spied beautiful Cozumel. Suddenly, I knew how Christopher Columbus must have felt. What a relief to see land! Not long after that, we were touching down at the busy airport in Cancún. *Whew, I did it, and as long as I live, I don't think I ever want to do that again!* Nothing had happened. The flight was totally uneventful. It was all in my head.

That trip did, however, help convince me to trade up to a twin-engine aircraft and, not too long after that, to buy my first jet. It was right around then that Cliff, my friend Jim Jacobs (who worked at the Great Barrington Airport in Massachusetts), and some other friends started pushing me to get my regular pilot's license. "You can't be a student forever," Jim told me. "It's time for you to graduate." You can't fly jets until you at least have your regular license.

I had more than enough hours of flying time with Cliff and other licensed pilots. My skills were first-rate, they all told me. I certainly loved being up there. But to earn my regular pilot's license, I still had to meet two last requirements—take a flight test with a certified instructor and complete the required solo trip. I decided to do the test at Jim's airport in the Berkshire Mountains of Western Massachusetts. Jim Pelton, Jim Jacobs's right-hand man and an experienced pilot himself, agreed to fly up with me from New York. As he and I flew north, I practiced the various maneuvers I'd be expected to execute in the flight test. I followed his instructions. I did my S-turns. I did my thirty-degree turns. I did my sixty-degree turns. Jim said they were all flawless. He did have a word of caution, though: "The only thing he'll fail you on is your emergency landing. Be careful with that."

I told Jim I was prepared for it. I had studied emergency-landing techniques. I knew the drill. Pick out a safe landing spot. Circle once. Circle twice. Circle three times until you are low enough to glide gently in.

"Thanks for the heads-up," I told Jim. "I think I'm ready."

Once we landed in Great Barrington, the people at the airport couldn't have been nicer. They certainly lived up to the airport slogan: "The friendliest airport in the Northeast." The small facility, I knew, had a lineage all the way back to the 1920s, when a farmer's potato field was converted into a commercial aerodrome to serve the Gilded Age resort city, where wealthy city people came out for the cool summer air. The airport's modern setup featured a paved 2,585-foot runway and two instrument approaches—about as well equipped a general aviation airport as you would find. It was a perfect place to take my flight test. Plus, I knew one of the owners and his right-hand man.

Jim Pelton wished me luck as the flight instructor took his place in the copilot's seat. I wasn't nervous. I was eager to show the instructor my stuff. I pulled down the throttle. I let off the brake. We picked up speed down the runway until we were airborne. Once we'd gained sufficient altitude, I did my S-turns and thirty-degree turns and sixty-degree turns, all as smooth as glass. The puffy clouds reminded me how much I loved flying. I restrained my instinct to try landing on them. The Berkshire Mountains were off in the distance. The gentle valley was spread out below. This was flying the way it was meant to be, and the test-giving instructor seemed to think I was handling it all like a pro.

"Very nice," he said.

Then, as I began my descent, he reached over and turned the engine off.

"Emergency landing!" he called out, just as Jim Pelton had warned he might.

"Okay," I answered, keeping my cool. I was ready for this.

I picked out a spot for my landing.

I began my circles just like I was supposed to.

First circle.

Second circle.

Each time I made another circle and reduced my altitude, Jim's voice was in my head: "The one thing he'll fail you on is your emergency landing . . . The one thing he'll fail you on is your emergency landing."

And I kept saying to myself: *Don't screw up the emergency landing . . . Don't screw up the emergency landing.*

There was a lot going on inside my head. It wasn't until I was performing my third circle that I realized I was leaning a bit to the right.

Damn!

I was already too low to circle another time.

DON'T SCREW UP THE EMERGENCY LANDING!

The instructor was staring at everything I was doing and not saying a word. His job wasn't to help me. His job was to watch me. I got that. I did notice he seemed to stiffen a bit in the copilot's seat, though.

I gritted my teeth, banked the aircraft nearly sixty degrees, and aimed straight for the spot on the runway I had already picked out, slamming the plane onto the unyielding concrete, hitting the brake as hard as I could. It was a rough landing.

I could feel the wheels slam against the runway.

I could feel the pressure on my spine.

I felt two or three sharp bounces as the plane jammed to a halt.

We survived.

And for a solid minute, the two of us just sat there. The flight instructor said nothing, and I didn't have the nerve to speak. We just sat there. Collecting our thoughts and catching our breath.

Silence.

A minute and a half. Two minutes.

Finally, the flight instructor spoke.

"I should fail you for that," he told me. "I should definitely fail you for that. But if I fail you, I might have to fly with you again."

He didn't say the words, but I figured I had passed the flight test.

I wasn't totally done yet, however. I still had to do my solo fight, tracing a triangular route—150 miles by 150 miles by 150 miles—without anyone in the aircraft but me. Never having flown alone, I had some apprehension about this solo journey. But I knew I had to do it, and I was as ready as I would ever be. The first leg of three began in Portland, Maine.

My takeoff was as smooth as silk. I had no trouble getting airborne. Then I made the mistake of looking out the window and down below.

Oh, my God! I thought to myself. *I am ten thousand feet above Boston! There's nobody here but me!*

But I gulped hard and just kept flying. It was, in fact, a beautiful day to fly. And if I do say so myself, I was performing flawlessly. As I headed over Boston, I was reminded of all the things I loved about being above the clouds. The peace. The beauty. The soothing hum of the engine. But I still couldn't shake the other thoughts that were bouncing around my head: *What the heck am I doing up here all by myself? I am the only one who can bring this airplane down. Nobody else is going to bring it down. I'm the only one. My life is in my own two hands.*

I completed the mission that day, every last mile of it—three takeoffs and three landings without a hitch. That made me proud. And I recognized something fundamental about flying and something fundamental about me: I loved to fly. I would always love to fly. But no matter how much flying I did, I did not want to fly alone. The truth was I didn't like doing anything alone. I didn't like eating alone. I didn't like being in my apartment alone. When I was a little boy, I couldn't fall asleep unless my mother came into my room and put her arm around me. Why should I like flying alone? I wanted to be around other people, especially at ten thousand feet.

....

Nothing can bring you down to earth like family.

As the years went on, I still saw my father every day because he was working in the business. But that wasn't the case with my mother. My parents lived right next to the office, but my mother was spending more and more of her time alone at home. Over time, she and I spoke less and less often. No reason was ever articulated, but we really did seem to drift apart. I am not exactly sure why this happened. The cold shoulder my parents gave to Liba was surely part of it. That tension lingered in the air, not often spoken about but not easily ignored. My mother was still a relatively young woman. But for whatever combination of reasons, she was less outwardly focused, living more inside the apartment and more inside herself.

Margo noticed this before I did, and she didn't like it at all.

"You know what you should do?" she said to me one day. "You should let your mother cook lunch for you. Your father can bring it to the office. She doesn't want to come to the office. We both know that. But your father can bring it. Your mother puts you on a pedestal. She always has. You're her only son. She adores you. Give her some respect. Nothing would make your mother happier than fixing lunch for you. If you don't like what she cooks, throw it in the garbage. Then call your mother and say, 'I loved it. Thank you very much.'"

Margo had a point. She was talking, after all, about the woman who used to peel my grapes.

When I brought this up with my mother, she agreed immediately. "I can do that," she said. She started preparing lunch for me. Just as Margo suggested, my father brought it into the office for me. My mother was still sitting inside all day. But now she had something to do. It may sound silly, but cooking lunch for her son gave my mother a new purpose. She made lamb. She made fish. She made chicken. She made all kinds of things. And all of it tasted wonderful to me.

"Oh, my gosh," I said to Margo. "This food is so good. I didn't know my mom could cook so well." Just as Margo predicted, my mother beamed when I called and said that to her.

My mother got sick in her early sixties. This came as a terrible shock to me. She had cancer, and it wasn't one of the easier kinds. I made sure she began treatment at what I had always heard was the top cancer hospital on earth, Memorial Sloan Kettering Cancer Center. I could afford it. But even if I couldn't, I would have found a way. I was good with the practical stuff—finding the right doctors, getting quick appointments. But when we got the diagnosis, I felt like someone had just punched me in the chest. Really, really hard. And kept punching me. Though I had achieved many things in my life at that point, I was not prepared for how much I still defined myself in terms of parents, my mother especially. I could hardly imagine what life would be like without my mother—or even what my life would mean.

Again, it was Margo who sprang into action. Not me. Not my father. No one else. Margo. She was the primary person who looked after my mother in those dark times. She visited every day. She took my mother to her doctors' appointments. When my mother went into the hospital, it was Margo who spent by far the most hours at her bedside while also looking after my father's needs, which took a load off my mother's mind. My mother fell in love with Margo. My father did, too. Margo wasn't any more Greek than Liba was, but they'd had a chance to get to know her as a caring and compassionate person. I guess they didn't mind my having a non-Greek assistant, if she was as attentive as Margo was.

As my mother got sicker, Margo was always there. She was the only person my mother recognized in the final days of her illness, even when she stopped recognizing me. Margo never acted like this was any kind of burden. "It's what I was brought up to do," she said to me when I asked her about it. When she was young, she explained, she had taken care of her grandparents when they got old. She still looked after her mother and stepfather, who had moved to St. Petersburg, Florida.

But as my mother's health deteriorated further, the sadness of it all took a toll on all of us, Margo especially.

"Are you going to the hospital or going to work?" I asked her, knowing she needed a break.

"I'm taking care of your mother," she answered. "I think that probably comes first."

When my mother died at Memorial Sloan Kettering in April of 1977, she was sixty-six years old. I was four months shy of twenty-nine. By the end, I think my mother was ready. But I wasn't ready at all.

. . . .

I did what I could to stay focused on my work. I had stores to run. I had people to take care of. I had my father, who was still coming in to work every day and just pressing on. That is what he always did. He

ssed on. Me? I tried not to think about painful issues. I just took on ew projects and tried to stay as busy as I could.

I had been involved with the West Side Chamber of Commerce since the early 1970s. I was a West Side guy. I owned supermarkets on the West Side. It was only natural that I'd be active in the Chamber. But now seemed like the perfect time to turn up the volume on that.

The West Side Chamber of Commerce was a sleepy organization back then. The total budget was something like $28,500. The executive director, who ran the day-to-day operations, got a salary of maybe $15,000. The office cost $3,000 or $4,000. These numbers are from memory, but I don't think they're very far off. There were some incidentals. And that was the budget, and the budget reflected the organization's modest goals. Actually, I can't even tell you exactly what th goals were.

It seemed to me that the West Side business community need a little shot in the arm: something to be proud of, something to ra some enthusiasm, something the local residents and business peo could call their own. What we needed, I decided, was a major str fair. That's how the Columbus Avenue Festival was born. This v 1977—not the greatest time in New York City. But we decided would round up as many neighborhood businesses as possible and on a weekend-long party.

Margo helped organize this. So did John Campi, the marke director at the *Daily News*, New York's "hometown newspaper. few other business people also jumped on board. We had a highly m vated team. The time was right. People were ready for something. idea caught on spectacularly.

A million people turned out that first September weekend, pac Columbus Avenue from Sixty-Sixth Street all the way up to Ninety- Street. They came from the fancy doorman apartment buildings from the walk-up tenements blocks, too. We had merchant booth games for the kids. There were several stages of live music and ve lining both sides of the avenue. We had a huge Red Apple Supe kets stand. We sold red apples, three for a quarter. We weren't to make any money. We just wanted to get our name out anc

some fun. The festival had a great, friendly feeling—lik
small town plopped into one of the greatest urban neigh
earth. Everybody came, it seemed. And as dusk fell that Sa
Sunday, no one wanted to leave. People who'd been there on
came again on Sunday, they had so much fun.

"What are we doing next weekend?" they wanted to know. A
can't swear they were joking.

The Columbus Avenue Festival succeeded beyond our wildest dreams. It gave the neighborhood a little swagger and a sense of being cool. It was really the beginning of the retail revival of the Upper West Side of Manhattan. It was the neighborhood saying, "We're here. We're special. You should be a part of us." I felt like I was using my leadership skills from Brooklyn Tech again.

All of a sudden, the Chamber of Commerce budget went from $28,500 to $300,000. A few years later, the Columbus Avenue renaissance had progressed to a point that I felt comfortable looking one block to the east and asking, "Why not create an Amsterdam Avenue Festival? We could do that one every May." And that was almost as big. Eventually, Margo and I moved on from the Chamber of Commerce. The group was strong and energetic enough to welcome a whole new generation of leadership. But those festivals kept on roaring, and the Upper West Side never looked back.

....

Flying definitely broadened my horizons, even as I tried to keep my mind on New York. For the first time in my life, I started thinking seriously about all the amazing places I might like to go. Not idle fantasies. Actual imaginings. I had been to Greece as a teenager. I had visited Florida a few times. But since I'd started flying—well, the world felt a whole lot smaller to me. With a pilot's license in my wallet and my own airplane waiting for me, I could easily get to places I had only dreamed of, read about, or seen in the movies. Who said this had to stop with Cozumel or Great Barrington?

I bought my first jet from Roy Disney, Walt Disney's brother. It was a six-passenger, first-generation Citation—a very gentle aircraft. It was

a whole lot faster than the single- and twin-engine prop planes I had been flying. The tail number was N44RD, the last two letters for Roy Disney. If flying a plane was fun, flying a jet was fun times ten.

Cliff, who was still my friend and copilot, would fly down to the Bahamas on a prop plane, roaring one hundred or two hundred feet over the beach at two hundred miles an hour. The sails on the boats would sway beneath us. The surf would crash in. There weren't too many rules in the Bahamas. As far as I was concerned, there was nothing more exciting in the world than flying like this.

But owning a jet is expensive, even for someone with a lot of money. Fuel bills. Maintenance fees. Storage costs. And don't forget insurance. Not to mention the hefty check I'd written to Mr. Disney to cover the purchase price. There are all kinds of flying machines, but the nice ones are never cheap—and mine was very nice. As much as I loved flying, I was first and foremost a businessman. Once my head was out of the clouds, my mind landed right on the bottom line.

I said to Jim Jacobs one day, "I've been thinking about a way to make some money off this jet." I am good at solutions. If I have a problem, I can usually come up with a solution. That's what I do all day: find solutions.

I told Jim, "I know a couple of people in Atlantic City," executives at large casino hotels on the Atlantic City Boardwalk. "You know a couple of people in Atlantic City. Let's go talk to them about flying gamblers to the casinos."

I set up meetings. Jim did the same. We flew down to Atlantic City to pitch the idea.

"You already provide limos for your valued customers in New York and New Jersey, and that's great," I said when we sat down with the first casino executive in his spacious office overlooking the Boardwalk. "But what about your customers in Connecticut and Massachusetts and the other Northeastern states? The ones who are too far away for a reasonable limo ride?"

"We don't have many customers in that outer circle," the casino man said.

"Exactly," Jim piped in. "But you could."

"How would they feel about being flown to Atlantic City in a private jet? Would they like that?"

"They would like that," the executive agreed.

We kept going, laying out our plan. "If you draw a circle around Atlantic City—give it a four-hundred-mile radius. There must be fifty million people in that four-hundred-mile radius. We'll focus on the people in the outer ring of that circle."

The casino executive nodded. He seemed interested.

I proposed a deal and even suggested a sales pitch. "Tell those customers or potential customers, 'We'll fly you here in a private jet. You'll have dinner and play, and we'll fly you home that night or in the morning. You can tell your girlfriend you're going to take her to Atlantic City on a private jet.' They can make believe they're running with the large dogs for a night. You don't think people will like the sound of that?"

The casino would pay for the flights, I explained, the same way the casino paid for the limousine rides. "But," I added quickly, "you can more than make that up from the extra losses at the tables. These are customers you aren't getting at all now."

In fact, the arrangement made perfect sense for casino owners. They were already paying the $500 limo bill to fetch the close-in customers. That was worth it if the gambler would cooperate by losing $5,000 to $7,000 on the trip. Our jet was admittedly more expensive than a limo, but paying a $4,000 jet bill to bring in a high-rolling customer prepared to put $10,000 or more at risk was still a profitable bet for the casino. These companies keep amazingly close track of their customers' betting habits. With pinpoint accuracy, they know who is prepared to bet how much. They also know the odds of winning and losing. None of the chance business is left to chance. The gambling casinos aren't so different from life insurance companies predicting that most of their policyholders won't live to be ninety-nine, even though a few might. The casino bosses know how much, on average, a gambler will risk, as well as how many will win and how many will lose. Knowing how that works is the foundation of the casino business. Jim and I were just applying their data to private air travel. It was all in the numbers, and I knew the numbers could work for both of us.

So we made a deal. The jet started flying, and almost immediately, other casinos wanted in. Pretty soon, we weren't flying for just one casino. We were flying for three. Then four. Then six casinos. And it wasn't just one jet. It was five, then ten, then fifteen. By 1982, we had a fleet of twenty airplanes. We'd been calling the operation Turbine Air. Soon, we changed the name to United Jet Fleet, which sounded more modern, I thought. We would fly deep-pocket customers anywhere, but Atlantic City remained our most popular spot.

And we didn't stop there. We were doing so well that we bought a company called World Jet, plus a couple of other companies. All of a sudden, we had operations at Johnnycake Airport in Harwinton, Connecticut, and Bradley International Airport in Windsor Locks, Connecticut, and MacArthur Airport in Islip, Long Island. We took those three operations and combined them into United Jet Fleet. From that one jet and one casino, we grew the business to forty-eight airplanes, servicing an ever-widening area.

Even with our growing need, it wasn't hard to find talented pilots. Many were ex-military fliers with excellent training who'd retired young and still loved being in the air. They were eager to go to work for an airline or a charter service company. Like anyone in the commercial air industry, we had to deal with a lot of rules and regulations, but we always took that seriously. Safety was our top priority, and we insisted on maintaining the top industry-standard quality control. I'm not saying there was no learning curve. But once we got things up and running, the business side of it really wasn't difficult. We offered a service that people wanted and were willing to pay for. And we performed well. That's not a bad foundation for any business. Not surprisingly, the value of the company kept increasing. I'd done well stocking people's kitchens with groceries. But it wasn't long until I discovered there was a lot of money to be made flying people around.

When Jim, our team, and I had taken it about as far as we could, we sold that company to Richard Santulli, an associate of Warren Buffett who pioneered the concept of fractional jet ownership and used our newly acquired assets to help create NetJets in 1986. Santulli would eventually sell the company to Buffett's Berkshire Hathaway

Inc., where it remains a leader in that highly profitable industry. And all of it came from my looking to make a few bucks off the pricey jet I had just purchased from Roy Disney. It was a great business and also a lot of fun. But by the time we sold to Santulli, I had already met two gentlemen named J. Nelson Happy and Farhad Azima. My aviation dreams were flying higher than delivering high-rollers to the craps tables and roulette wheels. I was done with United Jet Fleet, but by no means was I finished with the aviation business. I knew that much. It was too much fun and far too profitable to pat myself on the back and walk away. In fact, by then, I was already wondering: *How hard could it be to run a full-fledged airline?*

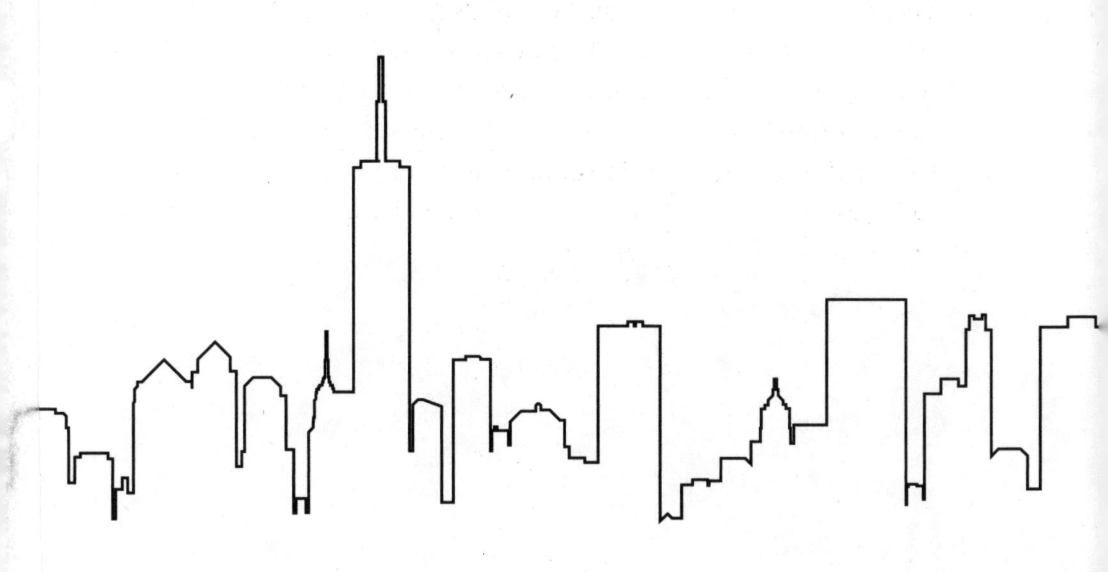

CAPITOL
CAPITOL

9

CAPITOL IDEA

J. Nelson Happy is one of the smartest people I have ever met in my life. He is a truly lovely man. But when we first met, Nelson was in a bit of a jam. He was Chairman of the Republic Bank of Kansas City and was struggling with a large investment he'd made in a charter-aviation company called Capitol Airlines. He'd teamed up with an Iranian-born aviation executive named Farhad Azima, and together they'd acquired 54.9 percent of Capitol. They installed John Jackson, a former Air Florida executive, as president of the airline. Farhad took the title of chairman. Nelson was still splitting his time between the airline and the bank.

Nelson showed up in my life in the first week of December 1983, offering to sell his share of the airline to me. He owed around a million dollars. After my cheerful experience with Jim Jacobs in Atlantic City, I was definitely open to being more involved in the aviation business. Capitol Airlines seemed like an exciting opportunity. Plus, Nelson was willing to sell his piece of the company at what sounded to me like a very reasonable price.

Before I dove in, I did my due diligence—or thought I did. The company had a proud history. It was founded at the end of World War II by a trio of former Army Air Corps pilots: Jesse Stallings, Richmond McGinnis, and Francis Roach. In the early years, the three of them operated a flight school and aircraft sales agency at Cumberland Field in Nashville, Tennessee. By the early 1950s, the company had acquired a fleet of piston-engine transport planes, including DC-3s and Lockheed Lodestars, and began carrying priority freight for the US Air Force and other customers. By 1956, adding twenty Curtiss C-46s, Capitol had become a primary civilian carrier for the military's Logistic Air Support program. Fifteen years later, the company had outgrown the little airfield in Tennessee and moved flight operations to New Castle Airport in Wilmington, Delaware, and entered the international charter market, carrying thousands of US vacationers to Europe and the Caribbean. Capitol Airlines was one of the first charter airlines to fly jets, mostly Douglas DC-8s, one of which set a world commercial-aviation record in 1984 by flying nonstop from Tokyo to Wilmington in twelve hours and twenty-five minutes. Soon, the company moved back to Tennessee, this time to the deactivated Sewart Air Force Base in the Nashville suburb of Smyrna.

With the Airline Deregulation Act of 1978, Capitol took another big leap forward, launching a busy network of regularly scheduled routes in the eastern United States and Europe. The company took over half the British Airways terminal at John F. Kennedy International Airport, plus additional hubs in Brussels and San Juan. From JFK, the airline served Los Angeles, Chicago, Brussels, Frankfurt, Paris, San Juan, and Puerto Plata. It was go, go, go at Capitol Airlines. That's how it looked on the outside, anyway.

Nelson and I settled on a price that was a little less than he was hoping for, and he agreed to remain involved in the company. As we'd been talking, I had really come to respect Nelson's intelligence and sound judgment. I was pleased to have him stick around. Before the deal could go through, however, he told me I would have to get the blessing of his partner—soon to be my partner, if all went well—Farhad Azima.

I didn't know much about Farhad, but I had a strategy for winning him over. The following Tuesday, Jim Jacobs and I flew out to Kansas City for a steak dinner with Farhad. People eat a lot of steak dinners in Kansas City. "I'm ready to buy more airplanes," I told him even before the Caesar salads arrived. "I want to expand the airline. We're just getting started here. Capitol Airlines should be everywhere."

Farhad's eyes lit up immediately. "Of course—I accept you, my brother," he declared.

A month later, in January 1984, Jim and I flew to Smyrna for our first Capitol Airlines board meeting. Nelson introduced us to the other board members, who included Fred Thompson, the future US senator. We also met John Jackson, the man who'd been installed as the airline's president. Right as the meeting began, the airline president looked at Jim and then at me, and said almost matter-of-factly: "So I think we're going to file for bankruptcy this week."

Bankruptcy?

What did he just say?

I looked at Jim. I looked at Farhad. Farhad looked at both of us. I looked over at Nelson, who was looking down at the conference table.

"Did he just say *bankruptcy*?" I asked.

This was our very first board meeting. The checks I had written for my share of the airline had just cleared the bank. And now the company was filing for bankruptcy? Not so fast! Was I about to get ten or twenty cents on the dollar for my investment? That didn't sound too good to me. Obviously, I needed to be more than a passive owner here.

We fired the airline's president. Farhad took over as Chief Operating Officer. I became Vice Chairman with a special focus on finances. I didn't trust anyone else to watch the money, so I watched it. All of us jumped into the deep end together without life preservers—actually, without any clue of how much water might be in the pool.

. . . .

So here was the real surprise: owning and operating an airline—a real, honest-to-God, major airline—was a total blast, even more than I hoped it would be. It put me in the middle of a fast-paced global enterprise with operations around the world. I almost had to pinch myself: look how far I'd come from 1Thirty-Fifth Street! Maybe we could actually save this airline! We could sure have fun trying. Aviation is a worldwide business. We had twenty-two offices around the world. Suddenly, I had a reason to fly to Brussels or to Frankfurt or to any other world capital that happened to strike my fancy.

I was still a Harlem guy. I still had the New York City supermarkets. I was still the boy from Nisyros who had climbed up from there. But suddenly, I was flying British Airways's supersonic Concorde to London and popping up in other major capitals around the world. Though the Capitol Airlines headquarters remained in Tennessee, I had a suite of offices in the Helmsley Building at 230 Park Avenue in Midtown Manhattan, just north of Grand Central Terminal. From there, my business territory was Planet Earth. Without even stepping outside, I could board an elevator in the lobby of the adjacent Pan Am Building and ride to the rooftop heliport. Even on Friday afternoons, as the city streets were choked with rush-hour traffic, I could chopper out to JFK in fifteen minutes and immediately board the Concorde. New York to London was three hours and eleven minutes, flying at 59,000 to 63,000 feet. It was a real experience. I must have made that trip fifty times.

We were part of the British Airways family. Let me tell you, that's not a bad family to be part of. Because of that partnership, we had full reciprocity. Our top people could take any British Airways flights. They could take any of ours, too, though to be fair I don't remember so many British Airways executives boarding our tourist-oriented charters or scheduled flights.

Commercial aviation, I learned in a hurry, is no business for the bashful. We were constantly adding new equipment, new destinations, and new routes. We were the first US airline to bring on the French-made Airbus aircraft. We leased them from Hapag-Lloyd, the German transportation conglomerate best known for cargo-container shipping. Operating globally, we had to be constantly aware of the business cultures of companies from different nations. For example, we had agreed to pay the Airbus lease fee every Friday at noon. Our German partner kept a close eye on the clock. If our wire transfer didn't arrive in Hamburg by 12:05 PM, my phones would be ringing in both New York and Tennessee.

That's the way it is in the international airline business. You deal with all manner of personalities and all kinds of characters. Some you learn to trust. Some become your friends. With some, it's all business, and with others, you have to run like hell.

Our company had chartered an aircraft to a charter operator named Nick. The flight was on a Friday afternoon, and it was supposed to take off from Miami at four o'clock. The aircraft was full of people, but just as they were taxiing to the runway, I had a hunch and quickly checked with my chief financial officer.

"Is the money in?" I asked.

"No, sir," he said.

"Then radio the captain," I directed. "Tell him, 'Turn that airplane back to the terminal.'"

That's how we had to operate.

It didn't take long. About two minutes later, the phone was ringing on my desk.

"What's going on?" Nick wanted to know.

"The wire transfer didn't get here," I said.

Believe me, if that plane had taken off without the money in our account, it could have been a very long time, if ever, before we collected a dime. But on this day, we were on top of it. By 4:30, Nick's people had wired the funds, and the plane took off.

I learned a lot about the aviation industry from Nelson, from Farhad, and from others we had in the company. But as interesting as all that was, you want to know what I really learned? I learned it's a great, big, exciting world out there. Filled with fascinating people and exotic locales. All just a quick flight away. Because of Capitol Airlines, I got around. I met people. I experienced cultures I had never experienced before. I didn't ever have to be a prisoner of the small Greek immigrant community where my family had first settled or even of the amazing city it was in—New York. New York isn't a bad place. In my experience, it's one of the most wonderful places on earth. But now I knew it wasn't the only place. The nation was my playground. The world was my playground. No disrespect to the supermarket business, but this was mind expanding. I hadn't realized how ready I was or how much I needed that.

Soon enough, we were expanding the airline just as aggressively as I had told Farhad we would. We added even more aircraft to the fleet. We kept expanding our route system. If we saw a profitable destination, we would fly there. Deregulation was still in full force, and we were well positioned to take advantage of it. Our costs were lower than at the so-called legacy carriers, who were stuck with pricey contracts, heavy pension obligations, and other expenses. And despite our rapid expansion into scheduled service, we never gave up our lucrative charter business, carrying people and cargo. Along with the vacationing tour groups, the airline got a big load of business serving the US military, one of Capitol's most important customers in the early days long before I arrived. One of our major trunk routes connected Rhein-Main Air Base in Frankfurt, Germany, to Charleston Air Force Base in South Carolina, with a refueling stop at Bradley Air National Guard Base in Connecticut.

That was good for us and perfect for the military.

....

Just because I co-owned an airline and had unfettered access to the flights of the Concorde didn't mean I had to stop flying my own plane. In fact, I flew more than I ever had. No surprise there. I had more places to go. I couldn't hopscotch across America in a supersonic jet. Often, that meant flying privately. But why is it when I start telling flying stories it's always the death-defying ones that jump first to mind? Over the years, I have flown thousands and thousands of hours, the vast majority utterly uneventful. Yet it's the bare-knuckle experiences that linger for me.

I will never forget one trip to the West Coast in 1984. Neither will Jim Jacobs, my copilot that day, or our four passengers. The jet was a Hawker 400, a midsize, twin-engine corporate aircraft that was just ten hours out of the shop, where it had gone for a full maintenance upgrade and a high-reliability engine check before our West Coast swing. Well, someone must have still missed something—perhaps not replacing or not fully tightening some very important screws. That's the best that I could figure. Back in the 1980s, engine reliability wasn't quite what it is today.

We were flying west from Denver to San Diego. From there, we'd be flying back to Nashville. I was in the captain's seat. Jim was beside me. We had four passengers with us that day, including Nelson, Farhad, and Farhad's lawyer. We were at 31,000 feet above the Rocky Mountains when something went *boom*!

I looked at my instruments. I could see right away there was a problem with the jet's right engine. I could hear it, too.

Ding! Ding! Ding!

All of a sudden, the airplane started shimmying. I could feel strong vibrations on the right side of the aircraft. One thing I knew? I had to shut down the right engine, and I didn't have time to waste. If the right engine fell off and hit the tail, it'd be *Good night, Charlie*, for all of us.

I shut down the right engine. The plane kept flying and the vibrations eased—but the shimmying did not.

The good news was that a Hawker jet can fly on one engine. The bad news was that the plane's maximum single-engine altitude was rated at nineteen thousand feet. We were at thirty-one thousand, and the Rocky Mountains peaked at about twenty-four thousand feet. How was I supposed to drop twelve thousand feet? How was I supposed to drop to seven thousand feet below what I was certain were some very rocky mountaintops? That didn't sound too safe to me.

Panic was not an option. I did what a pilot is supposed to do. I followed my training. I got on the radio and declared an emergency. Then I had to figure out where we were going to land. The closest airport was in Phoenix, Arizona, about one hundred miles away.

For the first time since the trouble started, I turned around and looked at the guys behind me. I thought they'd be pale as ghosts back there. But no—everyone seemed calm, almost jovial. Did they not understand the danger we were in? "We have an issue," I said in a firm voice. "We're going to Phoenix to make an emergency landing."

I assumed my passengers understood the meaning of the word "emergency." They were all grown-ups, after all. Hadn't they been feeling all the shimmying and turbulence? How could they not? I assumed they'd be in a state of genuine terror by now, maybe even saying their final prayers.

But no! They were irritated. Primarily, it seemed, at my choice of an emergency-landing destination.

"Phoenix?" one of them called up to the front of the plane. "Why Phoenix?"

"Las Vegas is just as close," I heard another voice call out.

I was dumbfounded. Suddenly, in an actual emergency, these guys were playing back seat navigators and travel agents? "We're going to Phoenix," I repeated.

"No! No! No! We want to go to Las Vegas."

You can't make this stuff up. "We're going to Phoenix," I said again. "It's closer."

But as I raked all this over in my mind, I did soften a little. I figured that, actually, Las Vegas might not be such a bad idea. And not just because after we landed—*if* we landed—I could probably use some time at the craps tables to calm my nerves. Vegas was a straight shot. It wasn't much further than Phoenix. I knew Vegas runways were long and wide. And I also knew that that the control tower and the ground crews there had plenty of experience handling distressed private jets.

I shared none of that with my rowdy passengers. The last thing they heard from me was about Phoenix. But I exchanged silent glances with Jim in the copilot's seat and pointed the nose toward Nevada, pressing gamely ahead. As we got closer to Vegas, I slowly reduced altitude. I made contact with the tower and declared an emergency landing. By the time I could see the broad runway, fire engines and ambulances were already lined up on both sides. They hadn't laid down the safety foam, though they were prepared to order that if they had to. They would have done it in an instant on my request.

It was perfectly possible to land this jet with one working engine. I knew that. The trick was that I couldn't afford to miss. I couldn't afford a missed landing where I would have to go around again. I had to land successfully the first time.

The landing was actually pretty smooth. A bump or two on the concrete, and we were down. As I taxied toward the gate, all four of my passengers had their noses pressed up against the windows. I'm not sure when these people came to their senses. But before we landed, I guess it hit them that we were in genuine distress. Now, with good reason, they all seemed very relieved to be on solid ground.

"This is Phoenix?" Farhad asked. "The buildings got a whole lot bigger since the last time I was in Phoenix."

"This isn't Phoenix," the lawyer said.

Somewhere between the runway and the tarmac, one of them noticed a sign for the Howard Hughes terminal. It was only then that my passengers realized that I had delivered them exactly where they wanted to be.

I had saved their lives *and* flown them all to Sin City, USA.

They let out one loud cheer. From the copilot's seat, Jim Jacobs complimented me on staying calm under pressure and making the executive decision that I did. Only one piece of uncomfortable business remained.

Checking into the Dunes Hotel for the evening, we had to call our wives and explain what the six of us were doing in Las Vegas.

I couldn't hear both sides of the conversations, but I could certainly imagine them. *Emergency landing? Las Vegas? A matter of life and death?* I'm sure all the wives had heard something like that before.

. . . .

Oliver North was a former Marine Corps colonel with a job on President Reagan's National Security Council, where he ended up at the center of a scandal that became known as the Iran-Contra affair. The basic allegation was that North hatched an illegal plan to sell weapons to Iran to encourage the release of US hostages then held in Lebanon, using the profits to fund the Contra rebels who were trying to overthrow the Sandinista government in Nicaragua. Unbeknownst to me until later, Capitol Airlines played a cameo role in that.

This shouldn't have been a big surprise, I suppose. Since its very early days, the company had done contract work for various agencies of the US government, both military and civilian. Flying in and out of international hot spots. Transporting equipment overseas. We had airplanes. The government needed airplanes. It was business for both of us.

By the mid-1980s, Capitol was doing a fair amount of US government work in Central America, flying in and out of San Pedro Sula and Tegucigalpa, Honduras, and San Salvador, El Salvador. We weren't running any operations. We were the airborne taxi drivers. And President Reagan was eager to stop leftist rebels from undermining America's friends.

Farhad was the one who handled all the details. Some of our planes were used in that effort. When I learned about it later, I saw nothing wrong with any of it. Why would I? All we knew was that a colonel named North was calling from the White House, where he was on the National Security Council staff, and ordering airplanes from us, presumably with the blessing of the Commander-in-Chief.

Our government was asking for help. We gave it. Plus, it was a longtime customer who always paid its bills.

As everyone is now aware, North's clandestine efforts became a huge story in Washington. Major hearings were held. Reagan took a lot of heat. Criminal trials were held. Even the name of the story sounded sinister: the Iran-Contra affair.

As the controversy blew into the public, Farhad was summoned to Washington.

"What do I do?" he asked me.

"You tell the truth," I said. "You got a phone call from the White House. You believed that Oliver North was working for the Commander-in-Chief. You're an American citizen. You did what you had to do. You did what your nation asked of you."

....

The 1980s were just a wild time to be in the aviation business. Fresh adventures were flying at us every day. Our flight from San Juan to Miami was hijacked to Cuba—three times. Thankfully, the hijackers were taken into custody all three times, and no one was hurt.

We also had a pilot kidnapped when he was delivering a plane to Africa.

And we kept finding new business opportunities, some of which took flight, some of which didn't. We bought twenty BAC-111s from USAir—twin-engine, sixty-six-passenger, British-made jets that were ideal for short-range flights. My associate wanted to fly West Coast gamers to the casinos along the Las Vegas Strip the way I had flown their East Coast cousins to the Boardwalk in Atlantic City. I thought the better play was in Greece, flying tourists to the islands. Those BAC-111s were perfect for short island flights. Neither one of those ideas got off the ground for us, but I still think the Greek-island hops were a good concept because of their close proximity.

We bought thirteen Boeing 727s and leased them to Pan Am, Northwest, and Trans World Airlines (TWA). During the first Gulf War with Iraq, Pan Am went into bankruptcy, and nobody rescued the company. So we got those airplanes back. But Carl Icahn, who owned TWA, didn't want to pay his bill, even though TWA at that time was sitting on a billion dollars in cash. I met with Icahn. We had a great conversation. After the meeting, he expressed his own frustrations about the airline industry, which both of us were sensing was becoming increasingly squeezed.

"John," he said to me, "if you and I can't make it in the airline business, nobody can."

We did eventually make a deal with TWA. It was a typical Icahn negotiation. They wanted to pay one fourth of what they had agreed to pay us. We did a whole lot better than that, but we didn't get to 100 percent.

Then real trouble flew in. Its name was PEOPLExpress, spelled funny, just like that.

With PEOPLExpress competing against us, Capitol Airlines was doomed. Founded in 1981 by Don Burr and several other refugees from Frank Lorenzo's Texas International Airlines, PEOPLExpress focused first on no-frills flights from Newark to Buffalo, Columbus, and Norfolk, routes that were decidedly second tier. But they added and added and added, and they kept their prices absurdly low—as little as $21 for short-haul domestic flights, $99 coast to coast. Next thing, they were advertising a cheap $149 fare from Newark to London. Some fliers, it turned out, didn't care so much that the boarding gates were mob scenes, that the leg room was just a rumor, and that the planes sometimes smelled like commuter buses with wings. The super-low fares were unbeatable.

History proved that PEOPLExpress was shiny on the outside and rotten at the core—"Enron before Enron" is how I like to describe it. It was never going to be a sustainable business. With huge debt from an overleveraged purchase of Frontier Airlines, PEOPLExpress was hardly a business from the start. They weren't making money. They couldn't make money with fares so puny, no matter how low their expenses went. But before they went under, they managed to suck the life out of quite a few of their competitors, including us.

Capitol Airlines was an operational success but a competitive failure, which is not so far from the hospital joke that goes, "The operation was a success, but the patient died." That's no way to keep a business afloat. By October of 1984, we'd decided that we'd better sell the airline.

Our buyer, Nicolás Nogueras Cartagena, was a hotel and real-estate owner and a politician in Puerto Rico who'd been the majority leader of the Puerto Rican Senate. His properties included the El San Juan and Americana hotels. And he had financial backing from Drexel Burnham of Puerto Rico. Despite the obvious challenges, the airline had a special attraction to him and his investors. Puerto Rico had long been one of our busier routes, with frequent flights from New York, Boston, and Philadelphia. As Cartagena saw it, those routes carried a lot of bodies he could lodge in his empty hotel rooms.

So we sold the airline to him and retained ownership of the airplanes as collateral. But sadly, before we knew it, Senator Nogueras's aviation dreams were also kaput. The company filed for bankruptcy, which meant we had to go into bankruptcy court to recover our fleet of planes.

We managed to get the airplanes back and sent them up to Canada, where they were used to launch that nation's third-largest airline, Nationair. But since we were US citizens, we weren't allowed to own more than 25 percent of any Canadian airline. So we teamed up with a Canadian partner who was in the airline business, Robert Obadia, and settled for collecting rental payments on the planes. I returned to New York to lick my wounds.

United Refining Company in Warren, Pennsylvania.

10

FULL TANK

Saying "see y'all" to the folks in Smyrna in December of 1984—that was a huge letdown for me.

One day, I felt like I was running the world. The next day, I was back on the West Side of Manhattan, operating my thirty grocery stores. I wouldn't be zooming around on the Concorde anymore or making deals in top international capitals. I was back in the produce department, deciding how much to charge for heads of lettuce and garlic. I had no issue with lettuce or garlic, of course, but I thought I was made for something bigger than that—farther away, at least. I wasn't sure I would ever claw my way into the big time again. Was the high flier permanently grounded? Were my round-the-world adventures over and out? Still in my thirties, was I already a has-been? Planet Earth wasn't my playground anymore. I was the neighborhood grocer again.

I was tempted to do nothing other than sit around, run my stores, and mope. Believe me, that's how I felt. But thankfully, my blues lifted quickly. I was still the same guy I had always been, right? The big time, I reminded myself, didn't have to be a one-and-done opportunity. If I'd expanded my empire once, couldn't I do it again? Pretty soon, I was sniffing around for something new to buy.

I didn't particularly care if it was a business I knew anything about. Heck, I didn't know much about aviation when I turned one jet into a charter business and then parlayed that into a major international airline. Going forward, I just wanted something I could get my head around so I could apply my insights and common sense. I didn't care if it had anything to do with the supermarket business. In fact, bonus points if it didn't. New is always invigorating. I liked expanding my mind.

As I thought about all this, I could see that I was well positioned to take on some new challenges. That's because I owned real estate. Quite a bit of it. Through the late 1970s and early 1980s, I had been quietly scooping up New York properties, often at very reasonable prices. This was a tough time for New York City. Crime was rising. Racial tensions, too. People who could afford to were moving to the suburbs and not looking back. City Hall had overspent and mismanaged its way into a fiscal crisis. Many people, in and out of the city, were certain that New York's glory days were entirely in the past.

I didn't happen to believe that. Or maybe I was just naive enough to overlook the depressing evidence. Or I just couldn't let a bargain pass me by. For whatever combination of reasons—slices of all three, I suppose—I had always kept my eyes open for good real-estate buys. Because of the city's shaky condition, the bargains weren't that hard to find, especially on commercial buildings in the Upper-Manhattan neighborhoods that had always been my territory. How things have changed, right?

When I found a solid piece of property at a reasonable price, my general philosophy was, *Grab it! If I can't find a find a tenant, I'll put a supermarket there.* Either way, I was bound to come out ahead. I could own a building with a rent-paying tenant. Or if for some reason I couldn't rent the space, I would have another location for a supermarket without the headache of a greedy landlord raising the rent on me. And all the while, I figured it was only a matter of time before New York got back on its feet and those depressed property values started rising again.

Real estate is an ideal backup plan for someone in a thin-margin business like supermarkets. I felt like I always needed a backup plan. Now, whether or not I made a lot of money selling groceries, I would also have real estate to rent or sell as I saw fit.

This also meant I was building a portfolio of assets that I could turn into collateral if I ever wanted to walk into a bank and seek a loan. Bankers like collateral, something of value to cover the money they are lending in case you fail to pay them back. They are much more comfortable lending money if they can tell their loan committees: "Don't worry. He owns a lot of buildings. We can always take one or two of those if he tries to skip out on the debt."

That's how bankers think.

So even in my post-Capitol funk, an important realization was shoving its way to the front of my brain. If I could find a company worth buying but would need to borrow some money to finance the deal, I wouldn't have much trouble getting a loan. The trick was keeping my eyes open for the right company. And wouldn't you know it: the company found me—in bankruptcy court, no less.

As the new owners of Capitol Airlines were trying to salvage what they could and we were working on getting our airplanes back, the federal bankruptcy trustee who was handling the matter was also overseeing the liquidation of a regional chain of gas stations. That would turn out be to an unexpected and wonderful coincidence.

The gas station company had an impressive history and a serious-sounding name: United Refining Company. Until 1979, United Refining was publicly traded and listed on the New York Stock Exchange. But it ended up in the hands of some clever operators from Houston. They sucked so much cash out, they drove United Refining into bankruptcy. That's when I stepped in.

Using my real estate as collateral, I borrowed some money and wrote a check. It wasn't even that large of a check. The company was in distress, and there weren't too many other potential buyers lurking around. This wasn't a glamour business, but I thought it might be a steadily profitable one. The company's main assets were more than three hundred Kwik Fill gasoline stations in Pennsylvania, Ohio, and Upstate New York, and a small oil refinery in Warren, Pennsylvania—an old lumber town on the Allegheny River about twenty miles up US Route 62 from Jamestown, New York. This was part of the old Northeastern manufacturing belt. Hardworking people. Close-knit families.

Not much manufacturing left. Lucille Ball came from Jamestown. So did naturalist Roger Tory Peterson, singer Natalie Merchant, and NFL Commissioner Roger Goodell. I'm not sure if anyone famous came from Warren. But damned if United Refining didn't have a refinery there!

I'm not kidding when I say I didn't know much about the oil-refining and gasoline-retailing businesses. To me, those three hundred gas stations looked like three hundred little grocery stores that happened to have pumps out front. I figured I'd buy the company and get a nice return on my investment from the pip-squeak grocery stores. People would pull in. They'd grab some soda, some beer, a bag or two of Doritos or potato chips—and then fill their cars with gasoline. It would be a nice little business.

Little did I know that retail gasoline stations have even slimmer profit margins than supermarkets do. Price matters a lot when people decide where to fill the tank. A penny or two a gallon is often enough to lure the customers into your station or send them across the street. You have to sell a lot of gasoline to do well at the pump, and you'd better think twice before jacking up the price.

Ah, but oil refining! That's a totally different story. Who knew that oil refining could be such a gold mine? Turning crude oil into gasoline and other petroleum products—that's when the cash registers really start to ring. Ninety percent of our profits, it turned out, would come from the refinery, not the retailing.

The refinery had its own pipeline from Canada. Canada is a huge producer of oil, much of it in the province of Alberta. In those years, Canada was producing about 1.5 million barrels of oil a day. (It's been twice that in recent years.) We'd buy wholesale Canadian oil, then pipe it down to the refinery in Pennsylvania, where it would be processed into gasoline and other fuels. I began to learn a lot about refining oil, starting with how big a barrel of oil is.

The answer is forty-two gallons. That's been true ever since August 1866, when several of America's earliest independent oilmen met in Titusville, Pennsylvania, forty miles southwest of Warren, and agreed on that number. The forty-two-gallon barrel was officially adopted by the Petroleum Producers Association in 1872 and has been the industry standard ever since.

Things get a little complicated from there, but not so complicated that it couldn't be learned. When that barrel of oil is refined, it produces about twenty gallons of gasoline, twelve gallons of diesel, four gallons of jet fuel, and about seven gallons of other products, like liquefied petroleum gas and asphalt.

If you've been adding on your fingers, you might have noticed that all that comes out to more than forty-two gallons. How is that possible? Easy. There is something called "cracking" that occurs in the refining process. Because of cracking, that forty-two-gallon barrel of crude oil produces forty-three and a half or forty-four gallons of refined product. You get a nice little bonus at the end.

Owning our own refinery gave us a tremendous advantage over other independent gasoline retailers—for much the same reason I liked owning the buildings where I had a supermarket. We weren't dependent on paying someone else to do our refining for us. We didn't have to wait in line behind their other customers. We didn't have to cover their profits. We weren't at the mercy of their rate increases. We had more control over the quality of our product and our own destiny. And every drop of that oil, by the way, came from right here in North America—not some distant nation that seemed to despise us.

When we were ready to open new gas stations, we made sure to pick locations within a two-hundred-mile radius of the refinery—a reasonable trucking distance from Warren. That's how it works. The crude oil came by pipeline to Warren. After it was refined, most of it arrived at the pump after a short tanker-truck ride. That was just about the perfect production and distribution scenario. And we did one other thing that might have been the most important of all: we came up with a way of differentiating our gas from the gas being sold at all those other stations across the street and down the block. In other words, we marketed.

The basic idea came the way any good marketing idea arrives. It started with a question and an open mind: "How can we sell more gasoline?" For us, the answer wasn't too difficult. All we had to do was focus on where our product came from.

In those years, people across America were feeling frustrated with the Middle East. The Israelis were constantly threatened by their neighbors. The Arabs couldn't seem to get along with each other. The Saudis were throwing their petro-dollars everywhere. Islamic fundamentalism was on the rise and, with it, some very scary terrorism, too. The Organization of the Petroleum Exporting Countries (OPEC) had a stranglehold on Middle Eastern oil prices and supply. This was all over the news at the time, and all over the coffee-shop and barroom conversations, too. It left a bad taste for many Americans.

Well, we weren't selling any Middle Eastern oil. One hundred percent of our product came from North America. Canada, to be precise, but that's still North America. And every drop of that North American crude oil was processed in our refinery in Pennsylvania by hardworking Americans in the proud Northeastern manufacturing belt.

That was the story. It was true. And we told it as loudly and as often as we could. Kwik Fill! You couldn't get much more American-sounding than that. I knew that a patriotic marketing campaign would give us a real competitive advantage if we could plant that reality in our customers' minds.

So we went on television with an advertising campaign that was unapologetically red, white, and blue.

"As an American, there's something I feel you should know," the commercial began. "We don't have to send our money overseas when we buy gasoline."

The ad featured a diverse group of Americans—White, Black, Latino, Asian, male, female, young, and old—speaking plainly to the camera, seamlessly finishing each other's thoughts about the importance of buying American. "United Refining Company in Pennsylvania makes its gasoline with 100 percent North American crude oil," the ad continues. "When we buy United Refining Company gasoline at Kwik Fill, we keep jobs in America. We keep businesses in America. We keep American families strong."

And then came the kicker:

"Make America stronger. Buy American-made gasoline at Kwik

Fill." I think Donald Trump may have gotten his famous campaign quote from us—with a very minor wording switch!

I dreamed up the ad and wrote the copy myself. It was brilliant, if I do say so myself. We doubled our sales in the next five years.

The message was very straightforward. It wasn't complicated at all. It was as diverse and unifying as America is. The American flag was flying. No one in the ad was embarrassed to express American patriotism. And it spoke right to a feeling of the moment. People were anti-OPEC, anti-Middle East, anti-terror, and anti-dictatorship. We capitalized on that.

Our message was unmistakably clear and tugged at the patriotic heartstrings. Buy Kwik Fill gasoline. Our stations serve Middle America, Buffalo to Pittsburgh. God bless America. You want to give your money to the Middle Eastern despots? You want to buy some Saudi prince another limo? We didn't think so. Buy American gasoline.

United Refining was my first big hit after returning to New York all sad and blue about Capitol Airlines. I still own the company. It's proven over and over to be a home run. Once I understood the value of owning our own refinery, once I saw the advantage of getting our oil close to home, I never looked back and never wanted to.

* * *

The mid-1980s, prior to the stock market crash of 1987, were Wild West days in the financial markets. Corporate raiders were targeting each other's companies. Highly leveraged buyouts were the order of the day. Any risk that wasn't excessive was considered a sign of timidity. These were the times captured so vividly in the movie *Barbarians at the Gate*. The titans of American capitalism were like Pac-Man, gobbling up everything in sight. Wharton Business School graduates who didn't believe in gravity seemed to be taking over the world. Back in New York, I wasn't deep in the middle of all that craziness. But I was close enough to experience some of the head-spinning drama and even profit from it. I may still have been a humble grocery man, even if my eyes were cast far away. But I'd like to think I more than held my own.

In the fall of 1985, the corporate raider Ron Perelman was staging a hostile takeover of Revlon, Inc., the iconic beauty products conglomerate. Revlon was a typical target for one of these assaults: a proud American business that had gotten a little soft over the years. The company was started in 1932 by brothers Charles and Joseph Revson. Working with chemist Charles Lachman—the L in the Revlon name—the Revsons created a new type of nail enamel that used pigments instead of dyes. From that humble beginning, Revlon grew into one of the top cosmetics houses on earth. But by the time Perelman showed up, the company (then in the hands of President Michel Bergerac) seemed to have lost a step or two to archrival Estée Lauder. Perelman's final bid of $58 a share—a total of $2.7 billion, including assumed debt—was enough to leave the other potential buyers crying in their rouge dust.

To pull off the Revlon deal, Perelman used an odd corporate vehicle—a troubled supermarket company that he and his junk bond lenders had taken over just a few months earlier: Pantry Pride. Perelman's plan was to acquire Revlon, then liquidate some of Pantry Pride's assets, which included forty-seven supermarkets in Florida, southern Georgia, the Tidewater region of Virginia, and the Bahamas. Under the pre-1986 law, he could still keep $300 million to $400 million in Pantry Pride losses on the books to offset his profits and bulk up his equity in the heavily leveraged $2.7 billion Revlon deal.

Got all that? Nothing was ever simple when Perelman was involved.

He certainly didn't care about grocery stores and their famously narrow margins. He just wanted to carry forward the Pantry Pride losses as tax-free equity in the Revlon deal.

I knew the supermarket business. I liked the idea of keeping the people employed. And Florida had always been a good place to make an investment.

Chemical Bank, Perelman's lender, said to him: "You've got to prove that you can sell something—how 'bout making a deal to sell those supermarkets before we close Revlon?" In fact, the bankers were downright insistent. They would not approve the Revlon deal until Perelman closed a deal to sell the Pantry Pride stores. And there I was, interested in buying and ready to negotiate. He was a super-aggressive, deep-pocketed corporate raider. But at that moment, I knew he needed to consummate a deal. Yes, it's always more fun negotiating from a position of strength.

Perelman's initial asking price was $100 million for the Pantry Pride supermarkets and the shopping centers they were located in—scattered like Florida seashells from Riviera Beach to Key West. I told him I liked the store-and-real-estate-combo idea, but I thought the price was a little high.

So the negotiations began. I dealt mostly with his closest adviser, Howard Gittis, whose title was Vice Chairman of MacAndrews & Forbes, Perelman's diversified holding company. They were still in the swirl of trying to buy Revlon.

I would go up to their office on East Sixty-Third Street. But we wouldn't talk there. Howard and I would go downstairs and walk around the block in one direction. Ron and whoever he was talking to about the Revlon deal would walk around the block in the other direction. We'd meet each every few minutes on one side or another, going opposite ways.

Every three or four days, they'd raise their Revlon offer by another $100 million—and they'd come down by $5 million or $10 million on what they wanted for the Pantry Pride assets. My strategy was to keep the conversation going and not agree too quickly. The number that I cared about, what I'd have to pay, kept going down. I'd like to think both of us got a good deal.

....

A few months after I made the Pantry Pride deal with Perelman, I had another potential purchase in my sights. Only this time, the seller wasn't a hard-charging New York corporate raider. It was the Dallas-based Southland Corporation—deep in the heart of Texas, the world's largest operator and franchisor of convenience stores, and the people behind 7-Eleven.

Was I ready for American capitalism, Lone Star style?

At that point, Southland had thousands of 7-Elevens around the world and, for reasons no one could quite explain, a small chain of upscale supermarkets in and around New York City. Southland had bought the supermarkets in 1968 from the descendants of Charles and Diedrich Gristede, two German immigrants who opened their first Gristede Brothers store at Second Avenue and Forty-Second Street in 1891. As the New York area grew in the decades that followed, so did the number of Gristedes family stores. They caught on especially well with more affluent shoppers, people who wanted gourmet items and personal service and didn't mind paying extra for it. By the early 1970s, when I first came into the supermarket business with Cousin Tony and Uncle Nick, Gristedes was one of the big boys of the industry. They had corporate backing and family know-how. I had respect for what they had achieved.

By the 1980s, however, the Gristedes operation was facing a new set of challenges. The New York supermarket business was changing quickly, and I'm not sure the 7-Eleven folks in Texas really knew how to respond. City rents were rising. Compared to the massive layouts of other stores, New York supermarkets were relatively small. New York had something called unions, which weren't such a factor in Dallas. And the New York competition, from Red Apple and others, was growing increasingly intense. Together, all this sent Southland's Gristedes division into a sharp downward spiral. In 1980, they'd had nearly one hundred locations—seventy-five Gristedes supermarkets, plus another twenty-four Charles & Co. sandwich shops. By 1983, the total had slipped to eighty-four. The following year, Southland closed another thirty-six stores and the main Gristedes warehouse, shuttering almost everything outside Manhattan. And no one seemed to think they'd hit the bottom yet.

I flew to Dallas on a Thursday afternoon in June 1986 to meet with Southland Chairman John Thompson. His family had been in the ice business back in the 1920s when one of their employees suggested, "Hey, maybe we should try selling eggs, milk, and bread, too." Having all that ice around made refrigeration a whole lot easier. And with that modest step, customers wouldn't have to travel long distances to pick up a few basic items. So was born the modern convenience store. You could say the idea really took off. But that didn't mean the

Thompsons or their Southland Corporation knew how to run supermarkets in New York.

I didn't fly commercial to Dallas. I flew my own jet. I wanted to look like a big boy to the Texans.

I walked into John Thompson's office. He couldn't have been more gracious or relaxed. I think he saw me as someone who might cure the headache he'd been suffering. He pulled out a piece of scrap paper. And then we went back and forth—but only briefly—on the terms of a deal. We agreed in a matter of minutes, and then he said, "Come on, let's go upstairs and have a drink while the lawyers type up the contract."

They had a terrific restaurant and bar on the top floor of the Southland office building. So we rode the elevator up and had a drink while the lawyers wrote up the deal. In just a few hours, we'd bought fifty Gristedes stores for a great price. They even threw in what remained of the Charles & Co. sandwich shops, which weren't worth too much. Altogether, the purchase was quite a bargain for someone with experience operating New York supermarkets. Thompson just wanted out.

With all the expanding we'd been doing at Red Apple, and now with another fifty stores, the Gristedes purchase made us one of the largest supermarket chains in New York City. The two brands remained distinct. They had different slices of the market and appealed, to some extent, to different customers. I didn't want to water down either brand. We did start remodeling some of the Gristedes stores, however—fourteen of them by the fall of 1987, adding in-store bakeries, delis, and salad bars. We put more emphasis on prepared foods and take-out items and upped the seafood offerings. These were all obvious enhancements that the Southland people could have done themselves, but I think they were just sick of the New York supermarket business by the time they sold to us. By contrast, the Charles & Co. sandwich shops were hopeless, as far as I could see. We pulled the plug on them as quickly as we could.

. . . .

What a run that had been! I came from Smyrna, Tennessee, in December of 1984, leaving Capitol Airlines. Almost immediately, I was negotiating to buy United Refining, which I heard about because we were working to get our Capitol jets out of bankruptcy court. We bought Pantry Pride in January 1986 and Gristedes in June. That was awfully quick. But that's how it happened—how we went from being a nice $100 million business on the West Side of Manhattan to a far-flung, multistate enterprise with $2 billion in sales.

Why did all these major players—the sellers and the bankers—want to deal with me? I wasn't the biggest or the richest or the best connected. I wasn't a pushover, either. We got great bargains on all three deals. I've thought about this a lot, and I keep coming back to the same two things: they knew I was an honest guy, and they knew that I had enough collateral to pay everyone back. The price we paid for Gristedes was chump change to Southland and to Chemical Bank. These numbers were petty cash to Ron Perelman, and my bankers had the solid in Florida in real estate. They knew that if worse came to worst, they could close those Florida stores tomorrow and turn the real estate into cash.

They never had to, of course. The business was going gangbusters. We paid back every nickel to everyone.

People still ask me: How did you do this?

One other factor, I believe, also came into play. I had no children yet. Even though I was married, Liba and I didn't have kids. That was liberating in a financial sense. The minute you have children, your sense of responsibility goes up twentyfold. All these deals had risk attached. I was playing in arenas where I was certainly lacking in expertise, but I had faith in my common sense. Nothing in business is 100 percent. But by not having children, I wouldn't have to worry so much if it all came crashing down and I went broke. I wouldn't have enjoyed that, I'm sure. But I could have lived with it, and I knew it.

But failure was never really an option. I was working twelve to eighteen hours a day. Nothing else was demanding my attention or my time. I could take the risk while devoting the time and energy necessary to make sure we succeeded. And that's what I did.

The only common ground between all these separate operations was me. I had a management team in Florida to run and oversee the

Florida operation, which ended up expanding into the Bahamas and the Virgin Islands. The oil company was run by a management team in Warren, Pennsylvania, where the refinery was. So I had an overhead view of Florida and Pennsylvania. The people there reported to me. But I wasn't responsible for all the day-to-day details. The people on the scene knew much more about those businesses than I did. I delegated to them. And the New York operation—Red Apple, Gristedes, and the real estate—was run by me in New York.

There was no other way to run a company on that scale. I gave my people the confidence to go forward, the assurance we were all going to win together. They looked at me as an open-minded, common-sense businessman who believed in them. That was all stuff I'd learned in my leadership experience at Brooklyn Tech. It was just as true in the business world.

You earn loyalty by picking the right people and letting them see that you have confidence in them. That's leadership. It's giving people the courage and the ability to win. I didn't need all the details. I had the right people in the right places.

That even worked when we bought by accident. In the Pantry Pride deal, we somehow ended up with a kosher food distributor in Florida. Zion Foods, the company was called. We ran that successfully for many years, even though I'd never claim I was an expert in kosher foods. We had a rabbi for that who kept me in the loop and reported to me. But I didn't second-guess his decisions on whether items should be certified as kosher or not.

Imagine if I'd stuck my nose into that! Oy vey!

I never got cocky. I never got overconfident. I just did what I had to do every day. I went to work and led my people and gave them the confidence to do their best. If you know a better strategy for succeeding in business, I wish you would share it with me.

John Catsimatidis with Fr. Alex Karloutsos at the 1992 Inaugural Parade on the balcony of Senator Daniel Patrick Moynihan's apartment in Washington, DC.

11

MY PRIEST

It was in the early 1980s that I began to find my way back to the Greek Ortho-dox Church, though saying I found my way *back* may be a slight exaggeration. I had been an altar boy a quarter century earlier. I had attended the Greek American Institute from fifth grade to eighth grade. I'd always believed in God. But, truthfully, I was never an especially religious person, not in any organized way. I just wasn't. I showed up at Mass on major holidays. I lit a few candles here and there. But churchgoing had never been at the center of my life.

It would be nice to claim that my triumphant return, if that's what you want to call it, was the result of some profound spiritual awakening on my part. But it wasn't. I never had one of those Saint Paul moments of being blinded by sudden light on the road to Damascus. Like so much else in my life, this was far more gradual and down-to-earth than that. I met someone I liked and admired, who happened to be a priest in the Greek Orthodox Church. He led me somewhere I hadn't planned to go.

He was Father Alexander Karloutsos, though everyone—and I mean *everyone,* from presidents to global business leaders to little Greek ladies in Queens—knew him as Father Alex. When Father Alex was a young priest in New York in the 1970s, a decade before I met him, he directed the youth ministry for the Greek Archdiocese. A friendly man with a natural charisma and undeniable charm, he quickly got to know the young people in the church and worked well with them. Soon, he was meeting their parents and their parents' friends. A natural networker, Father Alex started opening doors for his boss, Archbishop Iakovos, and for other church leaders—doors that had never been opened before. To local politicians. To potential donors. Even to the large and powerful Roman Catholic Archdiocese of New York, which in those days was run by Cardinal Terence Cooke.

Out of the blue one day, Cardinal Cooke called Archbishop Iakovos, who'd been the primate of the Greek Orthodox Archdiocese of North and South America since 1959. "My God," the Roman Catholic Cardinal said to the Greek Orthodox Archbishop, "you've got a young priest over there. He knows everybody, and everybody loves him."

Archbishop Iakovos summoned Father Alex to the Archdiocesan headquarters on East Seventy-Ninth Street near Central Park. "You know what?" the Archbishop said to the young priest. "I have some new duties for you. I'd like you be our liaison to Washington and various other leaders in this great country of ours."

The Archbishop had always liked mixing with national and religious leaders of all sides and faiths. He had gotten huge international attention in 1965 when he'd joined Martin Luther King Jr.'s famous civil-rights march in Selma, Alabama, including a photo with Dr. King on the cover of *Life* magazine. But in recent years, some of the broad acclaim had faded. In fact, not long before meeting with Father Alex, the Archbishop had received what he considered a less-than-enthusiastic invitation to Jimmy Carter's inauguration in Washington. It was one of those if-you-really-want-to-come-you-can invitations that leaves you not quite knowing how to respond. The Archbishop thought that Father Alex might be just the right man for the job.

"Would you be willing to help with this?" the Archbishop asked the young priest.

Father Alex said he'd be happy to. In the weeks and months that followed, mayors, governors, and other boldface names started dropping by Seventy-Ninth Street to see the Archbishop. Some of them Father Alex introduced as if they were old friends.

Then a few months after that, Archbishop Iakovos had a new request. "Can you take over fundraising?" he asked Father Alex. Money was another matter that needed attention, the Archbishop explained. There were many Greek Americans with money, the Archbishop pointed out. If they were approached right, wouldn't they be willing to give generously—or at least more than they'd been giving in recent times? "Our church needs an endowment fund," the Archbishop said.

Father Alex had no more formal experience in the fundraising field than he did in government relations. But it was clear that both areas needed attention, and no one else was offering to take charge.

"My responsibility is to be a priest shepherd," Father Alex told his Archbishop. "If that means improving relationships, if that means raising money, then that is what I will do."

Father Alex and I met on account of a meat strike. I'm not kidding. This was in the spring of 1981. By then, he was assigned full-time to the church's ornate headquarters on East Seventy-Ninth Street, where his official title was Assistant to the Archbishop for Public Affairs. He was handling fundraising and politics and bringing fresh energy to the staid Archdiocese. As a practical matter, he was quickly becoming the public face in America of the Greek Orthodox Church—mixing with politicians, dealing with the media, weighing in on the passing controversies of the moment, and building up his network of influential Greek Americans. He liked to host big dinners where people would meet and talk and eat and drink, often late into the night.

I was running my supermarkets, oblivious to all of this, when I got a call from Father Alex shortly before Greek Easter, which fell on April 13th that year. Father Alex told me he was planning an Easter supper to celebrate the holiest day of the Christian year. The guests were coming. The menu was planned. This being Easter, he would be serving lamb. That was the idea, anyway. As it happened, the union representing butchers in New York City was out on strike at the time. Father Alex had called all over Manhattan and Queens but could not find a single butcher shop or grocery store that had any mutton. But someone had told him there was a Greek American businessman on the West Side of Manhattan who owned some supermarkets, and—who knows?—he might know how to get his hands on some nice lamb chops for a needy Greek Orthodox priest, even in the middle of a butchers' strike.

"I hear you know a lot of people," Father Alex said to me. "I was hoping you might help me find some lamb."

I told him I thought I might be able to help him—I thought I knew who to call. "And I'll make sure you get a good price," I promised him.

Father Alex likes to joke that this was last time I ever made him pay for anything. After that, all I did was give and donate.

It wasn't hard to do.

I liked Father Alex immediately. He wasn't preachy. He was a priest, but he understood how to operate in the secular world. To me, he was like a bridge between the realm of God and the realm of man. He understood people, and he knew how to motivate them to support a good cause. When he had a project that he was raising money for, he would call me, and I would write a check. When he needed a contact or a phone number or lead of some sort, I would try to help him. He always sounded happy to work with me.

In 1984, Father Alex had a big idea. He announced he was forming something called Leadership 100, a special group of one hundred Greek Americans who would each promise to donate $100,000 to promote the social values of Greek Orthodoxy and the many good works of our faith. The money would be used to establish a lasting endowment like many large institutions had, a steady stream of financial support. It wouldn't be enough to keep the mission going forever, Father Alex said, but it was a whole lot better than zero. Father Alex asked if I would join the group. I agreed immediately.

He'd already recruited some successful people, almost all of whom I had heard of when he mentioned their names to me but very few of whom I actually knew. There was Dennis Mehiel, whose Four M company was one of the nation's largest producers of corrugated shipping containers. There was Michael Jaharis, who'd taken an insolvent cough-syrup company and built it into a major pharmaceutical firm. By then, Jaharis was investing in biotech companies, far before almost anyone else was.

"These are self-made guys like you," Father Alex told me.

There was Jim Chanos. The Yale-graduate son of a Milwaukee dry cleaner, he'd risen through the ranks on Wall Street and was just then launching his own hedge fund, Kynikos Associates (in Greek, *kynikos* means "cynic"). A sharp-eyed short seller with a nose for the next financial meltdown, Jim had already earned the nickname of "Wall Street's most notable bear."

There was Alex Spanos, who'd begun his career as a baker before buying a panel truck with an $800 loan and selling sandwiches to Californian farm workers. Investing his profits in real estate, he grew his A.G. Spanos company into one of America's largest housing developers. At that point, he had just purchased 60 percent of the San Diego Chargers football team.

Father Alex was right. Every one of these men had an inspiring story of success.

Up until that time, my only Greek friends—other than my Greek relatives—were the kids I had gone to school with at the Greek American Institute. At Brooklyn Tech, at NYU, in the supermarket and aviation and energy businesses, I hardly knew any Greeks. Most of my mentors were Jewish. Other than me, there weren't many Greeks in the supermarket business. My wife, Liba, was a German and Jewish, not Greek. My assistant, Margo, was Russian and Polish. I lived in New York. We had people from everywhere. But as I began getting involved with Father Alex and Leadership 100, I was meeting people who told the same kinds of stories that I told and who shared some of my life experiences. I was hanging around with people like electronics manufacturer George Chimples; steel magnate Andrew Athens; Arthur Anton, whose family ran a dry cleaning empire; George Kokalis, who founded a major produce cooperative and the Sure Safe chain of supermarkets; John Ledes, the editor and publisher of *Cosmetic World* and *Beauty Fashion* magazines; and George Tenet, a US Senate aide who would go on to direct the Central Intelligence Agency.

These were substantial, smart, engaged, and generous men who had already made their marks on the world and were still brimming with dreams and energy. Suddenly, I didn't feel so alone in the world.

These were Greek Americans like me. They'd all accumulated wealth and influence. They'd mostly made it on their own. And like me, they were just now getting connected with people who shared their heritage and experience. And one other thing: like me, many of them had nowhere else to go. Father Alex brought us all into the Greek community and—since he was a priest, after all—into the Greek church. And he made it all so easy.

To be part of Leadership 100, Father Alex said, you didn't even have to pay the $100,000 all at once. Ten thousand a year over ten years—that was all he was asking. I don't think the cash flow was a big issue for too many of these guys. Some of them were used to paying six-figure initiation fees just to join a golf club. And far more important than the easy-payment terms, Father Alex really seemed to get the psychology of people like us—successful business people, first- and second-generation immigrants, who'd risen from modest circumstances to positions of genuine wealth, power, and influence in America. He understood that, as a rule, we weren't big joiners. In fact, we often felt a little isolated.

"You are my eagles," Father Alex said to several of us one day, a comment I know he has repeated many times over the years. "Eagles don't flock, right? They soar. Once you are an eagle at this level, your natural tendency is to set yourselves apart, even from other Greeks."

Father Alex understood all that when he dreamed up Leadership 100. "To you, the assimilation process has meant more than being Greek. You want to say, 'I'm an American.' That's the number-one thing: being accepted and succeeding in America. But you came from somewhere—at least, your people did. And that is important, too."

You had to give it up for Father Alex. He could get things done.

If he could bring a bunch of us together, Father Alex understood, we might actually discover a connection to each other and therefore to our culture and our church. Thankfully, there are many successful Greeks in America. Who better than the church to bring them together? "This isn't about making money," Father Alex often said. "You guys all have money. Those of you who want fame, you already have fame. Up until now, you didn't have each other, and now you do."

He was right. I was meeting people through Father Alex who made me affirm my own Greekness, something I had hardly ever thought about before. For ten thousand dollars a year, this was far more fun and far more meaningful than joining a fancy golf club. I didn't even like playing golf. And one last point about Father Alex: he was given the Presidential Medal of Freedom by President Biden in July 2022 for his great works helping America.

There's a famous quote about university politics. Over the years, the quote has been attributed to Woodrow Wilson, Henry Kissinger, Harvard political scientist Richard Neustadt, Columbia political scientist Wallace Sayre, and probably half a dozen others, too. I don't know who said it first. My guess is that the line's been repeated, borrowed, and stolen so many times, no one has any idea who dreamed it up.

The quote goes something like this: "Academic politics are so vicious because the stakes are so low."

Well, I can say this much based on my own personal experience—those sharp-elbowed professors have nothing on the political combatants in church!

As the years went by, without a single heads-up from anyone, Archbishop Spyridon appointed me to be the highest-ranking layperson in the Archdiocese. My first instinct was to try to duck the dicey honor. My second was at least to consider it. My third thought was, *This might not be too much fun, but I suppose I'd better step up and try to help at this extraordinarily difficult time.* And suddenly, there I was. The title was Vice Chairman of the Archdiocesan Council, the equivalent of the church's board of directors. In our church, the Archbishop always holds the honorary title of Chairman, so I wasn't in line for that. Vice Chairman is as high as a layperson can get. As Vice Chairman, I didn't weigh in on theological issues. That was still the Archbishop's purview. But I was ultimately responsible for the business affairs of 526 churches across eleven metropolitans and dioceses.

Like it or not, I was suddenly in the middle of everything, and I became a leader throughout the international community in church affairs.

Top: John Catsimatidis with President George H.W. Bush. *Middle:* John and Margo Catsimatidis with New York City Mayor David Dinkins. *Bottom:* Massachusetts Governor Michael Dukakis, Democratic Candidate for President in 1988, with Margo and John Catsimatidis.

12

POLITICAL ANIMAL

The word politics derives from the Greek word *polis*, meaning "city" or "com-munity," and the related word *polītēs*, which is Greek for "citizen." When Aristotle called us "political animals," he was not referring to the animalistic nature of politics. What he meant was that we human beings have a natural love for being in the agora, the marketplace, the central public space in ancient Greek city-states where people liked to gather and where ideas were vigorously exchanged.

When Father Alex reminded me of that one day, I was pretty sure Aristotle was talking about me. Get me to the agora at once!

I had been interested in politics since I was in knee pants and my father would come home from the restaurant with the *New York Post* and the *Journal-American*. I loved the characters. I loved the issues. I especially loved the back-and-forth debates. I was a registered Democrat since I was twenty-one and old enough to vote. In those days, just about everyone in New York City was a registered Democrat, especially in immigrant neighborhoods like West Harlem and liberal bastions like the Upper West Side. But I was never a rigid ideologue or a real party man. On some issues—civil rights, education, taking care of the less fortunate—I definitely leaned toward the Democrats. But on other topics—budgets, taxes, keeping the government out of peoples' lives—I was more in tune with the Republicans. As a businessman,

I was almost always in favor of whatever it was that worked. I was never quite sure what the correct label was for someone like me. Independent? Free-thinking? Commonsensible? Those were all fine descriptions. But whatever you wanted to call me, the more I dove into the world of politics, the more fascinated I became.

Ever since the 1970s, I had been making small contributions to political campaigns. I'd give a thousand dollars here, a thousand dollars there. I gave to people I liked, Democrats and Republicans, and I didn't ask for anything back. No favors. No contracts. No legislative earmarks. Nothing. Really, I just gave and left it at that. I think some of these candidates were confused or at least surprised by my lack of an obvious agenda. They or their campaign managers sometimes cornered me: *Come on, what's your angle?* Eventually, they came to see I didn't have one. It wasn't about that. I wanted to see good people get elected. I truly just wanted to help.

Donating to campaigns did have one benefit that I suppose you could call personal. I did enjoy meeting and getting to know the various power players, up and down the political ladder and on both sides of the aisle, even if it did mean buying too many tables at boring fundraising dinners. One thing I can tell you 100 percent for certain: money does buy access in politics. If you make contributions or provide other help, politicians and their handlers will be happy to meet you, and they will always return your phone calls.

....

In the summer of 1984, I decided to get my hands dirty a bit. Instead of just writing checks and being friendly, I joined a political campaign. Not as a candidate. I didn't see myself as someone running for office—that wouldn't happen until much later. This was an entirely behind-the-scenes role. Being active in the community and a well-established businessman, I knew most of the local politicians. Others had hit me up for contributions, which I tended to oblige. One of those local pols was a man named Jerry Nadler, who by the mid-1980s was already a familiar face on the local scene. He was a real political junkie, even more into it than I was. Though he was born in Brooklyn, he graduated from

Manhattan's Stuyvesant High School a year before I graduated from Brooklyn Tech. His successful campaign for student-body president was managed by Dick Morris, the future Bill Clinton adviser and TV talking head. After graduating from Columbia University and Fordham Law School, Jerry was elected to the State Assembly and now had his sights on the Manhattan borough president's job.

"John," he said to me as he was putting his campaign team together, "I want you to be my finance director"—a fancy title for the person who goes around and tries to convince others to write generous checks. It's not the easiest job or the most glamorous in politics. But it's definitely one of the most important.

I had no experience helping to run a campaign. The closest I'd ever gotten was my high-school volunteer stint with Congressman Ryan—and all they'd let me run was out for coffee. But when Jerry Nadler asked, I was game.

"I'm not doing anything," I told him. "Why not?"

Scott Stringer, who would himself later serve as Manhattan borough president and city comptroller, was the campaign manager.

Our guy was a liberal Democrat, definitely more liberal than I was. But a job like borough president had almost nothing to do with grand political philosophies. The late New York Mayor Fiorello LaGuardia once said: "There is no Republican or Democratic way to pick up the garbage." That about summed it up for me.

The candidate we were running against was someone I had never heard of. His name was David Dinkins, and he was a lawyer who'd been quietly climbing the Democratic machine as President of the Board of Elections and city clerk. I had no idea that, four years later, this low-key gentleman would be elected mayor of New York, defeating three-term incumbent Mayor Ed Koch and an aggressive former US attorney named Rudy Giuliani to become the first African American to hold the city's top job. But in the summer of 1985, as far as I was concerned, he was just Jerry Nadler's opponent in the Democratic primary for Manhattan borough president.

When the votes came in on September 10, Nadler lost and Dinkins won. Dinkins then breezed to victory in the general election on

November 5. I was disappointed by the outcome, of course, but I loved being that up close to the whole political process. I knew I wanted to stay involved. And no one needed to feel sorry for Jerry Nadler. Though he lost a 1989 race for city comptroller against Brooklyn district attorney Elizabeth Holtzman, he remained in the State Assembly until 1992, when he was elected to the US House of Representatives, where he would build a long career and rise to Chairman of the all-powerful House Judiciary Committee.

Ten years after that long-ago borough president race, the three of us would be standing together at an event in Washington—Jerry Nadler, David Dinkins, and me. I remember drinking a Diet Coke. Jerry was also definitely drinking a Diet Coke. I don't recall what David was drinking. By then, I considered both of them friends of mine.

Out of the blue, David spoke up. "John," he said, "I never asked you. Why did you help run Jerry's campaign against me?"

I was surprised by the question, though of course he had every right to ask. I thought for a second and answered.

"He asked me," I said, nodding my head at the now-veteran Congressman. "I was bored. I didn't have enough to do. He asked me, and I said yes. I didn't do it to be against you, David. I just did it because I wanted to do something to help."

David laughed. He didn't seem upset at all. I think he appreciated my honesty. I had just given him the truth.

....

Politics became like a hobby to me. No, it was more than that—somewhere between a hobby and an addiction. That's how much I enjoyed being involved. In the decades that followed, I would come to know thousands of politicians and support hundreds of political campaigns—from newcomers seeking the lowliest local offices to presidents of the United States. Knowing Father Alex and working closely with him opened a lot of doors at the upper end.

Through my favorite priest, I got to meet Jimmy Carter, who was the first president I'd ever met in person and was exactly like he seemed on TV. Nice. Well mannered. Decent. Not too forceful. Through

Capitol Airlines, I got to travel to the White House and meet Ronald Reagan, who was just as warm and likeable as I expected him to be. I also got to meet Reagan's Vice President, George H. W. Bush. I really liked him. He was a smart, experienced man who seemed very level-headed to me. Conservative but in a kind, balanced way. Not extreme or excitable. Just solid. And when he ran for president himself in 1988, I was certainly planning to support him.

I was *planning* to.

But all of a sudden, a Greek American candidate showed up in the race. He was Michael Dukakis, the governor of Massachusetts, where he had presided over an economic revival that some people were calling the "Massachusetts Miracle." He had beaten several other solid candidates in the Democrat primaries and, that July, won the nomination at his party's convention in Atlanta. He chose Texas Senator Lloyd Bentsen to be his running mate and seemed to have a pretty good shot against the Republican ticket of Bush and Indiana Senator Dan Quayle.

As all this was unfolding, Father Alex came to me one day and said, "Vice President Bush is our friend."

"I know," I answered, not quite sure what the priest was implying. "I like Vice President Bush."

"We all do," Father Alex continued. "But we have an obligation to Michael Dukakis. We have to help him, too."

If a Greek American won a major party nomination for president, Father Alex seemed to be saying—how could prominent Greek Americans not be there for him? I agreed to do my part.

That didn't diminish my admiration for George H. W. Bush. His intelligence, his demeanor, his experience—any of it. To me, he was the class act of the remarkable and elegant Bush family, and I still feel that way. But when Father Alex asked me to help Michael Dukakis, I understood why that was important, and I stepped up. I raised some money from the Greek community and wrote some checks to do my part. I also joined the "inner circle" of the Dukakis campaign.

The inner circle was comprised of five to seven people who traveled with the candidate for a week at a time. We were expected to be present day and night, to give advice, to serve as a sounding board, to be helpful in whatever ways we could. As a member of the inner circle, I experienced my first truly intimate view of life on the presidential campaign trail. *The circle was a great idea*, I thought. It was also loads of fun. I spent a week on the road with the candidate and came away with the feeling that I was witnessing democracy in action, right up close, the profound and the trivial. I came away with a healthy respect for the professionals who keep a national campaign on the road.

We met at six o'clock every morning in the candidate's hotel suite. By then, the reporters would already be waiting outside in the hall, wondering what we were doing on our side of the door. In fact, what we were mostly doing was watching their reporting on TV, trying to figure out what to say next. True story. I've lived it. They wanted our comment on whatever was the news of the moment. We listened to their questions through the television, crafting the candidate's answers as the reporters waited just a few feet away. A symbiotic relationship, I believe that is called.

The reporters needed something fresh for the morning TV shows and the afternoon newspapers, something beyond what the morning papers and the prime-time news shows had. Social media wasn't yet part of the equation. There was CNN but not yet Fox News Channel or MSNBC. Still, the competition was fierce and, along with paid advertising, the news media was the primary way to get our message out. It was a great lesson in the sausage factory of American politics, and I ate it up.

All days are long days on the presidential campaign. Motorcades. Airplanes. Strategy sessions. Rallies. Meetings with supporters. We went through cities like a hot knife through butter. I did that for one solid week. I was still young, and even I was exhausted. How fifty-four-year-old Michael Dukakis had the stamina, I did not know. But he did, day after day after day.

We had to walk a careful line here. A church is not supposed to take political positions or endorse candidates, and yet I was at least informally representing the Greek church. We helped Dukakis. And we also helped Bush. It wasn't that the Greek church in America had special demands of either candidate. It was more important that we be at the table, that we be in the conversation, that we be on the trail. And we were.

One of these candidates was going to win the 1988 presidential election. One of them would be in the White House. Going forward, the church needed to have open lines of communications, no matter which side ended up in the Oval Office. I was part of making sure of that. It made total sense to me.

John Catsimatidis proposes to Margo Vondersaar in the Grand Ballroom of New York's Plaza Hotel.

13

SUNSHINE GIRL

Life often has its own ideas, whatever alternate plans you might have made.

That's a lesson I kept learning over and over again. I'd achieved far more financial success than I ever could have imagined, and it came to me at a far younger age than I had any right to expect. I got into industries I never dreamed I'd be part of. Aviation? Oil and gas? Really? I met people I probably had no right to meet. Presidents, church leaders, business titans—are you kidding me? I'm hanging out with *them*? I certainly never planned on being a player in the national political world. The future is tough to predict sometimes—I do know that much. That goes for my personal life, too.

Liba was a wonderful person—smart, hardworking, focused, and down-to-earth. That's how she was when she first showed up at my apartment with her soon-to-be ex-boyfriend. That's how she was the day she died in January 2018. She was a loving, supportive wife to me and always a friend. And yet, since we'd gotten married so haphazardly, neither one of us really knew what being married was all about. It was something Liba thought was the natural next step for us at the time. The way she described it so matter-of-factly—I figured she could be right. Did we lack understanding and commitment way back then? Probably. Did we lack maturity? Absolutely. And then there was the issue of my family. The sad fact of the matter is that my parents never fully welcomed her into the family. Liba wasn't Greek, and that was hard for them to swallow, no matter what else she was. Obviously, she couldn't change her own ethnicity.

Over the years, some of the romance had undeniably faded. In 1986, when Liba asked me for a divorce, I understood where she was coming from. I was so focused on my work and other things, I hadn't given her the attention she desired. She, too, had grown distant from me. Since she and I had no children, getting divorced wasn't nearly as complicated as it might have been. I didn't want to fight with her about anything. She'd been there with me for so much of the journey. I wanted her to have whatever she needed to live comfortably for the rest of her life. And although our marriage was coming to an end, I didn't see any reason for her to leave the job she'd performed so well for so long. She kept working for me, which I was thrilled with. I was happy for her when she found a new love, and I felt her pain when her daughter died three days before her twenty-first birthday. Nice people all around.

....

When Liba and I got divorced, I had no idea where that part of my life would lead. Would I stay single? Would I marry again? I didn't want to rush into any rash decisions. And I told Liba I'd wait a year until I did anything.

Successful thirty-nine-year-old businessmen have dating opportunities, even if they don't look like George Clooney, sing like Bruce Springsteen, or dance like Fred Astaire. That's just the truth. And I'd been married since my early twenties. I'd been out of the New York singles scene for a good, long while. Actually, I'd never really been *in* the singles scene. In the days when I was single, I was juggling school and work, and then Liba came along. But now that I was an adult and word got around that I was freshly divorced, friends of mine started introducing me to their female friends. As a well-off newcomer in the grown-up dating world, I was surprised how some women didn't even wait around for a proper introduction. They were more than happy to introduce themselves. But I was still clueless about what I wanted. I wasn't sure exactly how to react. Not knowing who else to talk to and not quite sure how to bring it up, I broached the subject with Father Alex.

I told him I was having trouble figuring out what I wanted to do next. Not with my business. My business was going fine—better than fine, even. It was my personal life I was thinking hard about. My marriage was over. Did I want to jump into another one? Was I better off single? Who, if anyone, did I want to share the rest of my life with? I told Father Alex I was genuinely confused and could really use his advice.

"John," Father Alex said to me, sounding very serious all at once. "Success can be a dangerous place for you. A lot of people want things from you."

"I know," I said.

"A *lot* of people," he emphasized. "Women included."

I nodded.

"When you are in that situation, you have to be clear about what's important to *you*—what *you* really want."

I knew that Father Alex was right about that, and I also knew I wasn't there yet. "I'm not sure I know what's important to me," I said.

As the years had gone on and my business life had become more successful, people did ask me for things. I didn't mind it. Often, I was happy to help. Donations to worthy causes. Business opportunities. Personal connections. Political backing. Professional advice. When I could help, I would. It brought me pleasure. It did some good.

But now I also noticed that women were paying more attention to me. Some women, anyway. I don't think I was any better looking than I used to be or any more charming. But now that I was single again, women who had never given me a second look were suddenly eager for my companionship. In a way, it was flattering. But it also made me suspicious. Was it my sex appeal or my checks appeal? I hated to question anyone's motives, but the attention did make me think twice. Thankfully, I'd always had decent instincts about other people's behavior. Generally speaking, I could tell the users from the trustworthy ones—and keep my distance from the user crowd. But watching all that swirl around me did give me an extra level of appreciation for my old friends and colleagues, people who'd been with me when the potential advantages were not nearly so obvious.

I was very blessed in that way.

Father Alex was right. Before I committed to another serious relationship or thought about getting remarried, I would have to be clear on who had my best interests at heart and what was important to me.

He didn't try to tell me what to do. He pulled out of me what I needed to know.

"What do you want more of in your life?" he asked.

One word came out of my mouth.

"Sunshine."

Father Alex gave me a quizzical look—was I was planning on moving to Florida? "Sunshine?" he asked.

"Not that kind of sunshine," I said. "I am very blessed by the people in my life. But at the end of the day, Margo is the sunshine. She makes me happy. She is the one who makes me smile. If I ever have children, I would want my children to always enjoy sunshine in their lives."

"That's important," Father Alex told me. "Very important."

Father Alex seemed happy for me. He wasn't strong-arming me or pushing me. He never did that. He didn't try to make me feel guilty for getting divorced or getting remarried. He just seemed to want me to be happy and to succeed. What more can you ask of your friend? What more can you ask of your priest?

"Go with the sunshine," he said.

• •

HANAC, the Hellenic American Neighborhood Action Committee, is a wonderful community service group. Founded in 1972 by George Douris, a former newspaper reporter who became a politically connected public relations executive, the organization focuses on job training, adult literacy, affordable housing, and similar good works. HANAC's annual fundraising gala, held each fall in the Grand Ballroom of the Plaza Hotel, is attended by everyone who's anyone in New

York's Greek American community. Every year, I reserve a table, which I fill with a group of my favorite relatives, business associates, and friends. HANAC is a worthy cause, and I've always been happy to do my part.

At that year's gala, George took the stage like he always did, singling out the major donors, thanking everyone for coming, describing the new programs HANAC had in store. And then he made a special announcement. "Margo," he said, "will you come up on stage, please?"

Margo looked around the Plaza ballroom. She glanced in my direction and shot a suspicious look at me. She glared even more sharply at George. But she couldn't exactly refuse his invitation. He was on stage and calling her name. She certainly couldn't hide in this crowd. Slowly, Margo walked up the center aisle to the stage.

"George," she half-whispered when she got up there, "what are you doing?"

He didn't answer. What could he say? He just waved me over and held out the microphone. I joined both of them on the stage.

The room was suddenly quiet. All eyes were on the three of us. People who'd been talking stopped talking. They were trying to figure out what was going on. Was there some new program George forgot to mention? Was there a large donor who still needed to be recognized? Word may have leaked a little. I'd given a quiet heads-up to a couple of my closest friends. But I don't think anyone had broken anything to Margo.

"Well," I said, stalling for time and trying to find the appropriate way to put this.

"You know," I continued, "I've been walking around for the last couple of weeks, and I had a ring in my pocket."

"A ring?" Margo said.

I pulled out the ring.

It was a nice ring.

She looked at me, not even glancing down at the ring. "Yes?" she asked. It was a question, not an answer, urging me to go on.

"Well," I answered. I'm not sure what I was waiting for. I honestly didn't know what words to use. Margo could see I was struggling.

Then, like the kind person that she's always been, she tossed a life raft to a man who was drowning, just when he needed it most.

"You have a ring," she said. "And what does that mean?"

I took a deep breath.

"Okay," I said finally. The relief must have sounded obvious to everyone in the ballroom. "Will you marry me?"

And despite my meandering presentation, despite my mumbling tone, Margo Vondersaar delivered an answer that was both loud and clear.

"Yes!" she declared.

At that, the whole ballroom erupted in cheers and applause.

George came over and hugged the both of us. Father Alex did, too. So, did a couple hundred other people, including most of my relatives and many of my closest friends. They were happy for us. I could see that. And I was even happier.

On October 2, 1988, Father Alex married Margo and me at the Greek Orthodox Cathedral of the Holy Trinity on East Seventy-Forth Street. He had a lot of help from his friends. They included, by my count, one archbishop, six bishops, an assistant to the patriarch, and more priests than I had fingers. We had Russian Orthodox clergy and Roman Catholic clergy and a couple of rabbis. I'm not sure if they thought our marriage needed the extra blessings, but Margo and I were both happy to accept whatever grace might be tossed our way. We had a reception for four hundred people at the Pierre hotel fourteen blocks to the south on Fifth Avenue. Joining us were Margo's mother and father, Albert and Jane "Tatiana" Vondersaar, as well as her brothers Chuck, Edward, and Victor and sisters Jeanette and Tammy.

Plenty of my aunts and uncles and cousins were there. My father beamed like the proud papa of the groom that he was. But when Margo danced with her father, the thought hit me: I should have been dancing with my mother that night. In fact, it had been more than a decade since we lost her, far too young. It was a hugely celebratory night. We were surrounded by all these people we loved who loved us back. But I couldn't help it. Thinking of my mother, I choked up for a moment. I had to look away and compose myself. My mother had loved Margo so much, and Margo had loved my mother. Margo had been there for her in my mother's final days when my mother needed it most. I just wished my mom could have been there to share the day that her son finally had a proper Greek church wedding, even if the bride didn't arrive from Nisyros or anywhere close. I know my mother was smiling down at us.

Ultimately, though, I was really proud of how everything had turned out. I'd had a choice to make. I chose the sunshine. And I was so glad I did. As events unfolded, it vindicated my good judgment.

On December 2, 1997, Margo's birthday, my father died. It wasn't sudden. He wasn't young. He was ninety-three years old and had lived an extraordinary life. Born and raised on Nisyros. Spending all those years alone on an island lighthouse with no one and nothing to keep him company but a handful of goats. Embarking on two bold adventures almost at once—into marriage and fatherhood and then off to America with a wife and a child. Making a life for himself and his family in the land of opportunity and never once looking back. My father had taken immense pride in me, his only son. I know he did. It was a special blessing, all those decades after he retired from the restaurant, that he could come to work for me.

My mother had died twenty years earlier. And still, I wasn't prepared to lose him. My dad and I had gotten especially close during those two decades. I dreaded the thought of sharing the news with seven-year-old AJ and four-year-old John that their beloved *Pappoú* had gone to heaven. There were many tears in our apartment that day.

Dad had been terribly lonely after my mother died. Eventually, he met a lovely woman named Anthoula, who was also from Nisyros. I was surprised but happy for him when they married. He was getting older, and it was a comfort to know he had a kind woman looking after him. When we got the call that Dad had passed, it was Margo who took charge of notifying our family and friends. She made arrangements for the wake at the Frank E. Campbell Funeral Chapel and the funeral at Holy Trinity. After the service, we all climbed into a limousine and followed the hearse along beautiful, winding roads through the hills of Westchester County to Mount Hope Cemetery.

Everything had been done perfectly. My father had the beautiful goodbye he deserved. When we got back in the limo, my head was filled with the warm words of condolence, the extravagant flowers people had sent, and the many generous donations made in his name. I leaned over to thank Margo for everything she had done. I knew that December 2 would never again be the same for either of us.

Top: John Catsimatidis with American Labor Leader and Civil Rights Activist Cesar Chavez.

Middle: Margo Catsimatidis in the Camp David Library.

Bottom: John Catsimatidis swims with daughter, AJ, and son, John Jr.

14

LITTLE ONES

After George H. W. Bush defeated Michael Dukakis for president in 1988, I got more, not less, involved in national politics and in other larger issues, sometimes involving my business, sometimes not. I felt bad for Dukakis, my fellow Greek American, whose intelligence and sincerity I'd come to admire. But I was also perfectly comfortable with Bush in the White House. He was our president. From the day he took office, January 20, 1989, I was happy to help him in any way that I could. Again, my goal was to give, not to take—to find some way I could be useful and then pitch in. I wasn't quite sure what that might entail. It's amazing how open people are to your assistance when you aren't asking for anything in return.

It was in this spirit that I connected with Cesar Chavez, the legendary founder of the United Farm Workers union. Chavez was very frustrated at the time. For five years, he had been trying to convince California growers to quit spraying pesticides on their grapes. Chavez was trying to sustain a California-grape boycott. His union printed up bumper stickers: "NO GRAPES" and, in Spanish, "UVAS NO." Chavez even went on a thirty-six-day, water-only fast. He shed thirty-five pounds. But the big California growers kept on spraying their grapes with pesticides, insisting there was nothing for anyone to worry about.

Cesar Chavez certainly wasn't convinced.

In the summer of 1989, he came to New York to meet with the owners of the city's supermarket chains. He figured we were his last and best shot. If the supermarkets would put some muscle behind the grape boycott, he hoped, the growers might finally cut back on those pesticides.

I think I surprised him when I agreed to help. Most of the other supermarkets weren't even returning his calls.

To me, the issue was bigger than grapes. By the late 1980s, shoppers in New York and across the country were becoming increasingly concerned about the chemicals in their food. People wanted natural food, clean food, organic food—food that was grown the old-fashioned way. They didn't trust those chemicals any more than Cesar Chavez did.

Even the names sounded scary: methyl bromide, captan, phosdrin, parathion, dinoseb. Could that stuff possibly be good for you? Did anyone really want to eat it?

On June 29, Chavez and I stood together on the steps of City Hall with a host of local officials, touting the national boycott. "Give us your vote at the marketplace," Chavez pleaded that day. "It is where we are going to win."

He also praised our "courage" for standing with him.

I thanked him for that. "Those chemicals aren't just bad for your workers," I said. "They are bad for our customers, too. Our customers are no longer going to buy these products if the growers continue to use pesticides. We have to draw the line someplace."

We quit advertising California grapes. We put up signs in our stores urging customers to buy grapes from other places. During the week of July 4, we didn't stock any California grapes at all, and we vowed to keep up our weekly boycott until the growers relented.

I'm certainly not taking all the credit. I'm sure there were many other factors. Chavez was a tireless fighter and a savvy advocate. But having a major New York supermarket chain standing at his side gave the grape boycott a giant boost. The media paid more attention. Other businesses did, too. And even the California grape growers, who were losing a major customer, decided to sit down with the farm workers and hammer out a deal. They just had to be a little more open-minded about how to grow their grapes.

The whole nation benefited as a result.

. . . .

This was a busy time in my business and a busy time for politics. I had planted all these seeds, and they just kept popping up. But truthfully, I had no idea what busy was. That didn't happen until Margo and I decided we were ready to bring a new Catsimatidis generation into the world. I was ready to start a family. Margo was ready, too. You can't accuse either of us of rushing into it. We were certain we had waited long enough.

Our dreams were answered on April 17, 1990, when our daughter, Andrea John Catsimatidis, was born. She was named for my beloved father, of course, with my own name tossed in the middle, and we call her AJ. I was forty-one years old. Margo was thirty-seven, the same age as my mother when she had me. Some people might consider these ages too old for brand-new parents, but it all seemed natural to us.

AJ was a beautiful little girl and so tiny. She looked more like her mother than her father. That might have been a good thing. She had expressive eyes and the sweetest little laugh you've ever heard, and I could tell from the very beginning that her willpower was made of iron. She would focus on something, and she wouldn't turn away. I wonder who she got that from.

Margo and I both felt so blessed.

"Look at what we did," I said.

"Look at what we did," Margo agreed.

AJ was baptized at the cathedral by Archbishop Iakovos. Father Alex and his wife, Xanthi, agreed to serve as godparents. Getting Father Alex to agree wasn't an easy sell. Priests are not normally allowed to play that role. But I pressured his wife with phone calls, letters, and visits. I would not stop until I got the answer I was looking for.

"Do you know how the Greeks conquered Troy?" Father Alex asked with a drawn-out sigh. "They never gave up trying. When you have a principle of value in your mind, you are relentless."

I'm not sure whether he meant that as a compliment or not, but I took it as one. I couldn't exactly deny I'd been persistent, though in my defense it was in pursuit of a very worthy cause.

....

George H. W. Bush was a lifelong Episcopalian. He'd always had warm relations with America's religious groups. As his presidency was up and running, he invited representatives of the major religions to participate in an informal advisory group. Catholics. Jews. Various Protestant denominations. The Orthodox churches. Father Alex representing the Greek Orthodox Church. The religious leaders got involved in various issues of importance to their faith communities and also agreed to take on some more practical projects.

One of them was at Camp David, nestled in the wooded hills of Catoctin Mountain Park about sixty miles north-northwest of the White House. Camp David has been a retreat for US presidents going back to Franklin Delano Roosevelt, hosting such world leaders as British Prime Ministers Winston Churchill and Margaret Thatcher and Australian Prime Minister Harold Holt. This is where, in September 1978, Jimmy Carter helped to hammer out the Camp David Accords, a sweeping peace agreement between Egyptian President Anwar el-Sadat and Israeli Prime Minister Menachem Begin. But when presidents and their families or their staff members or distinguished guests wanted to attend religious services while visiting Camp David, they had to find a house of worship in a nearby Maryland town. Sometimes services were held in a corner of the Camp David gym.

There had been talk for years about building a chapel at Camp David. Ronald Reagan even kicked in $1,000 to help the cause. But for whatever reason, no one had been able to get the project done. So President Bush asked the religious leaders to help, and Father Alex recruited me. My job was to write some checks, recruit others to write checks, and make sure all the good intentions got translated promptly into reality. Father Alex did most of the work on behalf of the Greek community.

The result of all our effort was the Evergreen Chapel, a beautifully rustic, octagonal building made of wood and stained glass, a short walk from the Aspen Lodge, the cabin that has served as the presidential residence. I was so proud of what Father Alex and I accomplished. This was not a chapel for any one faith. It was an ecumenical, nondenominational place for all faiths. Everything in the chapel had meaning. The stained-glass windows were created by Rudolph Sandon, an Italian immigrant who came to the States after World War II and wanted to donate the windows, he said, because America had been good to him. The window on the side of the chapel where the president sits was named the Tree of Knowledge, including depictions of a dove, a sheaf of wheat, and the presidential seal. On the opposite side of the chapel was the Tree of Life, containing symbols purposely open to interpretation by people of varying faiths. And the pipe organ, built by the Moller Pipe Organ Company of Hagerstown, Maryland, was outfitted with two keyboards and 827 pipes ranging in size from six inches to twenty feet.

The chapel bell, which came from the Navy destroyer USS *Endicott*, was named for Archbishop Iakovos. The chapel's small library was named for my one-year-old daughter—the Evergreen Chapel's Andrea Catsimatidis Library.

On April 21, 1991, President Bush invited us to the Evergreen Chapel's first worship service. Cardinal James Hickey, the Roman Catholic Archbishop of Washington, delivered the homily. Sandi Patty, a stirring gospel singer, filled the chapel with song. A wonderful, interdenominational crowd filled the chapel's 150 wooden pews. Archbishop Iakovos came. So did Rabbi James Rudin, the interreligious affairs director for the American Jewish Committee; Bishop James K. Mathews, a retired bishop of the United Methodist Church; and Bishop A. Theodore Eastman of the Episcopal Diocese of Maryland. I should also mention Kenneth Plummer, an active United Methodist layman and semi-retired construction contractor who'd been pushing the idea for an on-site place of worship since the day that JFK was shot—well before any of the rest of us showed up. He was an integral part of everything.

In his remarks, President Bush called the chapel a special gift not just to him but to all future presidents. "I accept with joy and gratitude this magnificent gift on behalf of those who shall use this chapel and extend my profound thanks to God and to all those whose generosity and labor have made this possible," he said.

President Bush then invited us outside for a barbecue, where he grilled hot dogs for everyone. It was the first time a president had ever cooked for me.

In June of the following year, the Evergreen Chapel would hold its first wedding, showing just how important it was to the whole Bush family. The president's only daughter, Dorothy Bush LeBlond, exchanged vows with Bobby Koch, a former Democratic congressional staffer just then starting a job as a lobbyist for the wine industry. As the bride's father, President Bush agreed to pick up the bill. Some things don't change, even when you are the president.

I never heard if the happy couple had time to linger in the Andrea Catsimatidis Library.

....

By then, our second child had already arrived. Why stop with one? Didn't AJ need a little brother? That was my thinking—and Margo's, too. John Andreas Catsimatidis Jr. was born on February 12, 1993, twenty-two months after his older sister. With hardly any prodding, Father Alex and his wife, Xanthi, agreed to be godparents. This time, I didn't have to pressure or beg—or hear any war stories from ancient Greece.

We never called our son Junior. He was John or Yiánni. What a wonderful child he turned out to be! Easygoing. Affectionate. Extremely precocious from the start. AJ took to him immediately—no resentment that she was losing her status as an only child. Truly, both of them were always surrounded by love.

I absolutely loved being a father, and Margo was a wonderful mom.

We understood from the start that our children would be raised in conditions very different from the modest circumstances Margo and I had grown up in. They would have comforts and advantages that we never even dreamed of when we were young. Weren't they living on Fifth Avenue across from Central Park in the greatest city on earth? All of this would offer benefits to them—education, travel, contacts, experiences, opportunities, and worldliness. But it also carried risks. We had seen some children of prominent New Yorkers grow up to be whiny, entitled little brats with no work ethic and no understanding of how the world really works. We did not want that to happen to AJ and John. We vowed we would keep them as grounded as we possibly could.

They would learn to work hard. They would know the difference between right and wrong. They would understand that responsibilities come with the advantages they have received. All of this would require hands-on parenting. We understood that. I wanted our children—and Margo agreed with this—to be raised by us. And so that is what we did. Whatever I was doing, I always made time for AJ and John. As they grew older, I would go to AJ's school performances and John's basketball games, cheering loudly with the crowd. When either of them called the office, I would never be too busy to get on the phone.

One weekend, Margo and I went to Rome for a Greek state dinner. We were away for two nights and three days. AJ, who was three and a half, and John, who was still an infant, stayed home with a nanny. When Margo and I returned home, AJ was standing by the door with her hands on her hips and a scowl on her face.

"Daddy," she said, "don't you ever do that to me again!"

"What?" I asked. I honestly didn't know what she meant.

"Don't you ever leave me home again!" she said.

And we didn't. When Margo and I traveled together after that, we traveled as a family.

There is a line, I learned, that well-off parents have to walk. You're blessed to be able to give your children every opportunity available. But you're doing them no favors if they don't also acquire the tools to live productive, independent lives.

"I don't want our children thinking that everything comes to them automatically," Margo said more than once to me. "They need to learn and work hard like everyone else."

So from the time the children could walk, I would take them with me to the supermarkets every Saturday as I made my rounds. Together, we would greet the employees and check out the aisles, making sure all the cans were stacked neatly, the floors were polished, and everyone had what they needed. The workers loved giving hugs and saying hello to AJ and John. The kids felt like they had an army of new friends. As they got a little older, I'd weave little business lessons into our visits. How to compliment people when they did a good job. How to make sure the store looked just so. Both children were super bright. They quickly grew used to being around grown-ups, and it showed. From the time they could talk, they could carry on conversations with just about anyone.

I used to joke that the first word John ever said was "EBITDA," an accounting term that stands for "earnings before interest, taxes, depreciation, and amortization." That wasn't really true, but that's how advanced he was as a child. AJ scored the highest on every exam she ever took at all grade levels; she came out a genius. They both gave me so much reason to be proud. I wanted to give them everything—just not too much. I wanted both my children to have the tools they would need for wherever their dreams might take them in the years to come.

I would be remiss if I didn't tell you about Edna. While Margo and I can take some credit for how our children turned out so well, a key force in their development as caring, hardworking, ethical adults was Edna. A gracious, smart, and supportive member of our household and family, she was with us for many years. The kids were blessed to have her in our home. She has and had a special bond with each of our children, separately and together. She helped to instill in them key values such as courage, intellectual curiosity, and respect for people of all walks of life.When she recently retired and returned to the Philippines, the land of her birth, all of us—Margo, AJ, John Jr. and I—realized that we would miss her daily presence for the rest of our lives. Thank you, Edna, for all that you did for our family.

John and Margo Catsimatidis with President Bill Clinton and First Lady Hillary Clinton.

15

BEFRIENDING BILL

Every experience I ever had with George H. W. Bush made me like him more, though my loyalty was tested again in 1992 as Bush prepared to run for reelection. Was I in a time warp? I looked up one day and a Greek American from Massachusetts was running for president again. It wasn't Michael Dukakis this time. It was former Democratic Senator Paul Tsongas.

Another Massachusetts Greek aiming for the White House? Where did they all come from? Did Harvard or MIT have a cloning lab I'd never heard about?

As the Democrat challengers gathered for the 1992 race, Tsongas positioned himself as a social liberal who was also a plain-spoken fiscal conservative, a Democrat who would tell it like it is and not promise voters the moon. Tsongas had left the Senate in 1984, deciding not to seek reelection after being diagnosed a year earlier with non-Hodgkin's lymphoma. Following a successful bone marrow transplant, his disease was in remission, and his straight talk was what America needed in the White House, Tsongas said. As the early primaries grew near, many commentators were calling him the front-running Democrat, better positioned than the other leading candidates in the race—Arkansas Governor Bill Clinton, former California Governor Jerry Brown, Nebraska Senator Bob Kerrey, and Iowa Senator Tom Harkin.

"What do we do now?" Father Alex asked me. "Are we going to support Tsongas?"

"We're supporting George Bush!" I said. I could swear we'd had this conversation before.

"I hear you," Father Alex said, obviously a little torn. "Well, let's see what happens in the Democratic primaries."

Thankfully, we never really had to choose.

We gave Tsongas what I would call minor support. He was a very decent guy. His campaign started strong with a victory in the New Hampshire primary on February 18, as Bill Clinton stumbled over issues of marital infidelity and draft dodging during the Vietnam War. But Clinton managed to rebrand himself as the Comeback Kid and stomped past Tsongas and the others on Super Tuesday. Tsongas did grab delegates in Delaware, Maryland, Arizona, Washington, Utah, and Massachusetts. But he was having trouble matching Clinton's fundraising and wins in other delegate-rich states. Tsongas's last, big hope was the April 7 primary in New York. But when Clinton grabbed Michigan and Illinois, that, too, seemed out of reach. After those Midwestern losses, we met the Greek American senator for dinner at Le Cirque on Park Avenue. It was Father Alex, Michael Jaharis, one or two others, and me.

"I'll be announcing that I will be suspending my campaign," he told us.

I knew he was disappointed. By leaving the race, he'd be clearing the way for Bill Clinton to claim the Democratic nomination at the party's convention in July. But Tsongas recognized he really had no other choice.

"The alternative," he told the media in his formal announcement, "was to play the role of spoiler. That is not what I'm about."

That was just the reality. We were zero for two with Greek American presidential candidates.

That fall, Father Alex and the rest of us did what we could for President Bush. But he had a problem, and I don't only mean a certain charming Democratic Governor from Arkansas who displayed surprising political skills. Bush could never figure out how to handle Ross Perot, the Texas billionaire who jumped into the 1992 presidential race as an independent candidate.

Perot had an array of issues and many easels full of colorful charts designed to distinguish himself from Bush and Clinton, the two major-party nominees. The Texan promised a balanced federal budget. He was against the outsourcing of jobs. He was an outspoken opponent of the North American Free Trade Agreement. Those were all fine. But what he seemed to care most about was the POW/MIA issue—his belief that hundreds of American service members were left behind in Southeast Asia after the Vietnam War and were still being held captive nearly two decades later. There was never much firm evidence of that. History says those fears were almost entirely overblown. But Ross Perot sincerely believed it, and it motivated him to run for president.

His campaign was certainly quirky. He withdrew from the race in July only to reenter in early October. His running mate, Admiral James Stockdale, wasn't quite ready for prime time. But give Perot his due: as a businessman-politician making an outsider's run for president, he beat part of the path that Donald Trump would follow a quarter century down the line.

It was Bush's job—or the job of his campaign strategists—to neutralize Ross Perot or, better yet, convince him to stay out of the race that he had already quit once in July. It really wouldn't have been that difficult, I don't think. What would I have done if I were President Bush? I would have called Ross Perot. I would have asked, "What do you need? Troops? Equipment? Logistical help? I'll send an aircraft carrier. Launch your rescue mission. Go get your prisoners. Let me fight Bill Clinton. Don't come back until after the election. Then, we bring those POWs home."

I think Perot would have gone for that. And when his rescue mission would find no POWs—well, at least he would have tried. But instead, Bush made an enemy. Perot ran against him, siphoning Republican votes away. With a solid plurality of the popular vote, Bill Clinton became President of the United States.

. . . .

Once the results came in, I figured that was it for me. Both my guys, Tsongas and Bush, had been beaten. Bill Clinton didn't know me from Adam, and I'd been against him twice. Generally speaking, that's not a very good way to generate dinner invitations to the White House. But soon after Inauguration Day in January of 1993, an invitation arrived in the mail. The return address was 1600 Pennsylvania Avenue NW in Washington, DC. It was from President Clinton, asking Margo and me to a reception at the White House.

I have to admit I was taken aback. Frankly, I was a little uncomfortable about saying yes. Was he confused about who I was? Had no one mentioned I'd written checks to his opponents? We made up some excuse about our schedule and sent our regrets.

But if Bill Clinton is anything, he is persistent. A few weeks later, a second invitation addressed to Margo and me arrived in the mail.

Again, we said, "Thanks, but no thanks."

Then, a third invitation came. Again, we didn't go.

It was only when the fourth invitation arrived that I said to Margo: "He is the President of the United States. I think we should just go."

We looked at each other and shrugged. "Okay," Margo said.

So we went.

The surprises had only begun. When we arrived at the White House in our evening clothes, I thought we'd be attending a dinner for three or four hundred people. Instead, there were four tables of ten. I was even more surprised when one of the White House stewards directed Margo and me to our assigned seats. I would be sitting next to First Lady Hillary Clinton. Margo's seat was next to Bill.

"Be nice," I whispered to Margo as we headed to our separate tables.

Hillary was a perfectly pleasant dinner companion. We talked about her daughter, Chelsea. I bragged about AJ and John Jr. We talked about how she was adjusting to life in the White House after her years in Arkansas. We talked about her desire to reform the healthcare system.

She said she knew it would be challenging, but she was confident she could get it done. Those were the heady, early days of the Clinton Administration, and I have to admit there was something a little infectious about all the optimism, even for someone who had backed the other side. It was definitely nice dining at the White House and sitting next to the First Lady, especially a woman as bright and informed as Hillary Clinton. I was raised by a smart woman, and I've always liked being around smart women.

While I was speaking with the First Lady, Margo was speaking with the President about patriotism and the importance of the American flag. A few weeks before the dinner, we had gone to an event for Fordham University honoring the university's president, Father Joseph O'Hare, with President Clinton present. Margo mentioned to the President that there was not one American flag. She noted that when one thousand people stood up for the national anthem with their hands over their hearts, there was no flag to face.

Margo said, forget that they didn't have pomp and circumstance. No seal for the president on the podium. No hail to the chief. But not to have an American flag is un-American. President Reagan always had American flags everywhere. Margo acknowledged that rich or poor, people need to believe in our country. She noted that the absence of flags, was not him but his staff, who were new to these things.

So after that, the President had American flags at every event.

After dessert and coffee, the guests started saying good night. Pretty soon, all the guests were gone except for Bill, Hillary, Margo, and me.

That's when Bill and Margo walked over to the table where Hillary and I were sitting and Bill asked cheerfully: "You wanna see the Oval Office?"

"Sure," Margo and I said almost in unison, a quick second before Hillary piped up: "Bill, it's almost midnight."

He didn't seem to hear her.

The four of us walked down the hallway to the Oval Office. I could hear Bill still talking to Margo about patriotism and the American flag.

And when we got to the Oval Office, I understood immediately why he wanted to continue the conversation there.

The President showed us a rare painting of the American flag, which hung proudly in the Oval Office.

Every President can put up artwork that is in the White House Archives. The President chose this particular painting.

The four of us sat down and kept talking for another hour.

I understand not everybody loves everything about Bill Clinton, but I'll say this much. Almost everyone who has ever spent time with the man has some genuine affection for him. He won me over that night. You might think of a hundred reasons to disagree with him or disapprove of him. But once you get to know him personally, you can't help but fall in love with the guy.

Margo and I got invited back to the White House many times after that night. President Clinton convinced me—he even convinced Margo—that he really did love America and was ready to do whatever he could to make life better for Americans. He's not a money guy. Money isn't what motivates him—it's the chance to be in the middle of the action, trying to get things done. That's what he lives for. That's where he gets his adrenaline. That's where he gets his sense of purpose in life.

Margo and I would spend the next eight years supporting Bill Clinton, promoting him and his agenda any way we could. He would seek my advice. He would send me on a few diplomatic errands when he needed an independent, outside hand. Some of my Republican friends scrunched up their noses and shook their heads at that, but I was happy to help. He was the president, and I also liked the man. Against all odds and expectations, he and I became genuine friends.

In 1996, I felt obligated to help him get reelected because that's what friends do. Plus, I wanted to. I would help him raise campaign money. I would round up support for him among New York businesspeople and my friends, whether Republicans or Democrats. Through Clinton, we would get to know his Vice President, Al Gore. When Gore ran against George W. Bush, we would help him, too. Gore's mistake,

I have always believed, was that he tried to distance himself from Bill Clinton. He was rattled by the controversies that swirled around Clinton, although Clinton's approval rating remained stubbornly high. He didn't ask Bill Clinton for help. Bottom line: he lost Arkansas and Tennessee. Bottom-bottom line: he ended up carrying his own luggage to the airport when all was said and done.

JOHN KATSIMATIDES

ANTHONY DEMAS

VASSILIOS HARAMIS

SHELDON KANTER

In memoriam of friends and family we lost on September 11, 2001.

16

UNDER ATTACK

I had been in my office on Eleventh Avenue for more than an hour when the very first bulletin came on TV. "A plane has hit the North Tower of the World Trade Center," the anchor said. "That's all we know so far."

This was at 8:46 AM on September 11, 2001, a clear, blue-sky day in New York. Rudy Giuliani was coming to the end of his second term as mayor. Across the five boroughs, voters were heading to polls to cast their ballots in the Democratic and Republican primaries, the first step in electing a new mayor and filling other city offices. Four candidates—Bronx Borough President Fernando Ferrer, Public Advocate Mark Green, City Council Speaker Peter Vallone, and City Comptroller Alan Hevesi—were locked in a hot race for the Democratic mayoral nomination. On the Republican side, businessman Mike Bloomberg seemed to have an easy edge over Herman Badillo, who'd been a congressman and Bronx borough president. The election was supposed to be the big news of the day.

There are always TVs on in the office, usually with the volume down until there is something I want or need to hear.

"A plane just hit the World Trade Center! Turn it up!"

My first assumption—almost everyone's first assumption—was that it had to be a small, private plane. *Stupidity*, I thought to myself.

Being a pilot, I knew that the pilots of private aircrafts flew up the Hudson River at an elevation of one thousand feet. That was a normal thing. It happened many times a day. But not this. *How could a pilot fail to see a 104-story building?* That was my first thought. And then: *This makes no sense at all.*

It wasn't until a few minutes later, as eyewitness reports poured in, that we learned this was no private plane. It was a 150-seat Boeing 767, American Airlines Flight 11. Definitely not a small plane. Things only got worse from there. A second commercial airliner, United Airlines Flight 175, slammed into the trade center's South Tower. The whole world watched that happen live.

Two airplanes. Seventeen minutes apart. This was no accident. This had to be a coordinated attack.

I wasn't born when Japanese fighter planes bombed Hawaii's Pearl Harbor, thrusting America into World War II. But all my life, I'd heard stories about how rattling that day had been for almost everyone. Suddenly, I understood how Americans felt on December 7, 1941. If anything, 9/11 was turning out to be worse.

No one knew all the details at the beginning. But the facts trickled in soon enough. Five hijackers had been on the first plane and another five on the second. Using box cutters as weapons, they had forced the flight crews out of the cockpits and locked themselves inside. The hijackers then flew the planes into the two tallest skyscrapers in New York, world-famous symbols of America's technical prowess and economic might, right down the West Side Highway from where I watched the carnage unfold on live TV. Before the morning was over, a third plane would strike the Pentagon outside Washington and a fourth would crash in rural Pennsylvania after the passengers courageously confronted the hijackers.

The human toll was almost unimaginable. In the four attacks, 2,977 people were killed. Over six thousand were injured. Untold thousands of rescue and recovery workers would suffer lingering illnesses and, often, premature deaths. The psychological impact on the living was impossible to calculate. We know this much: the death toll included 265 people on the four hijacked planes (there were no survivors), an estimated 2,606 people in or near the World Trade Center, and 125 people inside the Pentagon. Among those who perished were 343 firefighters, seventy-two law enforcement officers, fifty-five military personnel, and the nineteen terrorists. Given how diverse New York is, more than ninety countries lost citizens in that day's attacks.

One day, everything had seemed totally normal. The next day, the world was turned upside down. The night before the attack, I had been at Yankee Stadium, sitting with Harlem Congressman Charles Rangel, limousine titan Bill Fugazy, and Yankees owner George Steinbrenner. The crowd had a special buzz. Everyone was waiting for Yankees pitcher Roger Clemens to notch his twentieth win of the season. It should have been the perfect night. Clemens's old team, the Red Sox, were in from Boston. But it was raining in the Bronx. After a two-hour delay, the game was finally called off, and I headed home.

Then this: the Pearl Harbor of the twenty-first century. By any count, it was the deadliest terrorist attack in human history.

I was stunned. I was shaken. I was depressed. Everyone was. I had trouble absorbing the immensity of it all. I'd careened from bewilderment to sadness and then to rage. How could someone do such a thing to so many innocent people? What crazed ideology could justify the mass murder of civilians? The people who worked in those buildings, the first responders who rushed in, the passengers who were flying on those planes—what did they do to deserve their fiery deaths? Behind it all, we learned soon enough, was a radical Islamic terrorist group called al-Qaeda and its diabolical founder, a rich Saudi Arabian jihadist named Osama bin Laden. I know that all of America and much of the world was feeling the pain of New Yorkers that day. I was feeling it deep inside. How could I not take this personally? The worst of the carnage happened in my beloved, adopted city, the city that for more than half a century had loved and adopted me back.

When the towers came down, no one knew for certain who had lived and who had died. For the next few days, desperate people searched the local hospitals and morgues. Relatives posted photos of their missing loved ones on walls and windows around the city, praying that someone would have some news. One of those missing was my cousin John Katsimatides. He worked at the financial services firm Cantor Fitzgerald. He had been on vacation for three weeks. September 11 was his first day back in the office. It was horrible.

Every time his name was mentioned on TV or radio, Margo would get another call from someone thinking I might be dead. Friends were asking friends what they had heard. Forty percent of the victims were never recovered. My cousin John was one of those. His remains were never found.

He wasn't the only person I knew among the casualties. I had a good friend from Brooklyn Tech who had been working in the building. I had another friend from NYU. Neither one of them made it out. Manny Demos, a manager with international insurance broker Aon, also died. Manny had twin boys in my son's class. We used to take the boys to basketball practice on Saturday mornings, talking and cheering while our sons played. He made sure all his people got out of the building. He was going to be the last one to exit. He never got out.

The sadness was almost incomprehensible. But New York wouldn't stay paralyzed for long. I have never seen people so angry and determined at once. New Yorkers rallied around, vowing not to be fearful, not to be cowed. And they weren't. They did what they have always done in times of crisis. They refused to give in.

As an immigrant, I have always felt a special love for New York and a special duty to help protect the city that my family and I call home. I have never felt those feelings any stronger than in the days after September 11, 2001.

I felt proud and patriotic when President George W. Bush came to Ground Zero and helped raise the American flag. I loved what he told those first responders through his bullhorn: "I can hear you. The rest of the world hears you. And the people who knocked these buildings down will hear all of us soon." He set exactly the right tone that day. I was ready to back the President in whatever actions he chose to take.

There had been warnings, of course, for anyone willing to listen. In Bill Clinton's exit interview in January 2001, as he was handing off power to the incoming George W. Bush, Clinton warned Bush that

Osama bin Laden posed America's gravest security threat. A little over a month before the attack, on August 6, the Central Intelligence Agency presented President Bush with a daily briefing report entitled "Bin Ladin [sic] Determined To Strike in US."

The day before the attack, President Clinton was in Australia giving a speech to a business group in Melbourne. Clinton brought up the bin Laden threat again. "I spent a lot of time thinking about him," the former President said. He expressed what sounded like regret—mixed feelings, at least. "I could have killed him," Clinton said, "but I would have had to destroy a little town called Kandahar in Afghanistan and kill three hundred innocent women and children, and then I would have been no better than him. And so I didn't do it."

Hours later, planes were slamming into towers in New York.

Concerned about Clinton's safety, the White House arranged to fly the former President back home to New York in a US military plane, despite the fact that US airspace was still frozen. I got a call from Clinton's Vice President, Al Gore, who was frantic. He was in Vienna, Austria, when the planes struck and was now eager to get home to Washington. With the United States still a no-fly zone, Toronto, Canada, was the closest city he could fly to. He kept calling officials in Washington, but no one seemed willing to help.

When he finally landed in Toronto, he rented a car at the airport and started driving. He had flown for nine hours and had another nine to drive.

I got in touch with Clinton and explained the situation his former Vice President was in. I knew there'd been tension between the two of them over Gore's decision to distance himself from Clinton during the 2000 presidential campaign. But Clinton sprang into action immediately. He reached him on the phone just as Gore was passing through Buffalo. He invited his former Vice President to spend the night at the Clinton home in the northern New York suburb of Chappaqua, assuring him he'd still be up when Gore arrived at 3 AM. In times of tragedy, good people do good things.

That made me happy to hear. I think it made Al Gore even happier.

. . . .

In hindsight, it is easy to see that mistakes were made—both before the attack and after. Beforehand, our intelligence agencies weren't sharing information like they should have been. Afterward, we ended up in some international messes that would have been better avoided. Foreign wars, we learned again, are a whole lot easier to get into than to get out of.

You can make a strong argument that we were justified in attacking the terror forces in Afghanistan. There has to be some penalty for providing hospitality to mass murderers. The 9/11 terrorists got key parts of their training in that dysfunctional land. That said, I'd have certainly liked for us to get our troops out of there much faster than we were able to.

Getting embroiled in Iraq was an error on a whole different scale. I hate to be a Monday-morning quarterback, but there was a way to get in and get out. Except for the elite guard, the Iraqi forces hated Saddam Hussein—at least as much as we did. The invasion was the easy part. We could have kicked Saddam out and taken over the country like we did, then hired the Iraqi Army to run the place. Yes, hired. Pay the soldiers twice what Saddam was paying them. Keep a small American force in place to oversee things. Saddam would be gone. Iraqis would be running Iraq again. Our commitments would be small and manageable—not the decades-long quagmire we are trapped in.

That would have provided one other benefit as well: Iraq would still be a counterbalance to Iran. One of the clear tragedies of the war to emerge as we fought, beyond the American blood and money we spilled, was that Iraq's disintegration emboldened the radical mullahs in Iran as they continued to promote terrorism and inched toward nuclear armaments. It sure would be nice to have a solid Iraq next door. The approach we took left us with a problem in Iraq and a double problem in Iran. We are living with the consequences of those poor decisions still.

John Catsimatidis with New York City Mayor Michael Bloomberg.

17

MAYOR INTERRUPTED

I'd met so many politicians over the years at this point, I couldn't possibly remember them all. Once you become known as someone who makes campaign contributions, they have a way of finding you. More like a thousand ways. They send nice letters. They call to say hello. They show up at the office. They seek out mutual friends who can make introductions. They ask for guidance and advice. I didn't mind any of that. Most of the time, I enjoyed it. The word "politician" is often said with a sneer and intended as an insult. But I didn't look at it like that. I always believed—I still do—that running for elective office is a highly worthy calling, something our democracy needs good people to do. To paraphrase Teddy Roosevelt, I admire those who step into the arena, put themselves on the line, and offer to serve. There are some crooks and losers in the business of politics—no denying that. But I'm not ashamed to say it: a lot of politicians, I genuinely like. They are good and honorable people.

Still, after getting to know so many politicians over so many years, the thought did occur to me: maybe I should run for something sometime.

Really, why not? I had seen the system from inside. I was brimming with fresh ideas. I had a unique story to tell, a personal journey that others could relate to: coming to New York as an infant, growing up in an immigrant family in West Harlem, getting an education and achieving business success while demonstrating a commitment, over and over again, to an array of public-spirited causes and campaigns. And suddenly, it looked like there might be an opportunity to serve the city I loved on a whole different scale.

At the start of 2007, Mike Bloomberg was halfway through his second term as Mayor of New York. Under the city's term-limit law, two terms were the most a mayor could serve. The law was clear on this: two terms and out. Voters had twice cast their ballots for such term limits in city referendums—in 1993 and 1996. Come hell or high water—or even another terror attack like the one of September 11, 2001—New York's billionaire-businessman-mayor would be packing up his spreadsheets and management reports and saying goodbye to his City Hall bullpen at the end of 2009.

Bloomberg had been a successful mayor, as far as I was concerned. He worked hard and cared about the city. He had attracted some talented people to work for him, including Police Commissioner Ray Kelly. He had avoided major corruption scandals. No one owned Mike Bloomberg because he owed no one. He hadn't entirely succeeded at reforming the public schools. But who's perfect? Wall Street was humming. Crime kept going down. New people were moving into the boroughs. Most important of all, Bloomberg was a competent manager who governed mostly from the center like the talented business executive that he was. I liked all that. He had the same response to any new challenge: "Let's figure out what makes sense."

But who was coming next? New York was an undeniably tough place to govern. Not just anyone could thrive in that job. Independence and common sense—to me, those were the most important ingredients, along with some vision and a little pizazz. Not pizza, *pizazz*. The city needed someone who wasn't a captive of the unions, the political bosses, the race hustlers, the real-estate industry, or any of the other special-interest groups who thought they should run New York. We'd all seen in the bad old days what could happen when political hacks and patronage controlled everything in the city. We didn't need a repeat of that. If New York was going to keep moving forward, the city had to have a mayor who cared first and foremost about the *public* interest—not taking care of his cronies and looking out for his contributors, allies, and friends.

And what about Bloomberg's potential replacement, the ones who were starting to line up? They seemed like nice people—most of them, anyway. City Council Speaker Christine Quinn. Businessman Richard Parsons. City Comptroller Bill Thompson. Brooklyn Congressman Anthony Weiner. State Senator Martin Golden. A couple of other City Council members. Some current and former state legislators. But the whole situation definitely had me thinking: *Hey, what about me?*

Running for mayor, I realized, would be a huge undertaking. Just teaching people to say my name would take some doing, I knew. *Cat-see-muh-TEE-dis*! Even if we could squeeze all twelve letters onto a Catsimatidis campaign button, it still had five syllables! It wasn't easy for some people to remember or to say. How 'bout "Cats for Mayor"? Everyone could pronounce that. But I also knew that running wouldn't be cheap. If I were going to jump into the race to replace Mike Bloomberg, I'd have to jump with both feet—and also my check-writing hand. To get elected to his first term in 2001, Bloomberg had spent a huge pile, virtually all of it his own. The official report said $74 million, and that didn't include all the charitable donations he had made. If I wanted a shot at winning—and I didn't want to run just for my ego or my health—I knew I would have to pay up. I wasn't sure how much, but the numbers I was hearing were large, if not quite Bloomberg-ian. Thirty million. Forty million. Maybe more. The good news was I could afford it.

So in July of 2008, I set up an official exploratory committee. In a preliminary way, I began sounding out political pros, people who had experience running campaigns in New York City. Pollster John McLaughlin. Consultants Robert Ryan, Alan Bernikow, Lawrence Mandelker, and Joe Ithier. *What would it take?* I wanted to know. Their advice to me always began with a warning: winning is never easy for a first-time candidate. But, the experts added, that didn't mean this one was on the *impossible* list. With Bloomberg out of the way, the 2009 mayor's race was wide, wide open. Lots of people would run.

New York never suffers a shortage of ambitious politicos. But no one had this one locked up. With the right commitment and the right campaign, I might actually have a shot.

I was happy to hear that. It comported with my own businessman's analysis: eight years earlier, a billionaire businessman, a former Democrat running as a moderate Republican, had gotten himself elected mayor of this heavily Democratic city. Why couldn't that happen again? Like Bloomberg before he ran, I had never sought elective office. I had spent the last eight years as a Bill Clinton Democrat, meaning the moderate, middle-of-the-road kind. I concluded, as Mike Bloomberg apparently had, that a politically moderate businessman could never get the Democratic nomination for Mayor of New York City. The party had moved too far to the left for that. If I wanted a shot at winning, I would have to change my voter registration and seek the Republican nomination instead. One other thing was obvious: if I wanted to keep this possibility open, I'd better go out and meet some folks.

That part was time consuming but fun. Regrettably, it took me away from the family plenty of nights and weekends. Thankfully, the family wholeheartedly supported my effort. A lot of local politics is conducted in coffee spots and restaurants and not just from nine to five. I had lunch with Manhattan GOP Chairwoman Jennifer Saul Yaffa to discuss the future of the city. I began showing up at meetings of civic associations and local Republican clubs, especially in Brooklyn, Queens, and Staten Island. I bought a table at the annual fundraising dinner of the Queens GOP, where I was introduced as a "noted philanthropist." I didn't mind the sound of that. I made sure to attend the Lincoln Day dinner hosted by the Staten Island Republicans. I went to a fundraiser for Congressman Vito Fossella, a Staten Island Republican, where Newt Gingrich signed copies of his new book about Pearl Harbor.

I wasn't buying anyone's support. I was just out there getting to know people and, I hoped, making new friends. A lot of this was new to me. I was a Manhattan guy. I lived and worked in Manhattan. But the people in the city's other four boroughs couldn't have been friendlier or more welcoming to me. Like me, many of them had climbed from humble circumstances. Like me, most of them were worried about who might replace Mike Bloomberg. I think they liked my practical approach to city problems. In the months that followed, my name kept popping up in the New York media as one of the "plausibles," a long list of people who might possibly throw their hats (or their egos or their outstretched hands or their fortunes) into the 2009 mayoral race.

As the months rolled on, I even dreamed up an informal slogan for my unofficial campaign, a shorthand way of letting people know where I came from and what I stood for. I was the "common billionaire," a guy who had made a lot of money but had never lost touch with his immigrant family or his Harlem upbringing. Let all the other rich guys run their businesses from sleek glass towers in Midtown. I was happy operating mine above a Lexus dealership on Eleventh Avenue.

"I'm pro-business and pro-people," I explained to a *New York Times* reporter who called to inquire about my Cats-for-Mayor platform. "I love New York. Bloomberg has done such a good job that I don't want to take the chance of leaving it to some professional politician to be chief executive of this $53 billion corporation." (A few years later, that number would hit $88 billion and keep rising. At the time of this writing it is more than $100 billion.)

"New York is at a crossroads," I continued. "We could go backwards fast, back to the dirty, unsafe streets, without the right manager. Sometimes you've got to step out on the ledge and take a risk at something new; as an entrepreneur, that's what I did most of my life."

. . . .

Then, lightning struck. Political lightning with big claps of thunder. And a lot of people, myself included, got burned.

On October 2, 2008, Mike Bloomberg announced he wasn't leaving, after all. He wanted another term as mayor. He said he understood that term limits were the law in New York City, but he aimed to change that so he would be permitted to run for a third term.

This surprised a lot of people. Bloomberg had spoken frequently about serving two terms in City Hall and then returning to his financial media company, Bloomberg LP. He explained his change of heart by pointing to the mortgage crisis and national recession just then taking hold. "We may well be on the verge of a meltdown, and it's up to us to rise to the occasion," the Mayor warned ominously.

Bloomberg did not propose going back to the voters and seeing if they had changed their minds. It was too late for that, he said, and impractical to hold another referendum. He urged the members of the City Council to overturn the mayoral and city-council term limits, approving a one-time-only third-term opportunity for the mayor and themselves. Thirty-five of the fifty-one of them were currently serving their second terms. The minute Bloomberg proposed the idea, many of the council members reacted like they'd been floating at sea and had just been handed a life raft. The final vote on October 23 was twenty-nine to twenty-two, handing the mayor and two-thirds of the Council's own members four full years of bonus time.

• •

Bloomberg took stiff criticism for his rule change. But he had let it be known that he was prepared to spend whatever it took to ensure his reelection. By January of 2009, eight months before the September primary and ten months before the November general election, most of the other plausible candidates had dropped out of the race, including Council Speaker Christine Quinn.

I gave some thought to staying in. Bloomberg had incumbency on his side. He also had big bucks. But I had big bucks, too. And I figured my life story was at least as good as his. I knew this much: if I ended up running, I wouldn't let anyone, including Mike Bloomberg, outspend me. I'd been around politics long enough to know that you can't buy your way into office, but you should never let yourself be buried under the avalanche of someone else's cash.

That month, I wrote a $1 million check to my campaign fund. By doing that, I was talking in a language that political people and media people understood. *Maybe Cats is still serious!* "I am trying to show everyone I'm alive," I told the reporters.

They shook their heads a little, but they seemed to find my interest intriguing. Nothing is more boring for a political reporter than a race with only one serious candidate.

In the end, though, I decided it wasn't my year to run. This wasn't some grand, philosophical decision. It was common sense. Running against any incumbent is difficult. Incumbents have so many political tools at their disposal. Every city contract that is signed, every person who is hired at the Sanitation or the Parks Department, every ribbon-cutting the mayor shows up for—all that has political potency. Add in Bloomberg's billions, which stacked quite a bit higher than mine did, and I concluded that this was not a race I could realistically win.

On Tuesday, September 15, 2009, Democratic voters nominated Bill Thompson, the outgoing City Comptroller and a good and decent man, over City Council Member Tony Avella of Queens. The general-election campaign was a relatively sleepy affair. Thompson never ignited much passion, and Bloomberg, running on the Republican and Independence Party lines, never seemed to break a sweat. Voter turnout was light. On election day, November 3, 2009, only 1.2 million voters showed up—fewer than in most recent mayoral elections. The vote wasn't exactly a squeaker, but it was far closer than anyone had predicted it would be. Bloomberg got his third term with 50.7 percent of the vote to Thompson's 46.3 percent. Barely four points separated them.

Could my $50 million or $60 million have made the race turn out differently? I would never know.

The Catsimatidis family: Margo, John, AJ, and John Jr.

18

PROUD PAPA

Both my children keep making me proud of them.

It's true that I didn't have children early. But once I had them, I really hit the jackpot. Besides being charming human beings and successful young adults, AJ and John Jr. embraced the good parts of their privileged upbringing, avoided most of the pitfalls, and showed an early interest in business and politics. Their mother and I never pushed them in that direction. Margo and I wanted both our children to work hard, be happy, and find their own passions in life. But it's been a blast watching everything they've accomplished and imagining the amazing places they might be heading next.

These are extraordinary kids. AJ: bold, fearless, intuitive, outgoing, able to connect with just about anyone. John: warm, curious, driven, genuinely interested in everybody and everything. Both of them are deeply compassionate people and super, super smart.

Like me, AJ was always good with numbers and had a computer-like brain. Instead of just seeing numbers in a vacuum, she inherited my ability to take numbers off a balance sheet and bring them into the real world. I was amused by how competent she was at such a young age—year after year she beat the investment returns of all the big funds and banks. I remember having a meeting with one of those large banks, in which I asked the bankers why my twenty-two-year-old daughter had better investment returns than them. They didn't know what to say; she has a particular talent for leaving people speechless. She even has this effect on her dad sometimes. I remember when she was bought out of her first company at just twenty-two years old and made her first million. That day, I saw the reflection of a younger version of myself—like me she made her first million in her twenties and never looked back. She definitely inherited my ability to identify a home-run pitch and knock it out of the park. I couldn't be more proud.

From a young age, it was evident that AJ was brilliant. In high school she was not just on honor roll, but on high honor roll while enrolled in the most difficult classes.

She always had a love of math and science, however her all-girls school didn't think women needed science in lower school, and they certainly didn't consider having a class in robotics.

Like her father, she too does not believe in obstacles. So she taught herself how to build a robot and joined the science Olympiad team determined to compete in the Citywide robotics competition. AJ was the only female competitor in all of New York City, and, once again, left everyone speechless when she and her robot took home a medal. She even beat my alma mater, Brooklyn Tech!

It wasn't just robots she was interested in; we really bonded over science and outer space. Our favorite Saturday night tradition was to watch the featured movie on the Sci-Fi channel together. We were always two peas in a pod, so it was no surprise to me when she decided to go to New York University, as I did.

AJ was an outstanding student at NYU's Stern School of Business. Not only did she achieve high academic honors, but she demonstrated exceptional leadership skills in being the President of the NYU Republicans. AJ was bestowed with the high honor of being named one of the Most Influential Students at NYU. Her brother would follow in her footsteps a few years later. In that capacity, she was able to get more members for the College Republicans than was attained by the College Democrats, and believe me, at NYU that is a major accomplishment. She has built upon those early successes by becoming the Chair of the New York County Republican Party as well as the

Vice Chair of the State Republican Party representing all five counties in New York City. Her leadership there has led to the rebuilding of a two-party system in New York City and she has become a national figure in the Republican Party.

John took his childhood interest in computers and technology and really ran with it. Programming the PC in his bedroom. Building apps from scratch for his iPhone. Using more than twelve programming languages when he was in grade school. Offering tech advice to adults several times his age. He and I really bonded over computer science. Both of us are fascinated by that stuff. While I was upgrading our IT systems at the office, he had thoughtful questions and practical advice. You know that special moment when the student surpasses the teacher in some difficult field of study? Well, John keeps focusing me on new developments in the rapidly changing tech world. Both of us love staring into the future and trying to figure out what might be coming next.

While John was still a student at The Loyola School, a wonderful high school on East Eighty-Forth Street run by Jesuit priests, he was expertly analyzing raw data from our Kwik Fill gas stations and convenience stores. He set up a new system to detect trends and patterns and to carefully track the performance of each location. Did I mention he was still in high school? It was around the same time that John took an interest in the stock market. Pretty soon, he was making small investments on his own. How did he know so much? I'd like to think I helped to spark his interest, but he did most of this on his own. He really has a head for it. He's always been ahead of his years.

When it came time for college, I was happy that he chose my (and his older sister's) school, New York University, where he majored in business and dove into politics. I'm not sure whether the political part was from meeting so many politicians in our living room over the years. Or maybe, like me, he just wanted to know the political world from the inside. Whatever the motivation, he served as Vice President and then President of the NYU College Republicans—like his sister before him—hosting speakers, holding debates, and working to elect Republicans to local, state, and national office. For all his work on campus, he was named one of the ten most influential students of his class and was presented with the President's Service Award. John took his political activities statewide, getting elected Chairman of the New York State Federation of College Republicans. After graduating from NYU's Stern School of Business with a concentration in finance and management, John had his pick of great opportunities. But I was thrilled when he came to me and said he wanted to work with us at the Red Apple Group, focusing on our energy business then adding real estate and other projects to his growing portfolio. He has demonstrated the keen ability to analyze potential investments from a financial, operating, and strategic perspective. Since we are a conglomerate with diverse business interests, I deeply appreciate his ability to manage this varied portfolio.

When John first joined the company, he applied his programming and technology background to solve problems and make our businesses more efficient. I wanted him to have hands-on operating experience, so when we purchased a company out of bankruptcy in 2013, I thought it was a great opportunity for him to get involved on the turnaround team. He stepped up without hesitation. Thankfully that was a success. Fast forward to today and John built, and is responsible for, leading our investment team, spending significant time on high-level strategic decisions for our operating companies. At times, my son's willingness to dive into a variety of business challenges carries echoes of a younger me.

I really wasn't surprised. By joining the family business, he was also following in the footsteps of his older sister, who'd had a similarly impressive tenure at NYU's Stern School before joining the family firm. What Red Apple has is a rare combination in this day and age. We have this large, diversified company, but it's still Mom, Pop, and the kids—plus a lot of other wonderful people on the team! Like their mother and father, both our children are keenly interested in giving back, serving such groups like the Alzheimer's Foundation of America, the Police Athletic League, and the Emerging Leader's Council of The Federal Enforcement Homeland Security Foundation.

After college, AJ became engaged to Christopher Cox, who happens to be the grandson of Richard Nixon.

Margo and I got to know Chris throughout their engagement. He was obviously very bright, a graduate of Princeton University and the NYU School of Law. He had his own consulting firm, where he advised US companies on selling their products abroad. But he was also warm, funny, and totally unpretentious, despite coming from such Republican royalty and having Nixon as his middle name. I already knew and liked his parents—father Edward Cox, a successful Manhattan attorney who chaired the New York Republican State Committee, and mother Tricia Nixon Cox. The Coxes are talented, public-spirited people all around.

In 2011, AJ and Chris were married. It was a truly memorable day. The seven hundred guests, quite a few more than at my own large wedding, included friends of the couple and their parents, relatives from both sides, and quite a few familiar faces from the upper echelons of business and politics, present and past. Secretary of State Hillary Rodham Clinton and Police Commissioner Ray Kelly sat on the bride's side. Former Secretary of State Henry Kissinger and former Mayor Rudy Giuliani sat on the groom's side. Other guests included former New York Governor George Pataki; former New York Mayor David Dinkins; Pennsylvania Governor Tom Corbett; former Pennsylvania Governor Ed Rendell; Senator Chuck Schumer; Republican National Committee Chairman Reince Priebus; Congresswomen Nan Hayworth and Carolyn Maloney; Congressman Gus Bilirakis; *Washington Post* heir and renowned journalist Lally Weymouth; former Ambassador to the European Union Boyden Gray; CNBC's Larry Kudlow (who'd go on to be Director of the National Economic Council for President Trump); former American International Group Chairman Hank Greenberg; newspaper columnist Cindy Adams; Guardian Angels founder Curtis Sliwa; New York Supreme Court Justice Richard Weinberg and wife Elaine (a leading New York attorney); award-winning TV journalist Rita Cosby; Wall Street legend

Muriel Siebert; Jonathan and Somers Farkas; Francine LeFrak and her husband, Rick Friedberg; and, oh, the list went on and on. What they all had in common was that they were loved by AJ, Chris, and our families, and we wanted them there. You could have staffed quite a White House right out of those pews.

Archbishop Demetrios of America officiated with the Reverend Father Alexander Karloutsos, Reverend Dr. Frank Marangos, and Father Mark Arey. Father Alex and his wife, Xanthi—the bride's godparents—looked on proudly, but not everything in life turns out the way you expect it to.

They were married for three years and and while it ended in divorce, they promised to remain friends and they have. I still speak with Chris and see his relatives. Welcome to the modern family! I'd had an excellent relationship with my late ex-wife, Liba. I see no reason why AJ and Chris can't match or top that. And, in fact, they already have.

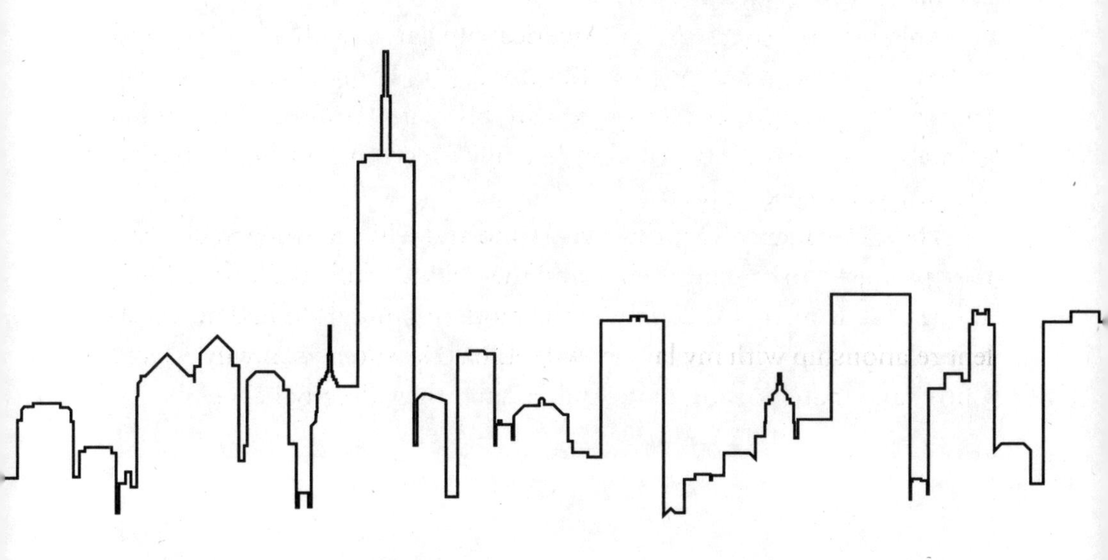

Top: John Catsimatidis announces his candidacy for Mayor of New York City.

Bottom: John Catsimatidis greets supporters during his run for New York City Mayor in 2013.

19

REALLY RUNNING

I woke up on the morning of January 29, 2013, and climbed into one of my very finest Jos. A. Bank suits. Then I headed down to City Hall, where I was joined on the steps out front by a few dozen friends, family members, and political allies. There, in front of a sizeable mob of news reporters, political people, and random onlookers, I announced I was running for the Republican nomination for Mayor of New York.

"I'm not a Mike Bloomberg billionaire," I declared. "I'm not wearing a $5,000 suit. I think my wife paid $100 for this." I grabbed the lapels of my wrinkled black jacket. "This is what I wear every day."

I got some chuckles from AJ, John Jr., and a couple of old friends, who all knew I'd never be mistaken for a clotheshorse. Margo shot me a look that I translated as, *Really? This is what we're talking about now?* Many of the supporters were holding red-white-and-blue signs that had my full name spelled out—JOHN CATSIMATIDIS FOR MAYOR—and also had our campaign web site, www.CATS2013.com. The CATS part was in bold red letters, larger than the rest.

CATS for Mayor. I liked the sound of that.

"I made it from that Greek island to 1Thirty-Fifth Street to the top of the business community," I told the crowd. "It's my turn to give back to New York. That's all I care about—making New York a little bit better every day."

I knew the reporters would be listening for a shorthand description of who I was and why I was running. Now I had it. It couldn't be much clearer. My story was my campaign.

After thinking about this day for so long, having gotten so close four years earlier only to step back, I felt like this was exactly where I belonged.

Standing on the steps of City Hall.

Running for mayor of New York City.

Ready for whatever might come my way.

I'd been around the game for decades—as a supporter, a donor, and a friend. But running myself, I understood, was a whole new ballgame, and I was committed to doing it right. That first day on the campaign trail, I vowed that I'd be transparent about everything—my views, my potential opponents, the political challenges I faced, and how committed I was to giving this a real shot. There are too many secrets in politics. There would be no secrets in the Catsimatidis campaign.

I understood New York City was a heavily Democratic city, and I was running as a Republican. But I didn't think Democratic voters needed to be put off by that. My parents were Democrats. I'd been a Democrat most of my life and still had plenty of Democratic friends. Many of my political heroes were Democrats. "I admired John Kennedy," I told the crowd that day. "I was fourteen years old when he got up in front of everybody and he had a vision. 'Let's go to the moon by 1969.' And we went to the moon. I admired Martin Luther King—he had a dream. He was a visionary. He dreamed that someday there would be a Black president. Well, thank God, his dream came true. I got my lessons from a lot of people. One of the people I admired was Bill Clinton. He wasn't a Republican. But businesspeople weren't afraid of Bill Clinton. He was pro-business. We all did well under Bill Clinton."

Running New York called for common-sense solutions, I said, not party extremism on either side. "I'm a moderate," I said. "In this city, you can't get the Democratic nomination unless you're extremely on the left. But do I have issues where I'm on the left? Oh, yeah."

I let it all hang out.

I got many questions from the reporters, which I took as a positive sign. Someone asked if I was nervous running for mayor, being a first-time candidate and all. "You know what being nervous is? Flying my airplane with one engine out and knowing you have to land it with no mistakes. If I did that, nothing else makes me nervous."

One reporter asked about Joe Lhota, the former Deputy Mayor and Metropolitan Transportation Authority (MTA) Chairman who was also seeking the Republican nomination. "I like Joe Lhota," I said. "We get along. He's a very fine person." But, I added, "I'm a visionary. I've hired tens of thousands of people. Visionaries are very hard to find."

The reporters seemed especially interested in how much I was prepared to spend. When I tossed out the number $20 million, they all scribbled it in their notebooks. And maybe more if I had to, I added. I would decide that based on need. "Whatever you decide to spend on a campaign, you go in increments," I said. "Look, if it's going in our direction, we'll spend whatever we have to spend. Like I said, it's an investment in New York, *my* investment in New York."

And by the way, I added: "I'm going to work cheaper than Mayor Bloomberg," who had made a point of accepting $1 a year in salary from the city. "I was a grocer," I said, meaning I understood how to attract customers with an enticing deal.

"I'll work for 99 cents."

. . . .

As our campaign got rolling, it was funny how often people compared me to Mike Bloomberg. Sometimes in a good way: "He has the business background to pick up where Bloomberg leaves off." Sometimes not: "He's no Mike Bloomberg." Either way, I took it as a compliment. Two business guys running as Republicans in an overwhelmingly Democratic city, promising to bring the expertise of the private sector into City Hall. We had that much in common, though our styles could hardly have been more different. Bloomberg had gained his early business experience trading bonds on Wall Street. I gained mine selling groceries on the streets of Harlem and the Upper West Side. But I wasn't looking to trash Bloomberg any more than I wanted him trashing me. And I'd like to think there was some mutual respect there. I believed he made New York a better place. The economy was humming again. Foreign investment was pouring in. Race relations were far calmer than they'd been in the Giuliani years, and crime kept going down. I didn't plan on undermining any of that. But four years after Bloomberg had changed the term-limits law to squeeze in another four years, the future belonged to whoever was coming next. I was planning on that being me.

I knew from the start I'd have plenty of company in the 2013 mayor's race, though the vast majority of the potential candidates would be lining up on the Democratic side. They included half a dozen current and previous officeholders. The usual suspects, I would call them. City Council Speaker Christine Quinn. City Comptroller John Liu. Former Congressman Anthony Weiner. Public Advocate Bill de Blasio. Former City Comptroller Bill Thompson. There were also a lot of other names floating around, *some* of whom were plausible candidates. Actor Alec Baldwin. Bronx Borough President Rubén Díaz Jr. Businessman Leo Hindery. Brooklyn Borough President Marty Markowitz. Charter schools advocate Eva Moskowitz. Manhattan Borough President Scott Stringer. *Daily News* owner Mort Zuckerman. Former Port Authority Director Chris Ward. Even Hillary Clinton's name popped up at one point. I think someone might even have mentioned Bill.

And that wasn't all. There was also former Bronx Borough President Adolfo Carrión Jr., as well as Malcolm Smith of Queens, who had been President of the New York State Senate. Really, the crowd was big enough to fill a rush-hour subway car. Manhattan Media Chairman Tom Allon. Pastor A. R. Bernard, TV commentator S. E. Cupp, Staten Island District Attorney Dan Donovan, State Senator Marty Golden, actor Kelsey Grammer, former stock-exchange Chairman Richard Grasso, Citigroup Chairman Richard Parsons, former Bloomberg Deputy Mayor Ed Skyler, and former State Banking Commissioner Diana Taylor, who had the added credibility (or was it the baggage?) of being Mike Bloomberg's girlfriend.

What explained this mob scene? It was simple, really. It had been twelve years since we'd had a race for mayor of New York City that didn't feature an incumbent mayor. People come out of the woodwork for something like that.

In the end, the Democratic race consisted of Quinn, de Blasio, Liu, Thompson, Weiner, and a small number of others with little money and less chance. The Republican field was smaller—Lhota, homeless advocate George McDonald, and me.

The media focused most on the Dems, assuming that whomever won that primary would probably be the next mayor of New York. I'm not saying we three Republicans grabbed no attention, but it was definitely less than what the Democrats got. And they were really going at each other. Quinn, the Council Speaker, was at the top of the Democratic polls. She had tons of endorsements, though not a lot of excitement. De Blasio was further to the left and drew his strongest support from Park Slope, Carroll Gardens, and other rising Brooklyn neighborhoods. Liu and Thompson were running what looked to me like demographic campaigns—Thompson seeking African American votes, Liu pushing the point that he'd be the city's first Asian American mayor. Weiner, in more ways than one, was the odd man out. He'd already been driven from Congress in a lewd-tweeting scandal. He was hoping the mayor's race would be his ticket back to office. Were New Yorkers ready to forgive him? That was an open question that wouldn't be resolved until the Democratic primary on September 10.

Joe Lhota would be my toughest Republican opponent. I knew that from the start. I had known Joe for many years. He grew up in the Bronx and on Long Island. After graduating from Georgetown University and Harvard Business School, he'd become an investment banker before serving as Budget Director and Deputy Mayor in the Giuliani administration and, later, as Chairman of the MTA board. He was a bright guy.

George McDonald, the other candidate, was a good man, too. He ran the Doe Fund, a nonprofit organization that provides jobs, housing, and educational opportunities to people with histories of homelessness, incarceration, or substance abuse—often all three. The Doe Fund is a worthwhile program. I have supported it over the years. Like me, George used to be a Democrat.

And there was me.

I didn't dislike either of these guys. I liked them. I respected them greatly. I just wanted to beat them, then take my best shot at whichever Democrat was left standing when the November 5 general election finally rolled around.

I knew I had to find ways to stand out from Lhota and McDonald, but that didn't turn out to be so hard. My common-sense message seemed to resonate with New York's common-sense Republicans. It would appeal just as strongly, I hoped—maybe more so—to general-election voters in November. I was a proven leader. I had built several successful businesses in very different industries. I had created many, many thousands of jobs. I wasn't a creature of some political consultant's focus group. I was running as me. I was the guy who could keep the economy humming, bring new jobs to the city, and push the crime rate even lower. With Cats as mayor, I argued, the voters would get a candidate who had Bloomberg's business savvy with more of a common touch.

One thing that's important to know about New York politics, and I focused on it early: it isn't only Democrats and Republicans. Many other parties show up on the ballot every Election Day. Many Democratic candidates also seek the nomination of the Working Families Party. Republicans often run the Conservative Party line as well. I say "often" because nothing in New York politics is true all the time. Depending on various factors, there can be dozens of parties on the ballot, many sharing the same candidates. It's a strange, complex system, but it's the system New York has.

All that said, I figured I shouldn't seek only the Republican nomination. I would try to be the nominee of the Liberal Party, too.

Why not? Joe Lhota seemed to have the Conservative Party nomination. And the Liberal Party of New York had a rich history filled with crossover candidates like me. The party was founded in 1944 as an alternative to the American Labor Party, which was itself an alternative party for leftists upset at the Democratic Party for supporting

Franklin D. Roosevelt. The Liberal Party never achieved the dream of becoming a truly national party. Its first marquee leader, former Republican presidential candidate Wendell Willkie, died as Liberals were hatching a plan to run him for Mayor of New York in 1945. But the party did hold on over the years, keeping its place on the New York ballot and endorsing candidates like John F. Kennedy for President in 1960. Kennedy returned the favor by famously declaring in his acceptance speech: "I'm proud to say I'm a Liberal."

In the decades since then, the Liberal Party had backed quite a few successful candidates, many of whom weren't all that liberal. They included several prominent Republicans—John Lindsay and Rudy Giuliani for Mayor of New York and Jacob Javits and Charles Goodell for US Senator. The party also backed the independent presidential campaign of former Republican Congressman John B. Anderson in 1980. The Lindsay case is especially interesting, however. In 1969, as the incumbent Republican Mayor, he lost his own party's primary but was reelected on the Liberal Party line, helping to elect enough other Liberal Party candidates for City Council to replace the Republicans as the minority party in city government. Such Liberal Party maneuvers didn't always work out in the end, though. In 1977, Mario Cuomo lost the Democratic nomination for Mayor of New York to Ed Koch. In the general election, the Liberals endorsed Cuomo anyway, only to have Koch beat him a second time. Ouch!

I liked the idea of running as a Republican-Liberal, following in the footsteps of Lindsay, Javits, Giuliani, and the rest. And, a month or so after I'd announced my candidacy, that door opened to me when Tom Allon dropped out of the race. Somewhere along the way, he had managed to sew up the Liberal Party nomination. Now that Allon was out, I saw an opportunity.

I spoke to Marty Hassner, the party's Executive Director. He seemed open to backing me. He liked my common-sense, businessman's vision. He said that was very much in keeping with the party's proud traditions. He knew I would run a serious campaign, and I was prepared to fund it. On May 7, I headed back to meet the reporters outside City Hall, this time with Hassner. "This is a force of nature," said the

Liberal Party leader, putting his hand on my shoulder and announcing that I was the Liberal Party candidate for Mayor. He called me "a very uncommon common man" with the "yearning necessary" to win the race. "There's nobody else like him around," Hassner said.

I appreciated him saying all that. When it was my time to speak, I wanted to strike a grateful and confident tone. "Today is a game changer," I said. "We have the chance to create a fusion ticket for pro-business New Yorkers and the pro-people New Yorkers," I said. "That's what I'm all about."

With each press conference, I was learning more about the way that media people—the ones in New York, at least—reacted to candidates for public office. They'd usually give you a chance to say whatever you'd come to say. But they'd quickly start quizzing you about something they were interested in. They would usually ask a series of questions, but often, those questions felt more like jabs.

"Are you trying to buy the Republican nomination?" one reporter asked while the others stood expectantly with their notebooks and tape recorders.

The trick in answering questions like that is not to get rattled and not to take the bait. A bold comment is even better, I have found.

"Not at all," I said. "I will abide by the city's campaign-finance law. I will disclose all my expenditures. And I won't take a nickel of the city's money to finance my campaign. I won't cost the city anything. Instead, I will save the city a bundle."

....

I liked being out on the campaign trail. I liked talking to the people. I liked visiting parts of the city I'd hardly seen before. I especially liked getting to know the civic leaders and local elected officials. By and large, these people really care about their communities and neighborhoods, and they know *everything*. I was at a forum on Staten Island when a woman named Linda Dianto came over and introduced herself. She told me she lived in the Grasmere neighborhood and ran a small nonprofit group called the National Lighthouse Museum. She and her board were working diligently, she said, to revive a crumbling piece of the borough's nautical past, the former United States Lighthouse Service General Depot a few hundred feet south of the St. George Ferry Terminal.

"Where do you stand on reviving the museum project?" she asked. I don't think she had any idea about the role a lighthouse had played in the life of my own family.

I gave her a big hug, and I said: "I want to help you. My father was a lighthouse keeper in Greece." Then I told her the story of Andreas Catsimatidis.

Random connections like that one were a daily part of campaigning in New York, along with being grilled by the reporters and trying to differentiate myself from Joe Lhota, which sometimes meant seizing on unfortunate things he said. At one candidate forum, he referred to Port Authority police officers as "nothing more than mall cops." Thirty-seven of those heroic men and women had been killed on 9/11. I jumped all over that. At an MTA board meeting, he'd addressed a seventy-seven-year-old Holocaust survivor, Board Member Charles Moerdler, taunting him to "be a man." Lhota apologized after the meeting, saying, "I think my Bronx upbringing came out today."

Were these terrible things? No. More like thoughtless utterances. But in the heat of a mayoral primary campaign, there was no chance they would be ignored.

I questioned whether Lhota was running in the shadow of his former boss, Rudy Giuliani, constantly praising and quoting the mayor whose budget director and deputy he had been. Giuliani, who still carried some sway with Republican voters, returned the favor by endorsing his deputy's candidacy. In a thirty-second TV commercial, I hammered their connection. The ad, which starred everyday New Yorkers, didn't knock Rudy. That wouldn't be such a good idea in a Republican primary. And I had the greatest respect and affection for "America's Mayor." But the ad did basically suggest that Joe Lhota was no Rudy Giuliani. "Not even close," as the ad said.

Joe had no choice but to address this and fire back at me, even though addressing it made it almost worse. "I am not a tool of Rudy Giuliani," he insisted.

As the September 10 primary neared, things got increasingly testy. On August 24, the *New York Times* endorsed Lhota. I didn't like that. Judgment Day was coming, and the sharp elbows were out. This was really on display the Sunday before the vote, which also happened to be three days before the twelfth anniversary of 9/11. The three of us gathered for our final debate and, of course, the terror attack came up. I pressed Lhota on the massive communications problems that terrible Tuesday in 2001. He said the problems should have been addressed but that he'd helped to get New York "up and running" after 9/11.

"Joe," I told the debate audience, "is more of a technical person. I am a big-vision person." Therefore, I added, I'd have a much broader appeal in November against whichever candidate survived the Democrats' primary.

"I have gone to every minority neighborhood," I said truthfully. "They've all given me hugs."

You could tell things were getting extra personal at the end, which was unfortunate but is probably inevitable in any hard-fought political battle on issues large and small. At that last debate, someone asked Lhota whether he would have shut down a subway line like the MTA did when a kitten strayed onto the tracks. He said he wouldn't have. Asked if that made him the "the anti-kitten candidate," Lhota drew the line. "I never said I wanted to kill a cat," he shot back. "I grew up with cats," adding that he meant the furry kind, not the "Cats man" who was running against him.

I couldn't sit quietly for that. I said it sounded to me like Lhota hated cats—"this Cat, anyway."

Yes, everyone had grown a little punch-drunk by the end.

....

I came up short.

Joe Lhota finished ahead of me in the Republican primary, 52.7 percent to 40.7 percent, capturing the party's nomination for Mayor of New York. Not the result I was imagining, obviously. But not a bad showing for a first-time candidate. That's what I told myself, anyway. I made some important points on the campaign trail about the common-sense solutions that New York was in need of. I met some wonderful people along the way. I visited parts of the city I never would have seen before and learned about issues that had never previously crossed my mind. Garbage pickup schedules! You have no idea what a burning issue garbage pickup schedules can be! I finished well ahead of what the last two polls in the race had predicted, which had me at 22 percent (Marist) and 28 percent (amNewYork). What do the polls know? Back in April, Quinnipiac actually had me trailing McDonald, 8 percent to 11 percent, with Lhota at 23 percent. Even at the time, that one seemed like an outlier to me.

On primary day, McDonald trailed both Lhota and me with 6.3 percent, though his impact on the results may actually have been larger than the vote he got. I honestly think that if McDonald, a former Democrat like myself, hadn't joined the Republican field that year, virtually all his votes would have ended up in my column, which would have turned the race into quite a squeaker.

I won Staten Island, the city's most Republican borough, by nearly eleven points. I came within two points of winning Brooklyn, the most populous borough. The headscratcher for me was how badly I lost Manhattan. There, Lhota stomped me 70.5 to 20 percent. If you add up all the numbers in the outer boroughs, I almost won. But of the 12,350 Republican votes in Manhattan, I got only 3,139 of them.

There was one other disappointment inside the numbers for me. I did not do all that well among minority voters. There aren't huge numbers of African Americans and Hispanics who vote in Republican primaries in New York. But given my Harlem upbringing and my long support for equality of opportunity, I thought I would have done better there.

....

It was a big commitment, running for mayor, and I don't mean that just in the financial sense. Running for a major office like that one takes a lot of time. Away from my business. Away from my wife. Away from my kids. It was interesting and fun sometimes, learning how New York really was a lot like a hundred little villages spread across five boroughs. But it was also a sacrifice—a sacrifice I was willing to make for the city that had been so good to me, but a sacrifice nonetheless.

I tried to learn from my mistakes. How else do we ever get better in life?

One mistake I made was running against pot in New York City. It wasn't a huge issue for me. But when the reporters asked, I came out clearly against legalization. I even ran a full-page ad, saying marijuana hurts kids. That came out of my own life experience. Or lack of it. I had too much responsibility in my life when I was young. I was working all the time. I was afraid if I started smoking marijuana, I might hurt my responsibilities. So I never smoked it. I still believe almost everything I supported in the campaign, but that's one thing in hindsight I might have done differently.

One other fact did disturb me after the results were all in: how low the voter turnout had been. Only 13 percent of eligible Republican voters had turned out that day. *That's pathetic*, I told myself as soon as the totals came in. It's something our city and our country still really needs to deal with. If we are going to be a functioning democracy, more than 13 percent of the people have to participate. How can we get folks more engaged in the political process? That's a big question. Even as I tried to put the mayoral primary behind me, I knew my work on that topic wasn't done.

....

At the same time that Joe Lhota, George McDonald, and I were battling for the Republican nomination, the Democratic contest had all the ups and downs of a Macy's escalator. City Council Speaker Christine Quinn, who had the support of Mayor Bloomberg and boatloads of cash, stumbled badly in the final weeks of the primary, taking heat from animal rights activists and other special-interest groups. Former City Comptroller Bill Thompson puttered along but never managed to expand his base of support, a frustration he shared with his successor in the comptroller's office, John Liu. Anthony Weiner, the ex-Congressman who'd once been riding at the top of the pack, totally flamed out when word got out that he was compulsively tweeting again. Bill de Blasio shot to the top with a single TV ad featuring his charismatic biracial son and stayed there long enough to grab a commanding win: 40.8 percent of the vote to Thompson's 26.1, Quinn's 15.7, and the others that finished even further behind. Former front-runner Weiner finished a hair below 5 percent.

On a couple of levels, the results were maddening to me. For one thing, de Blasio, who I liked personally, was the farthest left of the major Democratic candidates. He ran on vague promises of affordable housing and a vow to end stop-and-frisk, Mike Bloomberg and Ray Kelly's successful program to take guns off the street. He seemed to have no real plan to achieve the former. And to me, curtailing stop-and-frisk was pushing the city in exactly the wrong direction.

I would have loved a chance to run against him in November as the Republican nominee.

I could have stayed in the race, carrying the Liberal Party banner. Quite a few people urged me to. In hindsight, I probably should have. But by that point, it seemed like a futile endeavor.

De Blasio ended up with 73 percent of the vote. Lhota got 24 percent. The crumbs were divided among minor candidates. No, it isn't easy running as a Republican in New York.

Turnout was a little better than it had been in the Republican primary. About 24 percent of the city's registered voters made it to the polls, barely over one million of the 4.3 million that could have turned out. It was the lowest percentage in a general election in many decades. The previous low, 28 percent, had come four years earlier when Bloomberg won his third term.

John and Margo Catsimatidis supporting our military (top) and at a Police Athletic League Christmas Party for children (bottom).

20

GIVING TIME

Like many great ideas, the Police Athletic League bubbled up from the fertile mind of a single individual, though he got a lot of help along the way.

This was 1914, the same year that Archduke Franz Ferdinand was shot to death with his wife by the Bosnian Serb nationalist Gavrilo Princip, sparking a tragic descent into world war. Arthur Woods, Police Commissioner of New York City, had a very simple idea. He decided to close a handful of city streets for a few summer afternoons and invite the local youngsters out to play. Play Streets, he called his experiment, which was centered in some of the city's poorer and rougher neighborhoods.

What made the program special, besides giving children a reason to leave their hot apartments and somewhere to go when their parents were working, was that police officers from the local station houses would come out to join the fun. Sports was something the kids and cops had in common. The natural connections they made over stickball, stoopball, and basketball in those closed-off streets—well, the whole thing had a certain magic. The kids and the cops kept coming back for more.

Some years later, the commissioner's program merged with a similar one, Captain John Sweeney's Junior Police Clubs in the Lower East Side, and formed what today is the Police Athletic League (PAL) of

New York City. Before you knew it, a cops-and-kids movement was spreading across America, producing encouraging results wherever it went. Since 1961, the New York program has been chaired by Robert Morgenthau, the longtime Manhattan district attorney, and it's still going strong, supported by private donors and some public funds. It's not an instant cure-all to all of society's ills. No single program can cure poverty, violence, substance abuse, lack of opportunity, racial prejudice, and the weakening of the family structure. But the Police Athletic League keeps sparking miracles one at a time—using safe, organized fun to support and inspire young people to realize their potential in life. And if some cops get to know some kids as human beings—and, yes, vice versa—that's a wonderful added bonus.

I have served on the organization's board of directors for more than three decades. I've written a stack of checks. It's one of the best programs like it anywhere. I love talking to the PAL kids.

"I came from Harlem," I tell them. "West 1Thirty-Fifth Street. You know where that is? It's not so different from the blocks a lot of you live on. I made it. I really made it. If I can make it, you can, too."

That's a powerful message: "If I can make it, you can, too."

It's important for these kids to meet people who've started where they've started and ended up somewhere far away, somewhere better, somewhere great. One speech alone will not save a young life any more than one basketball game will. But the story I tell them is real and true and can actually inspire young people. I've seen the looks on the faces of those PAL kids and heard the questions they ask. "Really? You're from Harlem? And you're a billionaire?" I'm not kidding myself when I say role models are important in life. I know how much I benefited from all of mine.

And the success stories speak for themselves. Dick Parsons was a PAL kid. He went on to run the Time Warner company. Singer Billy Joel, boxing champs Muhammad Ali and George Foreman, actor Jimmy Smits, pop star Alicia Keys, and Secretary of State Colin Powell, who always works hard to help inner-city youngsters—they were all PAL kids. Lots of other PAL kids, famous and obscure, have made extraordinary strides in their lives and in the world. I've hired quite a few of them in my supermarkets and other businesses. It takes a lot of generous people to keep the program up and running, people from all different backgrounds. Business owners to hire PAL kids. (I have hired quite a few.) Professional people to write checks. Media bigwigs to spread the word. One especially generous soul is longtime *New York Post* columnist Cindy Adams. Cindy has always been there for the Police Athletic League (and for many other worthy causes, too.) It isn't only media coverage that she gives. She shows up. She takes a personal interest. She cares. I wish we had a hundred more Cindys.

Programs like this one don't work for everyone. Nothing does. But I have stood at Police Athletic League functions with commissioners Ray Kelly, Bill Bratton, Robert McGuire, and James O'Neill as we asked each other, "How many of these kids do you think we can save?"

None of us has ever come up with a reliable number. These things are hard to predict. But each time we have had that conversation, we end up in the same place: "We'll save a whole lot more of them than if we don't try."

....

The Police Athletic League is just one of many charitable organizations I have supported over the years with my energy, my money, and my time. I've given to all kinds of groups. I give because people ask me to. I give because I am especially impressed with the work a particular group is doing. I give because I have a special concern about an issue the organization has taken on. I give out of gratefulness to schools, hospitals, and other outfits that have helped me and the people I love. I give because I have been extraordinarily blessed in life, and I feel a responsibility to spread some of those benefits around. But at the very core of it, there is something else, something that lives inside me, something I strive for every day, something that I hope will partly define me long after I am gone. That something is *philotimo*.

It's a Greek word, and it isn't easy to define in English. Believe me, many people have tried. *Philotimo* comes from the root *filos*, meaning "friend," and *timi*, meaning "honor." But *philotimo* goes a whole lot deeper than "friend" and "honor." The concept also encompasses pride in self, pride in family, pride in community, and an abiding drive to do the right thing for the right reasons, all the time. Elder Paisios of Mount Athos, the beloved Greek ascetic who was canonized in 2015, described *philotimo* as "that deep-seated awareness in the heart that motivates the good that a person does. A *philotimos* person is one who conceives and enacts eagerly those things good."

Well, I'm no Paisios. Not even close. But I try.

In early 2018, as we approached the fiftieth anniversary of the assassination of Reverend Martin Luther King, Reverend Jesse Jackson came to see me at my office. He brought a film crew along. He was there to interview me for a documentary he was making about game changers and the American Dream. I guess he considered me a game changer.

Back in King's time, Reverend Jackson said, people dreamed about Black people and White people sharing the same lunch counter. "But hasn't that dream progressed over the years?" Reverend Jackson asked.

Of course it has, I answered. It's gotten much bigger and much stronger than it used to be. Good people feel a deeper commitment to help. Then I told him about the concept of *philotimo* and how it has affected the Greek community's pursuit of the American Dream. "Of all the Greek virtues," I explained, "*philotimo* is considered the highest. It's an outlook and a habit that truly becomes a way of life." Reverend Jackson seemed to find that intriguing, a powerful way of advancing other important values like social justice, economic opportunity, and political equality. It's also a great reason to give more than money to good causes, I told him.

Why just write a check if you can give in even more personal ways? There are so many routes to making the world a better place. People need help everywhere you look. In that spirit, I founded and co-chaired the Brooklyn Tech Endowment Foundation, benefiting my alma mater. Here's a New York City public school that has done so much for so many. Brooklyn Tech was hugely important in my own development, just as it has been for thousands of other young people over the decades. We need to continue that legacy into the future. I am a committed donor to Denise Rich's G&P Foundation for Cancer Research, which is conducting cutting-edge research into a disease that still kills far too many. With One Hundred Black Men of New York, I created the annual Catsimatidis Family Foundation Scholarship. I also fund scholarships at NYU's Stern School of Business, AJ and John Jr.'s alma mater. Two scholarships have been awarded every year since 1988. For five years, I was President of the Manhattan Council of the Boy Scouts of America. I don't need to tell you who the Boy Scouts are or all the good they do. But it doesn't happen for free. I have been on the board of directors of the inspiring Drum Major Institute. Our Hellenic Times Scholarship Fund has awarded more than $1.7 million in scholarships to seven hundred students across the United States. I was Vice Chairman of the Ellis Island Honors Society, formerly known as the National Ethnic Coalition Organization, which also presented me with an Ellis Island Medal of Honor in 1990. Receiving such an award had been very moving, even though my immigrant parents and I happened to land at Idlewild.

In March of 2017, when a rash of anti-Semitic attacks swept the New York area, we teamed up with the Police Foundation, the Jewish Community Relations Council, and the man I call my rabbi, Arthur Schneier of Manhattan's Park East Synagogue. Rabbi Schneier is internationally known for his leadership on religious freedom and tolerance. For decades, that cause has taken him to Russia, China, Central Europe—you name it. But in this instance, the issue hit closer to home, and Rabbi Schneier jumped right in. We agreed we had to bring the perpetrators to justice and do whatever we could to discourage future hate crimes. We recruited other help. As soon as they were asked, Governor Andrew Cuomo and Mayor Bill de Blasio added their voices and their influence to the cause. Working together, we designed a special Crime Stoppers reward fund for hate-crime tips, giving New Yorkers an extra incentive to step forward and say what they knew about these terrible acts. That didn't end the incidents entirely, but it made a real dent and reminded me again the importance of finding strong allies. Thanks, Mayor, Governor, and Rabbi—and all the others who worked with us. The right people, working together, really can achieve anything.

Fresh issues will always be popping up, and we have to keep responding. When Hurricane Maria swept through the Caribbean in

September 2017, I knew we had to respond. The need was so enormous, and it's never easy delivering emergency supplies to small islands in the middle of the sea. You can't exactly truck in pallets of bottled water and ready-to-eat meals. We'd previously had three hundred employees in St. Croix and across the US Virgin Islands. Coordinating with Governor Cuomo, we flew down a planeload of supplies for St. Croix and neighboring St. Thomas, thinking maybe we'd be helping some of our former Red Apple family members and their neighbors. Soon after that, my daughter AJ led a mission to Puerto Rico, delivering another planeload of much-needed medical supplies. I learned long ago, and I'm proud to say my daughter has also come to know, that there is something special about being in a position to help others. I think AJ enjoyed delivering the help as much as the local people liked receiving it. Everyone was so appreciative.

There are lots of other groups and organizations I am proud to contribute to and assist in other ways: the National Kidney Foundation; the Juvenile Diabetes Research Foundation; the United Service Organizations; the Jewish Community Relations Council; the Manhattan Theatre Club; the Broadway Association; the Green Beret Foundation; the Young Men's Philanthropic League; the Parkinson's Disease Foundation; the Alzheimer's Foundation of America; the Diabetes Research Institute; Outward Bound; the Children's Tumor Foundation; the Federal Law Enforcement Foundation; HealthCorps; and the Soldiers', Sailors', Marines', Coast Guard and Airmen's Club. I'll stop listing them now, though these names don't include countless local efforts, one-offs, and smaller, personal requests. They are just as important as the well-known organizations, and often they need the help even more. I can't give to everybody, but I try. And I am constantly urging others to join me.

. . . .

One of the great benefits of making a lot of money is that you then get the opportunity to give a lot of it away.

No one gets rich alone. As much as some people don't like to admit this, success is always a team sport. And all of us who have done well have an obligation to assist people who are still struggling and to promote the many causes that will make the world a better place.

That's what I believe, anyway.

At West Point, they teach the young cadets "duty, honor, country." In case anyone ever forgets, those three words are right there on the school's coat of arms. That's a pretty good cheat sheet for getting into the habit of giving back. It's certainly a fine place to begin. More people should get involved in their local charities, in their religious institutions, in community affairs—yes, even in politics. And you don't have to be rich to do so. Everyone can give something, and we can all give according to our means. Once you start giving, you will not want to stop.

Find causes you can feel passionate about and help them as much as you possibly can. Whether you're running the bake sale, reading to senior citizens, or writing fat checks, you'll go to bed feeling like you did something with your day.

Top: President Barack Obama chats with John Catsimatidis.

Bottom: President Ronald Reagan and First Lady Nancy Reagan greet John Catsimatidis during a visit to the White House.

21

FEEDING FRENZY

"Money is the mother's milk of politics."

I first heard that expression many years ago. I didn't know who'd coined it. But the deeper I got into the political world, the truer I could tell it was.

I Googled the quote one day.

It came from a man named Jesse Unruh, a big Bobby Kennedy backer at the national Democratic Party who also served as Assembly Speaker and State Treasurer in California in the 1960s, 1970s, and 1980s. "Big Daddy Unruh," he was called back then. He'd been around Washington and Sacramento long enough to know something I was quickly discovering on my own: just how vital money always is in politics. Donors, lobbyists, special-interest groups—they are constantly buzzing around the political world. It isn't bribery, what they are doing. Mostly, they are trading for access. That's just the way the system works. After all, the First Amendment to the US Constitution specifically provides a right to petition our government and a right to free speech. Where would we be without those?

At the same time, the field is also crowded with strategists, consultants, pollsters, media buyers, and other so-called political pros, almost all of whom have their hands out. They whisper in the candidates' ears. They plant dreams of higher office. "I see a big future for you!" they'll say. And then there are the candidates themselves, navigating between the givers and the takers, constantly under pressure to raise more campaign cash.

Why do you think members of Congress spend so many hours every week "dialing for dollars," as they call it in Washington? They need the money, that's why. Except for a handful of wealthy candidates who are able to "self-finance," they need to get the money from someone else. And it isn't just congressmen. It's officeholders (and aspiring ones) up and down the political ladder—federal, state, and local—every day of the week, every week of the year.

"Follow the money," young journalists are taught, and that's a pretty good road map to the truth.

Like a lot of political people, Jesse Unruh was certain that he hadn't been personally corrupted by all the lavish spending that surrounded him. "If you can't eat their food, drink their booze, screw their women, take their money, and then vote against them, you've got no business being up here," he once famously said. I make no judgment on Big Daddy's personal integrity or lack thereof. But I do know this much from all my years in business and politics: for better or worse, not much happens until the checkbooks come out.

I have been writing checks to political candidates, Democrats and Republicans, for more than three decades. I don't regret it. I've supported some good people. On balance, I think my giving has done some good. But I am not blind. I can also see that there is something really destructive about the huge piles of money that keep our system nourished and alive—like mother's milk, to quote the man from California who'd seen how it operates.

Why is this bad? Well, for a number of reasons. It means that people without money don't get heard like they have a right to. It means that special interests get their way most of the time. It means that common sense and the greater good frequently take a backseat when they aren't thrown out the window entirely. I'm not saying all politicians are for sale. Some are—and at shockingly low prices. But most people who run for office start out with good intentions to serve the public interest. They want to make the world better or promote some worthy cause. Over time, however, they come to realize what generations of politicians have discovered before them: dollars twist everything.

It isn't that money always wins in politics. I can show you some rich guys who spent a bundle to lose. Rather, it's that without sufficient resources, even the best candidates or the best ideas won't ever get heard. Politicians are constantly talking about "reforming the system" and "getting the money out of politics." Various reforms have been tried over the years. Almost all of them sound promising. Almost all are supported by everyday people. Then they collapse. Despite all the good intentions, the winner in most elections or most policy fights is still the side that spreads the most money around. That's not democracy the way our forefathers imagined it. If that's the way we pick winners and losers, we're all the poorer for it.

. . . .

You may be surprised hearing me talk like this, after all the contributions I have made to candidates and causes. I've hosted fundraisers. I recruited other contributors and bundled their checks. I am one of the people that people in politics come to when they need to raise money, which is pretty much all the time.

But in at least two important ways, I am different from most of the people who donate. For one thing, my giving is utterly nonpartisan. I give to Republicans. I give to Democrats. I give to people who are aligned with no party at all. I don't care about party. I give to people I have faith in, people I like, and people I think might do some good. But that isn't the main way I am different from most of the other big donors.

Unlike almost all of them, I never ask for anything in return.

Never.

Not once.

Not ever.

I don't seek government contracts or jobs for my relatives and friends. I don't have pet issues I demand loyalty to. Literally, I ask for nothing in return. Some of the people I've given to don't quite know what to make of this. They keep asking, "What do you want?" "What can I do for you?" "What is your interest here?" And I keep answering, "I don't want anything. Just do a good job."

Some of them have looked at me like I must be hiding something or as if I am hopelessly naive. Many of them figured I had a secret agenda that would reveal itself eventually. They were confident that, after I'd curried enough favor, I'd return with a giant ask. But as far as I was concerned, there was no ask—giant, tiny, or in between. I started giving because I wanted to give. I also wanted to get to know powerful people in the world, and I liked being around other people who gave.

That meant doing what they were doing—ideally, doing it bigger and better than they were doing it. A lot of them were going to political fundraisers and donating to campaigns. I had the money. I figured, why not? So I jumped in.

Now, not a week passes by—sometimes not a day—that a politician or an aspiring politician doesn't call or come to see me asking for money. I don't always give, but sometimes I do.

....

At the same time that almost everyone in politics is playing this money game, many of them are also complaining about it and denouncing it. The negative influence of all this money is one of the few things that many Republicans and Democrats agree on. I'm not saying it's a good system. I'm saying it's the system. And I don't expect it to end anytime soon.

Good-government groups keep making efforts to improve this undeniable reality, trying to loosen the stranglehold that money has on politics. Each reform does some good—for a little while. Corporate donations are forbidden in federal elections. Limits are put on how much a single donor can give. Contributions must be reported to the Federal Election Commission so everyone can see how much is being given and by whom. These are well-intentioned reforms, but not one of them has made money less important in politics. If anything, I think it's fair to say that money has never been more important than it is today. Each new reform generates new loopholes. Super PACs are invented.

Soft money is separated from hard. Small donations are bundled into larger ones. No crackdown ever really turns the faucet off.

Just as soon as a new regulation is drafted, smart lawyers on K Street are dreaming up fresh ways around it. I suspect this will always happen. It always has.

I'm not saying we shouldn't try to improve the system—but I am saying we shouldn't hold our breath for these efforts to succeed. And until they do, people who care about our country may just be forced to keep on giving. The world will not be better if the forces of evil bury us in their dollars and good guys refuse to give.

That's a prescription for disaster, I believe.

Top: John Catsimatidis with President Donald Trump and Vice President Mike Pence.

Bottom: John Catsimatidis honored with a commemorative postage stamp in Greece.

22

CATEGORY CATS

Sometimes I feel like I am living in a hurricane. Does the National Weather Service have a category higher than five?

I know. This is the life I have chosen. I'd rather be super busy—running lots of businesses, supporting lots of charities, staying engaged with life—than sitting around all day staring out the window or playing golf. Some people might call that relaxing. I would call it "bored out of my skull." One of the great things about living in my chosen whirlwind is that I never, ever have the time to get bored.

There's no denying I've gotten to know some amazing people along the way. In politics. In business. In many walks of life. This is one of the true joys of being me, along with the pleasure that comes with having such a loving family, such loyal friends, and such an interesting business life. People call. They come by. Friends send other friends. We meet at political gatherings and charity functions and media events. It helps that I live in New York City. Lots of fascinating people live in or near the world's greatest metropolis, and many others pass through from time to time.

On top of all my other business ventures, and with dreams of elective office behind me—at least temporarily—I found myself thinking about how I could share this gift more broadly, the gift of having all these extraordinary people in and around my life. I can't invite the whole world to my apartment for brunch on Sunday—it's a New York apartment. Really, it's not that large. But what if I hosted my own radio show? I could invite interesting people to come on the air with me. We could talk like we talk in real life, focusing on whatever we wanted to talk about, whatever popped into our minds. Nothing scripted or rehearsed. It would be just like coming over to the Cats apartment for brunch, minus Margo's eggs Benedict and smoked salmon.

I shared this idea with Jerry Crowley, the general manager of New York's AM 970 The Answer station, which is part of the Salem Media Group. Jerry loved the idea. We kicked around a few possible names and decided to call the show exactly what it was going to be: the *Cats Roundtable*. It would run every Sunday morning right before the TV Sunday shows come on. Producer Frank Morano, a real talk-radio professional, would be my producer, helping me with some of the mechanics of hosting a radio show.

The *Cats Roundtable* debuted in March 2014. There is hardly a major figure in the political world—conservative or liberal, Republican or Democrat—who hasn't been a guest on the *Cats Roundtable*.

What an A-list it's been!

Washington luminaries like Hillary Clinton, Nancy Pelosi, Chuck Schumer, Paul Ryan, John McCain, Dick Cheney, Newt Gingrich, Kirsten Gillibrand, James Carville, Joni Ernst, Ed Rendell, Richard Blumenthal, Ronna Romney McDaniel, Reince Priebus, Joe Lieberman, Marsha Blackburn, Pat Toomey, Barney Frank, Scott Pruitt, and Steve Bannon. New York power brokers including Andrew Cuomo, Bill de Blasio, Rudy Giuliani, Cyrus Vance Jr., Ed Cox, Tony Carbonetti, and former Police Commissioners James O'Neill, Ray Kelly, and Bill Bratton.

And that's not all. Media personalities like Geraldo Rivera, Rikki Klieman, Judge Jeanine Pirro, Dr. Mehmet Oz, and Caitlyn Jenner. Diplomats such as Patrick Theros, Zalmay Khalilzad, and John Bolton. Former British Prime Minister Tony Blair and his barrister wife, Cherie.

When we first started, I never could have predicted how successful I'd be attracting guests of this quality. I'd met many of these people along the way, but I didn't know with certainty that they'd want to go on my program. But I could tell we were really up and running when such a large field of hopefuls turned out for the Republican presidential primaries in 2016, and every last one of the candidates felt a desire (or was it a need?) to come on the *Cats Roundtable:* Chris Christie, Rand Paul, Marco Rubio, Ted Cruz, Scott Walker, Mike Huckabee, John Kasich, Lindsey Graham, Jim Gilmore, Ben Carson, George Pataki, Bobby Jindal, Carly Fiorina, Rick Perry, Rick Santorum, Jeb Bush, and, of course, Donald Trump.

Who have I forgotten? The hits keep coming, as the music-radio DJs like to say!

These are unedited conversations. Anything goes. I don't try to nail the guests with "gotcha" questions. At the same, I'm not tossing softballs. I try to have an intelligent, civil exchange with some of the most interesting people in the world. You name 'em, we've had 'em. I think even Jerry Crowley was impressed with our lineup of high-profile guests and the sizable audience we were attracting every week. Soon, the show was added to the schedule at Washington's 570 AM station and at a growing network of other Salem stations. I think we out-booked *Meet the Press*, *Face the Nation*, *This Week*, *State of the Union*, and *Fox News Sunday*.

What I think took everyone by surprise was what big news these *Roundtable* discussions turned out to be. Major media organizations, broadcast and print, were paying close attention to our interviews. What choice did they have? My guests often came on the *Roundtable* and answered my questions in ways that made news. Before being chosen by President Trump to be his Secretary of Housing and Urban Development, Dr. Ben Carson told me on the *Roundtable* that one of Trump's virtues is his willingness to listen to other people, adding candidly: "He may not say that publicly because there is a humility issue there that could perhaps use some polishing."

That got picked up by media outlets across the country, but it didn't deter other guests from coming on and making statements that the morning papers almost had to quote. Roger Stone, the colorful and contentious political operator, came on to defend Trump's controversial trip south of the border by likening the journey to the famous expedition of another candidate Stone advised: Richard Nixon. If Nixon could go to China, the bare-knuckle political advisor asked, why couldn't Trump go to Mexico?

New York Senator Chuck Schumer came on the program and offered some rare bipartisan praise for the Republican President. "I'm a Democrat," Schumer said, "but Donald Trump did a very good job defending New York." Schumer wasn't the only one to surprise the political world with praise for a rival in the White House. Jeb Bush, who Trump had mocked as "Low-Energy Jeb," was downright effusive when he said, "Certainly, on the regulatory side, the President is off to a good start. He has made some pretty good progress . . . at the EPA, Department of Labor, and other agencies . . . He has made some good appointments."

Really? Did Jeb Bush just say that? On the *Cats Roundtable*, he did.

And there have been other newsworthy announcements made first on my program. Caitlyn Jenner (born Bruce Jenner), an Olympic gold medalist now of Kardashian fame, used the *Cats Roundtable* in June 2017 to tell the world she was considering running for the US Senate in California. The cable news programs jumped all over that one, as they did five months later in November 2017 when Trump strategist Steve Bannon declared on the *Roundtable* that he was launching a new tax-exempt social welfare organization to push his and Trump's agenda.

All of this was news. And all of it was made on the *Roundtable.*

I love Chuck Todd, George Stephanopoulos, John Dickerson, Jake Tapper, and Chris Wallace. But which one of them can match our lineup in depth, breadth, or diversity? Everyone—and I mean *everyone*—comes on the *Cats Roundtable.*

....

On Labor Day weekend of 2016, I did not host a barbecue at our beach house in the Hamptons. Instead, I flew with Margo, AJ, John Jr., and a few close friends to Athens for a very special ceremony. I was being honored by the Greek postal service, ELTA, with my own official Greek postage stamp. I have received some very nice honors over the years—but I can't think of anything that is cooler than having your own stamp.

I wasn't the only one being honored this way. Four other "Distinguished Greek Personalities" were summoned to the same ceremony in the main auditorium at the capital's Acropolis Museum: ABC's George Stephanopoulos, Greek-French filmmaker Costa-Gavras, XPRIZE Foundation founder Dr. Peter Diamandis, and singer-actress Rita Wilson, born Margarita Ibrahimoff, who is Tom Hanks's wife.

Such impressive company, I thought when I heard about my fellow honorees! Being part of this group reminded me how many extraordinary people of Hellenic heritage now live and work abroad. Almost all of us aspire to help our heritage and our fellow Greeks.

Over the years, I had made many donations to Greek-focused charities, both in Greece and around the world. I promised the officials in Athens that I would continue doing that and even step up my giving. In the summer of 2018, that meant helping the victims of the wildfire that raged through the coastal area east of Athens, killing more than ninety people and causing massive property damage—the nation's deadliest forest fire in more than a century. Just as important, I said, I would keep looking for potential business investments in Greece, new ways to help revive the nation's troubled economy. In recent years, Greece has struggled with one financial crisis after another. The Greek people keep being asked to endure fresh hardships. The government's response hasn't always helped. More than charity, what Greeks need most of all are decent, well-paying jobs. Shortly before I arrived for the stamp ceremony, I had joined a group of investors seeking to buy the Hilton hotel in Athens. Though another group of bidders ended up making the deal, I vowed to keep looking for job-creating opportunities in Greece.

These are complicated issues that are not easy to solve. In many cases, they are larger than Greece alone, encompassing all of Europe. The continent, diverse as it is, is having trouble forging sensible immigration policies. Special safety zones for immigrants still need to be set up. Ideally, I believe, refugees should be returned to their home countries once peace is achieved. By and large, Greeks love their homeland.

The main reason they leave Greece is for jobs in other countries, the same reason my father and his father left so long ago. If we want to help Greece, the very best way is with good, new jobs.

The ceremony was beautifully done. Our stamps were unveiled and projected in the auditorium, many times larger than life. All the honorees vowed to do what they could to help the land of their ancestors.

I was asked a lot of questions. I tried to answer them all.

Someone wanted to know if I was planning on running for office again in America.

"I'm thinking about it," I said.

There was an upcoming New York City mayoral election in 2017 and a gubernatorial one for New York State in 2018.

"I haven't made any decisions about either of those races," I cautioned. "But I do think I have one more run in me."

Someone asked me a question that was much more personal but quite appropriate at a once-in-a-lifetime honor like this: "Which of your dreams has not yet been fulfilled?"

I thought for a second, and then I explained.

"On this trip," I said, "I have been thinking about my father and my mother and my grandparents and how they would be so proud of this, me getting my own Greek stamp. I have accomplished a lot of things in my lifetime, I think. But that is what I am still striving for. I want my parents' spirits to be proud of me. That's my largest unfulfilled dream."

The post office printed up 2.5 million John Catsimatidis stamps, featuring my smiling face and my tie slightly askew. Before we left Athens and flew back to New York, I went to the main post office, hoping to buy three thousand stamps—enough to share with some of my friends back in New York. But that wasn't as easy as I thought it would be. Before the charge went through on my credit card, I got a call from the fraud department at Bank of America. The woman said they were going to reject the charge. They had never heard of anyone spending $5,000 at a post office.

. . . .

In the early part of 2017, I did give serious consideration to running again for mayor of New York. Bill de Blasio and I had a perfectly friendly personal rapport, but I believed some real improvements needed to be made at City Hall. More and more people had been telling me they thought the quality of city life was slipping. After four years of de Blasio, four years since Mike Bloomberg left, could it be time for fresh blood at City Hall? Cities need constant nurturing. Otherwise, they lose their edge.

When I looked closely at the race, however, I wasn't convinced the politics lined up for me. Taking on an incumbent mayor is always a heavy lift, especially in a big, diverse city like New York. Incumbents have many ways of slicing the city politically and building support. I decided upon reflection that 2017 wasn't the year for me. But that didn't mean some other year wouldn't be the right time. I would always be thinking about those possibilities. Plus, I had another political ascent to focus on—my daughter's.

AJ, who had been working diligently in our company, certainly knew her way around politics. Growing up in our family, how could she not? Politicians had been coming in and out of our living room her entire lifetime. During her courtship and marriage with Chris, she got even more drawn in, learning from the insights of various Cox family members and helping in Chris's congressional campaign. Somewhere in there, I think she got the bug. AJ set her sights on what many consider a difficult and thankless job deep in the machinery of politics: chairing the Manhattan Republican Party.

That's not a glamourous position. It's a post that requires technical knowledge, real dedication, and hard work. In a position like that one, more than a few egos need to be massaged. The demands are nearly endless. Recruiting candidates for local office. Raising money to keep the party afloat. Representing the Manhattan GOP with the state and national party organizations. New York Republicans, don't forget, are quite a bit more moderate than Republicans in most other parts of the country—fiscally conservative but socially liberal. Policies that might be popular with Republicans in Iowa or Mississippi just won't fly on the streets of New York. The five county chairs in the city need to finesse all that.

If AJ were to get the position, one of her constituents would be the President of the United States. The Manhattan GOP was Donald Trump's home party.

The Manhattan chairmanship came open when the previous chair, Adele Malpass, moved to Washington to be with her husband, David, who took a position in the Trump Administration as the Treasury's Undersecretary for International Affairs and later as President of the World Bank Group. AJ announced her interest in the position during the summer. She ran unopposed and was chosen unanimously.

I always knew that she would win. When she was eighteen years old, I turned to her at a cocktail party with a former chair, and said, "You will have her job someday." Every year since her big debut in politics, she and I have made the City and State Power List; we are always listed together!

It was a quite an achievement for her, and she got busy immediately, representing the Manhattan Party to the outside world and to itself. She gave her first interview to the *Cats Roundtable,* of course.

I'd interviewed governors, senators, and presidents, and now I was interviewing a rising political star who I had known since she was a baby. I was so proud. "The Republican Party needs to be a big tent," she declared confidently as I began my questioning. "We should attract every type of voter. We need an inclusive vision that can attract a wide range of conservative voters."

Social media had to be part of the equation, she said. So did modern polling, organizing, and fundraising techniques. She knew that it was important to be modern, but that you also can't forget what works, and to build on that.

To illustrate the point, she used a famous quote I'd been citing for years. "As Mayor LaGuardia once said, 'There is no Democratic or Republican way to pick up the garbage.' I think that having that philosophy will bring more voters into our party."

I didn't ask if she'd gotten that one from me. But I was pretty sure I was sitting witness to a new generation of leader, AJ style.

She must have been doing something right. During her very first year in office, she was named Vice Chair of the New York State Republican Party, representing the Manhattan, Brooklyn, Bronx, Queens, and Staten Island organizations in the statewide group. Clearly, others were noticing her prowess as well.

The Catsimatidis family—AJ, John, Margo, and John Jr.—celebrates the acquisition of WABC Radio at a reception in March 2020.

23

RIPE OPPORTUNITIES

Because I was born in Greece, I can't run for President of the United States. But I always say: everything else is on the table. Business, politics, media, real estate, philanthropy, fun—I'm not ruling out any of it. Why should I? Life is supposed to be lived, and there's an endless array of arenas for doing that.

I know I love being in the middle of the action, wherever and whatever the action might be. Many Friday nights when I'm in town, I grab dinner with two of my closest friends, brilliant economist (and government and media star) Larry Kudlow and talk-radio titan Mark Simone. We talk about what we've all been up to. We swap opinions about the news of the week. We discuss. We debate. We argue. We laugh. We do a lot of laughing. It makes me happy, hanging out with these guys. They have their fingers in all kinds of adventure pies. They never run out of interesting things to say. We were out at dinner one Friday in March 2018 when Larry got a phone call he said he needed to take. It was President Trump, asking him to become Director of the National Economic Council, the President's Chief Economic Adviser.

"The country needs you," I whispered to Larry when I realized who the caller was and what Larry was being asked to do. Mark and I both agreed Larry should take the job.

Just another night out with the boys!

I am always open to new business opportunities—so long as the price is right and the enterprise is something I can get my head around. Some of my most thrilling experiences earlier in my career—I'm thinking about Capitol Airlines—could not have been more different from the industry I started in, city supermarkets. Yet I loved every minute of my time in commercial aviation, except maybe the time when PEOPLExpress came in and took a butcher knife to our fares. That part wasn't too much fun. But a constant willingness to leap is what landed me in United Refining, my most profitable venture of all. What did I know about gas stations and oil refineries? I had mastered self-serve at the gas pump. That was about it. But I kept an open mind and hired talented people. I let them do their jobs. I learned as I went along. And that single, bargain-basement purchase from bankruptcy court has been paying me back ever since.

That's what our Red Apple Group is all about: a family of companies built on family values and run like a family business, with the next generation now assuming positions of leadership. I am so lucky to still have Margo's counsel. She's been there almost from the beginning. It's hard to imagine what I would have done without her. I am just as lucky to have AJ and John Jr. on the scene. All three of them have helped me build a diverse, modern conglomerate that is poised for even greater growth in the decades to come.

The way things are looking, we're only getting started now. The past couple of years have been a time of new opportunities and tremendous growth for us in three of the most exciting and fascinating fields around—media, real estate, and professional sports. All three are high-profile, high-profit, high-risk businesses. And all three have something else in common: they are loads of fun.

. . . .

Radio can be addictive. It didn't take long for me to figure that out.

As time went on, I kept hosting the *Cats Roundtable* on AM 970 The Answer, and I kept loving it. I enjoyed having a regular forum in which to share my insights. I treasured the chance to interview some of the most interesting politicians, celebrities, and thought leaders around.

There are so many different media platforms today, and each one has its own special niche. But there's still something unique and powerful about talking on the radio. It's intimate. It's personal. It's totally real. And you know me—when I find something I like, I want more of it. "Hosting a radio show is great," I said to myself one day in 2019. "But wouldn't it be even better to own a radio station?" And as long as I was thinking of buying a radio station, why not buy the number-one news-talk station in America's number-one market, WABC in New York?

I knew that the station's owner, Cumulus Media, was groaning under debt from a $5 billion buying spree. Since emerging from Chapter 11 bankruptcy, the company was looking to unload assets, and I offered to take one off their hands. Once we started talking, I discovered I could scoop up this 50,000-watt, clear-channel blowtorch at 770 AM for the rock-bottom price of $12.5 million. Didn't people pay that kind of money for Podunk stations that weren't much more than a couple of toilet-paper rolls connected by a few yards of kite string? I made the deal through my Red Apple Media company, got all the approvals we needed from the Federal Communications Commission, and became the new owner in early 2020.

Now all I had to do was run the joint! Thankfully, my head was packed with ideas, some from the heyday of radio, some from the very latest developments in the digital and social media worlds. And I had some creative broadcasting pros who were eager to join me on this wild adventure.

The station had a wonderful heritage to build on. Launched as WJZ in 1921, WABC helped to birth the exciting new medium of radio, got the country through two world wars, served as the flagship for the ABC Radio Network, and defined the "top 40" music format with superstar DJs Dan Ingram, Scott Muni, and the unforgettable Cousin Brucie. And then, starting in 1982, WABC led radio's revolution in conservative talk. Six years later, when Rush Limbaugh burst onto the national scene, WABC was his home station. Together, Rush and WABC helped turn conservative talk into a political force that would truly change the country. The station still had a powerhouse signal.

After sundown, you could hear it across much of the Eastern United States and Eastern Canada. But by the time I showed up, WABC was a business in steep decline. Ratings were down. Commercial billing was down. The audience was old and dying off. Worst of all, "77 WABC" was not on the minds or the lips of New Yorkers. Most of the shows were provided by national syndicators. No offense to Sean Hannity, Michael Savage, or those other national voices. They are all talented broadcasters. But in my view, New York needed a station that spoke *to* and *for* New Yorkers—and connected with the rest of the world from a solid New York base. That's the station I aimed to create.

The guiding principle? Live and local programming around the clock.

As far as I was concerned, live-and-local was the future of radio. That and realizing that a radio station isn't just a radio station anymore. It must also be a producer of compelling content for every other imaginable media platform—TV, streaming, internet, podcast, social, mobile, and future platforms that haven't even been invented yet. If someone figures out how to beam an exciting show through the fillings in your teeth, I want that show to be coming from WABC. The American railroads stumbled because they thought they were in the railroading business. They didn't think broadly enough. They failed to fully recognize that *transportation* was the business they were in—with its endless possibilities. Yes, there's a reason the company is called Red Apple *Media* instead of Red Apple Radio.

It's been a fascinating journey already, bringing this vision to life. We quickly moved the station into the Red Apple headquarters on Manhattan's Third Avenue, building a world-class production facility. Another key move: *Cats at Night*. Just like the Sunday-morning *Cats Roundtable* . . . but bigger, better, and five times a week, airing live in the busy afternoon-drive time slot. Same A-list guests. Same tell-it-like-it-is approach. But the daily show has its own right-now urgency and a lineup of provocative New York cohosts: former Congressman Peter King, former Governor David Paterson, former City Hall Chief of Staff Tony Carbonetti, former State Republican Chair Ed Cox, former Deputy Mayor Rudy Washington, former Brooklyn

Republican Chair Craig Eaton, and former State Supreme Court Judge Richard Weinberg.

These folks have street-smart reactions to everything, and they are just as happy setting *me* straight. I'm the boss? They don't care! The opinions start flying as soon as the on-air light comes up. If you don't have a sharp comeback on this show, you'd better duck! And all our A-list guests from the weekend *Cats Roundtable* were suddenly showing up Monday to Friday on *Cats at Night*, joined by a steady stream of popular newcomers, like Senators Dan Sullivan, Bill Hagerty, and Heidi Heitkamp, and superstar Generals David Petraeus and Jack Keane.

Soon, the station's whole lineup came alive. From *Bernie and Sid in the Morning* to *The Other Side of Midnight* with Frank Morano, the station is now the talk of New York again—with the Nielsen ratings to prove it. We've also beefed up the news division and added robust social media support. By mid-2022, our lineup of daily hosts featured the New York–accented voices of Greg Kelly, Rita Cosby, Rudy Giuliani, Bill O'Reilly, Brian Kilmeade, Curtis Sliwa, Dominic Carter, and former Rush producer James Golden (a.k.a. Bo Snerdley). You might agree with their opinions. You might not. But you can't call any of them wishy-washy, generic, or dull any more than you can apply those adjectives to the city they broadcast from. We're never afraid to take chances and let the sparks fly: What other radio station in America would pair Sliwa, the founder of the crime-fighting Guardian Angels, with the ex-con, ex-Congressman Anthony Weiner? Believe me, when those two are going at each other, there is no shy person in the studio.

After dark on the weekends, we're doing something that no other big-city talk station dares to. We produce party-time music shows where the fast-talking DJs are the real stars. *Cousin Brucie's Saturday Night Rock and Roll Party*, *Saturday Nights with Tony Orlando*, and *Dean and Deana Martin's Night Cap*, which airs on Sundays, are the good-times proof: though we love debating the issues, we also know how to have fun! And on weekend days, we feature the strong voices of Larry Kudlow, Joan Hamburg, Cindy Adams, and Judge Jeanine Pirro.

Guiding this whole new generation of New York radio is Chad Lopez, the visionary President of Red Apple Media. Chad starts each day inspiring the talent to create programming you just have to listen to and forging creative business solutions for our loyal advertisers. But that's just where Chad's days begin. He is also laser-focused on pushing WABC deeper and deeper into our listeners' lives. And that means delivering exciting programming anywhere and everywhere they are, by any and every means possible.

I don't care *how* people hear us, just so long as they hear us (and maybe watch us, too). And our media dreams aren't stopping now. We're already sharing our shows with other stations around the country, and we are constantly looking for new ways to expand. Soon after we closed the deal on WABC, I wasn't satisfied with the reception I was getting at our beach house in the Hamptons, where Margo and I were holed up as the coronavirus pandemic raged.

My answer? Buy eastern Long Island's WLIR-FM, broadcasting from Hampton Bays at 107.1 FM. Today we are simulcasting WABC shows and starting to add some local programs, too, such as the *Long Island Report* with my *Cats at Night* cohosts Richard Weinberg and Peter King and Suffolk County Republican Chairman Jesse Garcia. There's a template here with a big future ahead.

However we deliver the programming, I never want to beat people over the head with divisive ideology. We have enough of that in the world already. I simply want to tell the truth. I want to get people talking to each other in honest, interesting, common-sense ways. And I want to be in the middle of all of it. What could be more fun than that? Talk radio is uniquely positioned for the times we live in. It's a good business, and it's good for the city, the region, the country, and the world.

....

Real estate has been a part of my business from the very start. If you own supermarkets, you can't help being in real estate. Whether you rent or own the locations, you have to put the stores somewhere.

Early on, when I was first buying buildings that held my supermarkets, I learned an important lesson: real estate has enduring value as long as it's located in places where people want to be. In recent years, Red Apple Real Estate has been taking that to the next level, developing large, mixed-use apartment-and-retail complexes.

Back in the 1980s, I bought a four-acre piece of property from Long Island University on the corner of Myrtle and Flatbush Avenues, a scruffy area that straddled Fort Greene and downtown Brooklyn. The price reflected the area's rotten reputation back then: approximately $600,000. This was what some people liked to call a "two-gun neighborhood"—you might want to carry a second gun so you'll be prepared when your first gun runs out of bullets! Nothing much happened there for the next couple of decades, other than a false start or two and a citywide financial crisis. But I knew one thing for certain: the property was one subway stop from Lower Manhattan, and more than a dozen train lines ran nearby. Its day would come.

Fast forward to today. The area is a booming New York City submarket, packed with young professionals and hardworking families. The sprawling MetroTech office complex is close by. So is the Barclays Center, home of the NBA's Brooklyn Nets and also the highest-grossing concert venue in the United States. And look at that once-scruffy corner of ours: it's buzzing with four residential rental towers that stay close to 100 percent occupied—the Andrea, the Giovanni, the Margo, and the Eagle. Where do you think we got those first three names? Something about "the John" just didn't seem to work, so we added a touch of Euro to that one. The buildings are all top of the line, and we're getting close to Manhattan-level rents.

It was slow going at first. I opened a supermarket to give people somewhere to shop. CVS put in a drugstore. A zoning change by the Bloomberg administration and a couple of construction loans from Bank of America gave us some momentum. Our patience was eventually rewarded, and our vision really came to life. It's 970 units all together, plus sixty thousand square feet of retail and a parking garage, and people are clamoring to get in. Starting with a $600,000 piece of property, we now have a development worth somewhere in the high nine figures and cash flow like you wouldn't believe. I'd call that a development home run.

. . . .

With the same long view and a willingness to wait—that's how I'd been eying Brooklyn's Coney Island. Known for its Atlantic Ocean boardwalk, Nathan's Famous hot dogs, and the retro Cyclone and Wonder Wheel rides, the neighborhood had struggled for decades. The nearby blocks contained dreary walk-up apartment buildings, some higher-rise housing projects, and nothing that could remotely be called upscale. I wondered: How come? Why can't this stretch of Brooklyn waterfront have some luxury living, too? Doesn't Coney Island have the same salt water and same soft sand as the trendy Hamptons and Long Island's South Shore? Someone, I decided, just needed to invest there. I also decided that the someone should be me.

Our new Ocean Drive development on Surf Avenue is made up of two twenty-one-story, glass-sheathed residential towers with 425 apartments and twenty thousand square feet of retail, just west of the amusement area and near the Sea Gate community. These are the high-end rental towers Coney Island has always deserved, and we have two more on the drawing board. The amenities are unmistakably first-class: a twenty-four-hour concierge, a fifty-foot indoor swimming pool, a state-of-the-art fitness center, and a residents' lounge with a library, billiards, and oversized TVs. We will be bringing in direct ferry service to Manhattan.

A lot of local people are already moving in—teachers, nurses, transit workers, flight attendants, police officers, and firefighters—along with folks who never before considered living in Coney Island. It turns out almost everyone likes easy beach access and million-dollar ocean views.

How do we know it's working? I'll tell you how. The buildings are fully occupied, and half a dozen other developers are suddenly breaking ground on projects in the neighborhood. We like the added scale, so we welcome the copycats. And no one's calling Coney Island a "ghetto by the sea" anymore.

. . . .

I'll admit it: I'm not the best vacationer, not the sit-around-and-do-nothing kind. When I travel, I always have an eye out for opportunities. Over the years, Margo and I and the kids have traveled often to St. Petersburg, Florida, where Margo's mother lived for decades. On our many visits, I couldn't help but notice a shabby piece of property right in the middle of the vibrant Gulf Coast city's artsy downtown.

It wasn't easy to acquire that parcel. The longtime owners weren't so sure about selling. A complex ground lease was already in place. There were questions about zoning options and development rights. But we patiently navigated all of that, and soon, the tallest residential building on the west coast of Florida will stand on that long-neglected corner, soaring 515 feet into the sky.

The Residences at 400 Central, as the 1.3-million-square-foot mixed-use project is called, are like nothing ever seen in this part of Florida: 301 luxury condominiums built to the highest standards of architecture and design, supported by enough office, retail, and parking to help supercharge the city's downtown. This is not just another punched-window, stucco high-rise that passes for "luxury" with some Florida buyers. It's a cutting-edge, world-class building designed by the award-winning global architecture firm, Arquitectonica. We arrived with such strong praise and reviews, one quarter of the units were under contract even before the building came out of the ground—$150 million in signed reservations with deposits. Now that's a sign of confidence and trust!

One of my favorite touches: instead of stacking the rooftop with another layer of penthouse apartments, we are using that precious space for a 360-degree, amenity-packed observatory, where all the residents are welcome to gaze at the stars at night. That way, every single resident can have the best view in the house. We pushed through COVID-19. We pushed through hurricanes. We pushed through the inevitable gyrations of the local and regional economies. And here we are. They certainly love us at St. Petersburg City Hall: we'll soon be the largest property-tax payer in town. People are already calling St. Pete the Austin of Florida.

We're giving this wonderful city the skyline it deserves.

This development, along with the rest of the Red Apple Real Estate portfolio, has been pushed to a whole new level by our energetic Senior Vice President, Ralph Zirinsky. As Ralph keeps reminding me, "You're not here to squeeze every last dollar out of these projects. If we keep doing it first class, the people will keep coming."

. . . .

Every year, *Forbes* magazine cites our Red Apple Group as one of America's largest privately held companies. We're a long way from where we started, but we can never forget our roots. I sometimes joke that our supermarkets, the business that launched us, now account for 2 percent of our revenue but 95 percent of our headaches. That's mostly a joke. Mostly. The supermarket business is a challenging one. The costs are high. The margins are slim. The bananas go from green to brown in an awful hurry. And the profits can be just as perishable as the fruit. But I love supermarkets. That's where I started. That's where I grew up. A neighborhood really isn't a neighborhood without its own supermarket. I can't imagine ever not owning supermarkets. And the people—the people are a huge part of it. I love the people who work in my stores. Some of them have been there with me from the very beginning. Could I really walk away from them? That wouldn't feel right to me. My guiding instinct is to add new things, not subtract old ones.

. . . .

When Major League Baseball reorganized its minor-league system, the Class A Staten Island Yankees were one of the teams that got eliminated. That was in 2020, and it left a giant hole in New York City's "forgotten borough." Not only did Staten Islanders lose a professional sports franchise, the Richmond County Bank Ballpark, with its drop-dead views of New York Harbor and Lower Manhattan, a short walk from the St. George Ferry Terminal, was suddenly an empty, silent shell.

That had to change.

Everyone from the Yankees to Major League Baseball to the people and politicians of Staten Island wanted that 7,171-seat ballpark alive again. But who had the business know-how? Who had the capital? Who was willing to take the risk?

Yankees President Randy Levine had an idea: me. I had tried to buy the team some years earlier. That didn't happen. But now that the job involved starting almost from scratch, Randy put me together with Eric Shuffler, a veteran political consultant and obsessive baseball fan who was itching to run a sports franchise. It's been an excellent partnership. Shuffler is President. I'm Chairman of the Board.

We had to assemble a whole baseball team. Recruiting players. Hiring a manager and coaching staff. Forging a business plan. Whipping the stadium back into shape. Even dreaming up a team name. Thankfully, we got tons of suggestions on that last one and decided on the Staten Island FerryHawks. Anyone who's ever taken a ride on the Staten Island Ferry knows those bold and squawking birds. Keeping things Staten Island real, the stadium now features a Staten Island walk of fame (think local luminaries like *Saturday Night Live*'s Pete Davidson), a Little League Moments wall, and a food stand called the Taste of Shaolin, which serves favorite dishes from popular local restaurants.

Our FerryHawks play in the North Division of the Atlantic League of Professional Baseball against teams like the Charleston Dirty Birds, the Southern Maryland Blue Crabs, the York Revolution, and our fierce metropolitan rival, the Long Island Ducks. This is family entertainment that actual families can afford.

Our home opener, May 3, 2022, was a huge achievement for everyone involved. What a thrill it was! Standing behind home plate, staring into the outfield as the fireworks almost outdid the twinkling lights of Lower Manhattan—I dare you to find a more dramatic view anywhere. And then there was an amazing night of baseball.

I love Staten Island. I've always thought of Staten Island as the John Catsimatidis of boroughs: a little rough around the edges, perhaps, but full of heart and capable of amazing things. For all this to work as a business, we need to fill that ballpark not just on the days and nights the FerryHawks play, but all the time! So we are booking concerts, trade shows, festivals, other sporting events, and gatherings of every imaginable sort. I'm looking for the team to be a perennial champion and looking for the stadium to become a vibrant entertainment complex and a real hub of Staten Island and New York life.

Staten Islanders deserve nothing less.

....

And what about politics, you might ask?

For me, politics started as an interest and grew into a hobby before it became much more than either of those. I'm not sure if Father Alex knew the spark he was striking when he reminded me about the Greek origins of politics and wondered whether I might like to make a contribution or two. But I'm sure he realized soon enough. I didn't care about buying a boat or playing golf or doing most of the other things that guys start doing when they get a little money. Okay, I always liked to fly. But somehow, politics got a grip on me. That was the game I loved to play. Once I got on the inside of politics, I couldn't leave. I didn't want to leave. It was too interesting, too important, and too much fun. Who cared how many swings of a club it took to sink a little ball into a hole? Politics was far more thrilling to me, and it was *real*. I'm sure the seeds were planted in the early part of my childhood, hearing my father talking about a young Jack Kennedy who had a headful of fresh ideas. I have now spent decades talking about politics, arguing about politics, getting to know politicians, financing political campaigns, and—inevitably, I suppose—running for office myself.

I have zero interest in entering Greek politics. At various times over the years, especially as the economy in Greece has stumbled badly, Greek friends of mine have asked if I might consider returning to the land of my birth and running for president or prime minister. The answer has always been the same: no. The last time I lived in Greece, I was still sleeping in a crib. Greece needs leaders who have spent more time in the country than I have—and more recently. I still have the deepest love for the land of my ancestors. I still feel hugely connected to its culture, to its ideals, to its people, and to its future. Greece has given so much to the world and so much to me. And I am always happy to give back. Whenever I am asked to—and sometimes when I'm not—I try to help my homeland. When Prime Minister Konstantinos Mitsotakis asked me to help him form a better relationship with the *New York Times* editorial board, I did what I could. I've never gotten involved in promoting one Greek politician against another Greek politician, and I don't intend to. But I've always been there to help the country, and I always will be.

As for American politics—well, I don't have the same excuse of "I don't live there." As I look around my beloved New York these days, I still see all the things that make the city great. The energy, the drive, the hustle, all the different kinds of people trying to make better lives for themselves and their families. The friendliness and the random acts of kindness are still deeply embedded in New York. But I have also begun to see some worrisome signs. I hate the rise in crime that arrived with the COVID-19 pandemic. I hate seeing mentally ill people wandering the streets instead of getting the help they need. I hate watching leaders pull the city in the wrong direction. Anyone who lived through the 1970s and 1980s in New York City knows exactly what I am talking about. Those were the bad old days, a time of spreading disorder and dangerous decline. The lesson could hardly be any clearer: we have to do whatever we must to make sure days like those never come back again. Mayor Bill de Blasio's "progressive" abandonment of the NYPD's stop-and-frisk program put more handguns on the street—and in the worst hands imaginable. Albany's ill-fated bail reform law, a get-out-of-jail-free pass for countless criminals, undeniably made the city less safe. I've seen some encouraging signs from Mayor Eric Adams's administration. As a former police officer, he has an innate understanding of some of this. Still, turning a giant city in the right direction is never accomplished overnight, and we'll just have to see what comes next. I can promise: I'll be there to help in any way I can.

People will put up with a lot to live and work in a city as vibrant as New York. But there are limits to the abuse those same people are prepared to endure. The truth is we need a broad mix of people living here, including the middle class and the rich. We need successful businesses. They pay most of the taxes. We'd be in a terrible fix if they all packed up and moved to Florida.

So we all need to come together. We need to listen as well as talk. We need to respect other people's points of view and not suppress their freedom of speech. We need the healing power of common ground. We need to remember Abraham Lincoln's famous warning: "A house divided against itself cannot stand." Lincoln knew a few things about divided nations. He is still worth listening to. Times like these demand real leadership—politicians and community figures who can speak clearly, bring people together, and exercise some common sense. Leaders who can find real solutions and guide people there—not pander, scapegoat, or further divide.

Whether that means I will ever run for office again, I really don't know. As I say, I can't be president, but I'm not ruling out anything else. For now, I am very happy with the road I'm traveling. I see my role in the realms of business and ideas more than in elective office. If I can keep nudging my city and my country in the right direction, what could be better than that?

Afterword

EVER ONWARD

There is one last thing I want to mention before I get out of here, something important that I have come to understand over these past many decades. Success is wonderful. It opens a lot of doors. But it's still my responsibility to decide: Which of those doors do I want to walk through? And that question never goes away. Here I am, half a century into adulthood, and I am still looking for new opportunities. New companies to invest in. New political causes to get behind. New forums for sharing my insights. New ways of making myself and my loved ones happy. New projects for helping the world become a better place. After all these years, I am still trying to figure out what *I* want to do with the rest of my life. Every time I climb a mountain, I see another one I want to climb.

I know that's something young people are often asked: What do you want to be when you grow up? After all these years, I'm still asking myself exactly the same question. And the truth is I don't always know. I've tried a lot of things. It's important to try a lot of things. Some of them I loved, some of them not so much. In business. In politics. In culture. In travel. In philanthropy. And I will keep opening new doors to walk through. I'd like to think I've contributed something in every new venture and every new relationship. I know I have been enriched by all of them—and I don't just mean monetarily.

Life truly is a journey. It keeps going . . . if we're lucky. I see no reason to stop living it prematurely.

I have never forgotten what my plain-spoken mother used to say to me: "When you're in the middle of the dance floor, keep dancing."

Thanks, Mom.

The music's still playing, and I'm still on my feet.

COUNSEL BY CATSIMATIDIS

People often ask me, "What's the secret to your success?" It's a flattering question, and I appreciate it. Now I can tell them, "Read this book. It's all here." But some people prefer a bite-sized version, a quick and easy rundown of the key guiding principles. This list is for them. It's my own personal cheat sheet should I ever forget what got me here. I've been compiling it quietly my entire life. Feel free to borrow, steal, embellish, or ignore.

1. You can't win if you're too afraid of losing.
2. Know your products, your customers, and your vendors better than they know themselves—and treat them all like family.
3. Hire people who know more than you do, and inspire them to do their jobs.
4. People do what you inspect, not what you expect.
5. Mentors are hugely valuable—but take only the best from each of them.
6. Always be seeking the next opportunity.
7. Own the real estate.
8. Great success comes with great effort—outwork everyone.
9. Take reasonable risks—somewhere between reasonable and risky.

10. The right time to negotiate is when the other person needs the deal.
11. Seek allies in unexpected places, and dream up mutually beneficial ideas.
12. Time is the most precious commodity—use every second purposefully.
13. Failure is not an option—ever.
14. Help others at every opportunity. You'll benefit as much as they do.
15. Dedicate everything to the people you love the most.
16. Have fun.

ACKNOWLEDGMENTS

This book could never have been done without the tireless and wonderful contributions of Ellis Henican, a renowned journalist and author, who worked with me from start to finish.

Others who contributed major efforts include my two General Counsels, Judge Richard Weinberg and Nick Katsoris; my agent Laura Dail; Sherry Diamond; and our wonderful publisher, Matt Holt.

A COLLECTION OF MEMORIES

Top: John and Margo Catsimatidis with former Soviet Union Leader Mikhail Gorbachev
Bottom: John Catsimatidis with New York State Governor Mario Cuomo.

Top: John Catsimatidis with former United State Senator Daniel Patrick Moynihan.
Bottom: John and Margo Catsimatidis with Fidel Castro